The Evolutionary
Psychology Behind Politics

How Conservatism and Liberalism
Evolved Within Humans

Anonymous Conservative

Federalist Publications

Macclenny, Florida

Published by Federalist Publications, Macclenny, Florida
All text and artwork, Copyright© 2012, 2014, 2017 by Michael Trust
Cover Artwork by Betterbookcovers@Gmail.com

Revised July, 2014, May 2017

www.anonymousconservative.com

Printed in the United States of America
ISBN-13 : 978-0-9829479-4-4 (Cloth Hardcover, Jacketed)
ISBN-13 : 978-0-9829479-3-7 (Softcover)
ISBN-13 : 978-0-9829479-5-1 (Amazon Kindle)
Library of Congress Control Number: 2012931464

Library of Congress Subject Headings:

Psychology.
Psychology and religion.
Good and evil -- Psychological aspects.
Psychopathology.
Religion and Psychology.
Social problems -- United States.

Dedicated to all those who helped.

"Conservatives think like lions. Liberals think like lambs."

-Unknown

Table of Contents

A long time ago, I read a book titled *Games People Play*, by Eric Berne. The book's premise was that many of the behaviors which people engage in while dealing with others are repetitions of behavioral patterns that they engaged in as children. In other words, they are behavioral responses which their brains were conditioned to engage in, in a Pavlovian fashion, when presented with various stimuli during early developmental periods. As such, these behaviors were related to their childhood environment and psychology, and would often seem unrelated to the logical adult environment in which they were evoked.

At the time, the ideas that book contained seemed far too revolutionary for my teenaged thinking. Though I read it from cover to cover, and in so doing committed its contents to memory, I dismissed its theories as applying only to an extremely small, mentally damaged portion of the population. The vast majority of people had to be logical, and most behaviors had to be simple logical responses to the unique circumstances which precipitated them.

As the years and decades passed, and experience intruded upon assumption, I found myself perceiving patterns of behavior in the people around me, which I recalled from that book. In my youth, I had no compunction about disregarding the experience of a trained, practicing psychiatrist with decades of experience, and substituting my assumptions. As I grew older, I realized that there can be knowledge anywhere, even when you can't see it at all. Sometimes those wholly immersed in a discipline will see an underlying mechanism which will appear highly implausible to the novice.

Though I do not now ascribe to all of Dr. Berne's work, *Games People Play* could have advanced my understanding of human behavior much faster, had I only taken the book more seriously at the time. The benefits of hindsight.

I don't ask that you finish this book, and ascribe to this theory. As Dr. Berne's work was to me, the ideas this theory is founded upon are likely far too advanced for you to absorb them completely from just one work, especially if you are not a scientist. Rather, as I did with Dr.

Berne's work, I only ask that you remember what you read. Perhaps with time, as Dr Berne's work grew on me, so too, will this theory grow upon you.

*On Religion, Morality, and Free Will*_____

There will be those who will take issue with this work, due to religious beliefs, or over concerns about the implications of this work upon the free will of man. It is unpleasant to view a conscious man as merely a slave to some clockwork mechanism of the mind, and even worse, I believe such a view is incorrect as well. Therefore, I would like to address these concerns regarding this work prior to delving into the subject matter of this book.

In addressing the religious issue, I myself believe in God. I see no conflict between my faith and my love of God, and this work. God created an incredible world. He created this world such that all of the best attributes mankind can embody would spontaneously emerge within the nature of our species. I cannot help but find His mechanism fascinating.

I also recognize the power of free will, as does this work. This theory is not a scientific theory that explains exactly why every person behaves as they do. It does not diminish man's free will, or the greatness of virtue. Walk through this world, and human unpredictability will always surprise you.

This work is a theory of group interactions, which explains how two groups within our population came to hold two divergent intellectual philosophies.

Just as the certainty of Newtonian physics breaks down into unpredictable chaos at the quantum level, so too will this theory offer a poor characterization of a specific individual's philosophy or psychology. This theory accurately describes how two different groups of thought came to exist, and even offers insights into their practical origins, as well as how historical events would affect them. But it cannot specifically describe the elusive and unique motives which will underlie each individual's personal choices.

As for concerns regarding the implications of this theory upon morality and one's responsibility for their actions, the urges described herein are merely urges. Humans are unique, in that we may process complex information, draw conclusions from that information, and then choose to change who we are. In so doing, we can actually consciously alter the very neurobiological structures which make us what we are. Whether an individual simply allows their nature to be molded by fate and immediate desires, or whether they take the initiative, and define who they are themselves, according to their own recognition of morality and decency is solely the province of free will.

Those who blindly cede to their urges, absent any respect for others, and absent any intellectual analysis of themselves and their actions, bear the sole responsibility for the evil they engage in. This theory is not an excuse for those who oppress, nor does it absolve anyone of any moral responsibility for assailing the freedoms of others.

Rather, it is hoped that this work will, in elucidating the origins of our political urges, make the embrace of freedom an ever more cherished virtue, and see to it that we all feel responsible for respecting each other's choices and protecting each other's freedoms.

Chapter One

The Theory of this Book_____

This is a book for those ideologues who find themselves puzzled by their political opposition. If you are one of those individuals who sees their own political ideology as wholly logical and you cannot possibly fathom why there exists an opposition party, let alone why its ranks should be, in part, filled with individuals just as intellectually capable as you, then this book will answer a lot of questions you have posed to yourself over the years.

John Jost, who studies the different characteristics of political ideologues at NYU, once said, *"I think it's a truly fascinating possibility that the left-right distinction, which emerged over 200 years ago in response to the French Revolution and continues to be the single best way of understanding ideological differences today, may be rooted in fundamental human needs for stability vs. change, order vs. complexity, familiarity vs. novelty, conformity vs. creativity, and loyalty vs. rebellion....It may be that conflicting tendencies in human nature play themselves out in the political sphere as the struggle between right and left."*[1]

This book will explain why unique evolutionary circumstances evolved these two different psychological tendencies within our species. It will explain where these tendencies can be seen in other, more primitive species in nature. It will even explain how these psychological tendencies convey survival and reproductive advantage on those organisms which adopt them, both in other species, and in humans. By the end of this book you will understand why political ideologies link such disparate issues as mating strategies and conflict-tendencies, why populations will trend leftward and rightward over time, how this occurs, and what it tells us about the future of our own civilization.

As we begin this journey we will first provide an overview of the theory which this book will attempt to explain. In later chapters, you will see strange names for brain structures, complex personality assessments, and other scientific terms and technical concepts. You will find yourself

1

thrust headlong into detailed analyses of current scientific understandings and debates, within a myriad of fields. As each piece of evidence is placed on those which came before it a crisp picture will emerge of just how and why political ideologies arose within our species.

Unfortunately, such a massive quantity of information, presented piecemeal, in such a coldly technical fashion, may fail to clearly convey the essence of the theory behind this work. The underlying premise of this book will be buried beneath the mountains of evidence supporting it before you ever gain a chance to see the theory clearly, in its totality. This would be a shame, because the premise of this book has real potential to alter not just how we govern ourselves, but to alter the very destiny of our species and its individuals. It is for that reason that this work will begin with a very short, clear explanation of the theory behind this book, absent evidentiary support.

The theory of this book is that there is a simple explanation for the origins of political ideology. Put most simply, our two main political ideologies are merely intellectual outgrowths of the two main reproductive strategies that have been described in the field of Evolutionary Biology for decades.

Biologists have long recognized that two different psychologies exist in nature. These two psychologies each guide the organisms which hold them to pursue behaviors which will be most likely to yield survival and reproduction. These psychologies are referred to as reproductive strategies, but they are really deeply imbued psychologies. They frame how an organism views the world, how it views its peers, and how it behaves as it moves through life.

The study of these psychologies is often described using the shorthand *"r/K Selection Theory."* Both the *"r-strategy"* and the *"K-strategy,"* as they are referred to within the field, are psychologies which yield behavior that is custom tailored to a specific environment. In humans, as in nature, the r-psychology is primarily an adaptation to the presence of copious resources, which do not require out-competing peers. This is a condition which reduces the advantages of producing fit offspring, in turn favoring the fastest and most prolific reproducers, regardless of offspring quality. By contrast, the K-psychology is an adaptation to a relative scarcity of resources, where only the fittest

2

compete and survive. This produces an increased selective pressure favoring the survival of more advanced and fit specimens. It also reduces the advantages of producing copious numbers of less fit offspring.

Although the presence or absence of resources may vary within a population over the short term, over the long term these two environmental conditions will usually accompany either the presence or absence of a constant, high mortality, most frequently predation. Predation lowers population numbers and prevents overcrowding, thereby increasing the per-capita resources available to each individual. This prevents the onset of resource shortage due to overpopulation.

It is for this reason that the r-strategy, which is the evolutionary origin of liberalism, is most often seen in nature within prey species. Meanwhile the K-strategy, which underlies conservatism, is most often seen in species which are not preyed upon. This is in fact, the biological underpinning of the oft heard maxim, *"Conservatives think like lions, liberals think like lambs."* Lions are a K-selected species which exists sans predation. As a result, each new lion must compete with its peers to acquire a share of the limited resources available to the population. As a result, lions evolved to exhibit a K-type, competitive/aggressive psychology that intensively rears offspring to compete. Sheep, by contrast, are a more r-selected prey species, surrounded by fields of grass they will rarely, if ever, fully consume. This is reflected in their less belligerent, more pacifistic, more freely promiscuous nature.

One species exhibits a psychology which is belligerent, competitive, and sexually restricted and selective, so as to compete for limited resources and produce the fittest offspring. The other exists as the exact opposite, simply trying to turn resources into offspring as quickly as possible, regardless of fitness. Each is perfectly designed to compete with peers in their respective environment.

The r-strategy entails five main psychological traits. Each trait is designed to help an organism out-compete peers in the r-selected environment of free resource availability. This psychology exhibits a psychological aversion to both, competition with peers and the competitive environment. It also exhibits a tolerance for, or embrace of, promiscuity, low-investment single-parenting, and early onset sexual behavior among offspring. It will also tend to not exhibit any group-centric urges, such as loyalty to in-group, or hostility to out-group.

3

Of these five traits, (competition aversion, promiscuity, single parenting, early onset sexuality, and aversion to group-centrism/ethnocentrism), political leftists exhibit a tolerance of, or an embrace of, all five. Indeed, as we will show, these five urges explain the entire liberal platform of issue positions.

Liberalism seeks to quash competitions between men (from capitalism, to war, to citizens killing criminal attackers with privately owned firearms). Liberalism also adopts a lax attitude towards rampant promiscuity, if it is not actively embracing it. Liberals tend to support single parenting, such as was seen in the debate over the TV show Murphy Brown's glorification of single motherhood. Liberalism exhibits a tolerance for, or an embrace of, ever earlier sexual education for children as well as an ever more sexualized media environment to which children are exposed. Liberals tend to reject ethnocentrism, and view any tendency towards a pack mentality as an odd and foolish evolutionary throwback.

On top of all of this, at the heart of most liberal policy is a fundamental perception that resources exist in limitless quantities, and that any shortage is not inherent to the finite nature of the world. Rather, any shortage must be due to some specific individual's greed altering the world's natural state of plenty, which would otherwise be able to easily provision everyone with a comfortably high level of resources. This is a psychology designed to avoid danger, and focus the individual on reproducing as fast as possible. In our ancient evolutionary environment, absent birth control and abortion, this would produce large numbers of offspring, beginning early in life, and it would be perfectly adapted to r-selection, where every offspring would have food and survive.

The K-strategy entails an embrace of five opposite psychological traits. K-selection favors an aggressive embrace of competition and the competitive environment, where some individuals succeed, and others fail, based on their inherent abilities and merits. It tends to reject promiscuity in favor of sexual selectivity and monogamy, and it will strongly favor high-investment, two-parent offspring-rearing. The K-strategy also favors delaying sexual activity among offspring until later in life, when maximally fit. Finally, in its most evolved form, K-selection will tend to imbue individuals with a fierce loyalty to their in-group, to facilitate success in group-competitions. Competition,

4

shortage, and conflict are the evolutionary origins of the pack mentality, and they are ever present in the extreme K-selected environment.

Clearly, conservatives favor competition, from capitalism, to war, to armed citizens fighting off criminals with personally owned firearms. Conservatives accept that such competitions will produce disparate outcomes which will be based on inherent ability and effort. Conservatives favor a culture of monogamy over promiscuity, and they tend to desire a culture which favors high-investment, two-parent child-rearing, as evidenced by the conservative uproar over Murphy Brown, as well as the growing debate over "family values" within our culture. Conservatives also tend to want to see children protected from sexually stimulating themes or sexual education until later in life, so they will be more likely to delay the onset of sexual activity until they are mature. Of course conservatives have always viewed liberals as exhibiting diminished loyalty to their nation and its people because to a conservative, patriotism, and support for "one's own," is a vital moral quality in peers and its expression can never be too exaggerated.

Again, this is a psychology, designed to house one's genes in carefully reared, highly fit, competitive machines. It is perfectly adapted to confront conditions of resource limitation, where one's only means of acquiring resources is to be better at competition than your peers, and to do whatever it takes to not be the individual who failed to succeed.

Why do the r and K reproductive strategies exist? How exactly does each strategy offer advantage to the individual who exhibits it? Let's take a closer look at r and K in nature. Suppose you have a field, and it produces enough grass to support 100 r-selected rabbits. A group of owls moves in however, and keeps the rabbit population at only 20 rabbits, in a field which produces enough food to support 100.

Now this environment offers specific advantages and disadvantages to each rabbit. The owls will shorten each rabbit's average lifespan. As a result, Darwinian selection will favor rabbits which reproduce fast and early. If a rabbit waits to mate, it will be eaten, and that sexually procrastinating trait will be culled. As a result, those rabbits that produce the next generation will have no compunction about mating as early as possible. In this environment, "teenagers" and "children" mating is simply normal, as anyone who feels otherwise is eaten prior to reproducing. Mating earlier also offers a numerical advantage in offspring production, which is advantageous when the competition is about producing as many offspring as possible.

Conflict is an unnecessary risk, since each rabbit already has vastly more food than it can eat. Those who compete will waste time and energy fighting for something which is already freely available elsewhere. Those who fight will risk injury and death, while those who do not fight will enjoy the same freely available food, absent any risk, simply by fleeing to another green pasture. The fighters and competitors will produce fewer offspring than those who avoid competition's risk and focus all of their time solely on reproducing. As a result, the competitive will find themselves numerically out-reproduced by the more prolific individuals who avoid conflict and competition.

Under r-selection, monogamy is disadvantageous, since to impregnate only one mate, and then see the few offspring you have with her eaten, is to see yourself fail, in Darwinian terms. Monogamy will also limit the total numbers of offspring produced, as a single female can only produce so many young. Thus in this environment, one is best served by producing as many offspring as possible, by as many mates as possible, beginning as early as possible. In that way, it becomes likely statistically that some of your numerous children will survive to reproduce. Since under conditions of r-selection, these are the traits Darwin rewards, these are the traits which will emerge within a species placed within an r-selecting environment.

Since producing high numbers of offspring is the goal, it is also advantageous to not waste too much time on rearing any one offspring. The goal in r-selection is mass production, as early and as often as possible. Those who produce more offspring, even less fit offspring, out-compete those who do not, since fitness is unimportant when resources are free and there is no competition. As a result, high-investment parenting for extended periods will give way to investing as little as possible in each offspring's rearing, so one may dedicate oneself to the actual act of reproduction, and produce as many offspring as possible. Since resources are freely available, and aggression and competition are rare, offspring do not require much education or protection anyway, and they may be turned out of the home relatively early to fend for themselves. Males will also abandon impregnated females with offspring so as to pursue their highly promiscuous mating strategy. You see how free resources can actually devolve a population, reducing greatness.

Since there is also no competition, there is no need to ally with anyone else to compete for resources. As a result, these rabbits will not evolve any group-centric urges, or emotional connections to their peers. Indeed, the very notion of in-group or out-group would be puzzling to them, if you could communicate the concept. Each rabbit is wholly on their own – at most a part of a global rabbit warren.

As a result of all of this, in this environment a population will evolve to avoid conflict and competition, mate with as many partners as possible, mate early, and not invest highly in any one child, while feeling loyalty to no one. The emphasis, as so many biology textbooks will assert, is to produce quantity over quality when producing offspring in an r-selective environment.

Now suppose we zoom out from the field, and zoom in to a nearby forest. There, several packs of K-selected wolves exist in harmonious balance with a deer population. Once these wolves reproduce, there will not be enough food to support the entire population of wolves, so some wolves will die due to starvation. This creates a different selective pressure entirely. Here, to survive, a wolf must aggressively compete with his peers for a share of the limited food available. Those who avoid conflict and competition, in hopes of stumbling on non-existent food elsewhere, will die from starvation. The wolves who survive will be those who go after any food they see, even if they have to try and take it from another wolf by force of violence. Thus, such a K-type psychology will evolve to exhibit a more aggressive, competitive nature, more accepting of violence, and more accepting of inevitable disparities in competitive outcomes between individuals.

Of course a wolf's success, in Darwinian terms, will revolve not just around surviving and mating, but also around producing offspring who survive and reproduce themselves. From a Darwinian perspective, if a parent survives and mates, but all of their offspring die due to competitive failure, the parent may as well have not bothered reproducing at all. As a result, K-selected wolves will evolve a psychology designed to invest heavily in a few, highly competitive offspring. This will produce a small number of offspring that are likely to outcompete their peers, rather than a larger number of lower quality, competitively incompetent offspring. Those wolves who mate randomly and often, with any mate they happen across, will see their numerous haphazardly produced offspring killed off by the fitter offspring of those

7

parents who carefully sought out the fittest mate possible, and then competitively monopolized their mate's genetic fitness through monogamy. As a result, this K-trait of careful mate selection, and competitive monopolization, will emerge spontaneously as Darwin works his magic.

Young wolves will evolve to wait before entering the competition for a mate, so as to make sure they are as competitive as possible and are not simply killed by their older competition due to their immaturity. Parents will also evolve to discourage such early sexual precociousness in their young, so their young will be maximally mature (and maximally attractive to highly fit mates) when pursuing their own lifetime mate. Likewise, parents will evolve towards high investment, two-parent (or even pack) rearing, so as to better protect their offspring until they are ready to compete, and to carefully prepare them for the rigorous competition with peers which awaits them.

Intense K-selection often evolves into groups of individuals competing with other groups, since this is a more effective way to acquire limited resources than working alone. As a result, K-type organisms will tend to evolve into groups of individuals who exhibit pro-social traits, such as loyalty to in-group and disregard for out-group interests. This is why K-selection produces packs of wolves, family groups of elephants, pods of dolphins, and prides of lions, all of whom care deeply for each other, while mice, antelope, deer, rabbits, and any other r-selected species will not exhibit any sadness should one of their ranks fall prey to a predator.

Since rabbits exist at the bottom of the food pyramid in nature, and are preyed upon fairly consistently by a wide range of predators (from owls, to hawks, to foxes), rabbits never truly experience the K-selected environment for any extended period. As a result of eons of fairly consistent r-selection pressures, they express a consistently r-type psychology throughout their species. Other species, which have existed for long periods under conditions of limited resources, will be highly K-selected in their psychology and behavior. Still other species can exhibit a mix of r and K-type psychologies, due to a variety of unique environmental conditions, among them having a history of living in varying environments with periodic resource abundances and resource shortages.

These r-selected and K-selected conditions are the two environments that conservatives and liberals are perfectly adapted to function within. It is almost beyond imagination to think that exposure to these environments in our past is not what evolved our two political psychologies today. In truth, I am still stunned as I look at this to think nobody has ever proposed this concept before.

This theory will be highly controversial within the biological sciences and our political debates. Biologists have long viewed r-type organisms as somewhat inferior to K-type organisms, for a few reasons. To begin with, humans are highly K-selected, and thus have not evolved to be morally tolerant of r-type behavior, as a whole. Promiscuity, child abandonment, instinctual cowardice in the face of threat, lack of loyalty to in-group, and the sexualization of children all clash with the K-selected mores and values of our species, and thus are rejected as morally inferior by most humans (Even as leftist intellectuals present these behaviors to the populace as marks of liberalism's superiority, modernity, and sophistication).

Moreover, due to the r-strategy's abandonment of sexual selectivity, in favor of a more random mate assortment that is less concerned with mate fitness, r-selected organisms usually exist as far less evolved organisms. Absent the fierce evolutionary force of competitive selection or the breeding of the fittest with the fittest, r-type organisms become less capable, less intelligent, less loyal, and less impressive as specimens as their r-selection goes on.

Pure r-selection will tend to devolve those species which adopt it, through the abandonment of this competitive selection - producing quantity over quality is not without cost evolutionarily. The quality of the product will decline, if there is no competitive test of fitness prior to mating. The fact that r-selected species will often be prey species, their evolutionary development trapped helplessly at the whim of a more impressive predator does not help. Leftists will not like this work, despite its clearly apparent veracity. Few of them will look at this work objectively, and assess it on its merits. Much more likely, those who do address this work will try to curtly portray it as unworthy of debate, thus allowing them to avoid debating any of its merits at all.

Regardless of how anyone might oppose the conclusions of this work, there is no denying that anyone who opposes it must run head-on into the fact that r/K Selection Theory revolves around five issues of behavior, while political ideology revolves around the exact same five issues, arranged in the exact same way. These five issues - attitudes towards free competition/aggression/protection, promiscuity/monogamy, high or low-investment child-rearing, age of offspring sexualization, and loyalty to in-group - are the intellectual bedrock of both. No matter what argument opponents might make, no matter how they may try to dismiss this insight, not a one will confront those simple five traits, or their presence in both ideologies and reproductive strategies.

Even worse, they must confront that a historical review will show that each ideology will arise in a society under the respective conditions it was designed to confront. Provide copious resources and a high degree of success, and a society will spontaneously trend leftist. Restrict resources, and watch confrontational, aggressive psychologies emerge, as leftism retreats into the shadows and the right-wing rises.

We will go further in our support of this work. We will present evidence that in humans there is a gene which is documented to be involved in producing a more r-selected behavioral strategy. We will show how this gene has been shown to be involved in the adoption of a leftist political ideology, and we will even show where a researcher examining this gene's behavioral effects (outside of the political realm) describes how it would naturally enjoy advantage in an environment of r-selection. To any reasonable reader's eye, it will be impossible to deny the relation between the well documented r/K Selection Theory, the well documented natures of political ideologues, and the substantial scientific evidence for their clear linkage biologically.

In nature, populations can exist as almost solely r-selected organisms, almost solely K-selected organisms, or as a bifurcated population, with sub-populations of each psychology to varying degrees. We maintain that this r/K bifurcation in humans likely has its earliest origins in our worldwide migration. For humans, a critical mutation was the loss of body hair, which allowed us to function well in the heat of an African day. This allowed us access to furred prey which was more adapted to the cold of the African night. During the day as we hunted, our furry prey was unable to flee or resist our predation, due to its inability to move about in the heat. As we pursued such prey, it would quickly experience heat stroke due to its warm fur coat, allowing us to kill it and acquire its meat with ease.

10

As time went on and we enjoyed this free resource availability, our populations multiplied. As they did, resources became diminished relative to population levels, competition began, and the environment turned K-selective. One group of humans stayed put, formed groups, and battled for the limited resources remaining in their territory. In return, they experienced the selective pressure of a K-selective environment. As a result, they evolved our tendencies towards competitiveness/aggression/protection, monogamy, high investment parenting, and sexual chastity until monogamous maturity. They also evolved an intense loyalty to in-group, and a preference for familiarity.

Another group fled the violence, and landed in a new untapped, uninhabited environment, filled with freely available resources. As this new environment became competitive, the descendants of these migrators fled again. This evolved into a strategy of avoiding competition by fleeing to a new environment of freely available resources. This group became the r-selected cohort of our species, prone to docility and anticompetitiveness, promiscuity, low-investment parenting, and early age at first intercourse. They also evolved further traits to motivate their exodus, such as reduced loyalty to in-group, and preferences for change and novel environments. (Even today, the gene associated with liberalism/leftism is found to be associated with both novelty-seeking and migration.)

Over time, we colonized the globe, as these migrators spread out and multiplied with the ferocity of an r-selected, invasive species. Closely behind them, as each new environment turned competitive due to overpopulation, would follow the K-selected psychology, which would then quickly advance the evolution and adaptation of these new populations. As time went on and populations grew established, variable resource availability in the environment likely began to favor individuals who could adapt their strategy on the fly, to present environmental circumstances. Now, not only were individuals innately predisposed to a strategy, they were also able to adapt their strategy to present conditions.

In this book, we will present evidence that will demonstrate that in such bifurcated populations in nature, where different strategies live side by side, the r-selected males adopt non-threatening, feminine appearances as a means of conflict and competition avoidance. Meanwhile their K-selected counterparts exhibit large, macho displays of aggression, as a means of promoting the conflict and competition they so readily engage in. In such populations, the feminine, r-selected, male individuals are wholly pacifistic and violence averse, even as their masculine K-selected counterparts fight violently, just feet away.

We will go on to examine how this K-selected/r-selected competitor/anticompetitor model of evolution has evolved within humans. We will first examine how the primitive r/K urges have been modified by group selection processes, how this group selection model molded our modern sense of morality and fair play, and how all of this has produced our modern political ideologies. We will even explain why both psychologies exist within our species together, and why our species has not evolved to exhibit solely one or the other.

We will then lay out all of the evidence which presently supports this theory. We will begin by citing examples of how these behavioral models in other species mirror those of our human ideologues. We will go on to examine research into the brain structures of ideologues, and show how the brain structures involved in ideology govern exactly the same traits that r/K Selection Theory governs. We will even examine experiments in monkeys in which ideology-related brain structures were damaged, and show how the monkeys then adopted every facet of the r-selected organism's behavioral tendencies, from docility, to hyper-sexuality, to promiscuity, to the adoption of low-investment child-rearing strategies.

We will go on to study the genetic origins of political ideology, and show how a gene involved in ideological predisposition codes for a neurotransmitter receptor which is involved in both, r/K psychological drives and the function of brain structures associated with ideologies. We will even show that the liberal-associated form of this gene is found in large numbers in migratory populations, and associated with an r-selected reproductive strategy in humans. We will examine research in the social sciences, and show how the psychological traits of ideologues correlate with documented human r-type and K-type psychologies. We will examine how early childhood experiences likely modify the adoption of r/K strategies in both humans and animals, and how this mechanism is related to the same gene that is associated with the adoption of a political ideology. We will even examine a pathogen which alters the function of the signaling system produced by the "political" gene, and show how this pathogen's disruption of this signaling system, and its physical alteration of the associated ideology-related brain

12

structures, produces many of the traits of both, the r-strategist and the modern liberal.

We will finally discuss how this analysis can explain many of the more subtle aspects of our modern political battles. We will show how evolution has not yet managed to catch up with the more modern selection pressures of today, such as birth control, democracy, and modern governance. We will even show how this theory may explain some important historical events in our species' history. By briefly examining the periods preceding historical events in the context of r or K-type selection pressures, we will show how the imposition of either r or K-selection on a populace has altered the psychology of entire populations, and thus altered the course of history - sometimes just one generation hence. Finally, we will examine what all of this may mean for the future of our species' evolution, as well as what this evolutionary model may tell us about future historical events yet to come.

r/K Theory has immense power due to it's veracity, as will be demonstrated once it is taught in politics courses in schools and colleges. When exposed to it, youth are subtly forced to identify, either with loyal, courageous, K-selected wolves, or with cowardly, selfish rabbits. Once exposed to that meme, then everywhere they look, every issue they are confronted with, will be seen through the prism of rabbits and wolves. Nobody will want to see themselves as a lowly rabbit, living just for themselves and their basest urges. Everyone will want to be part of the wolf pack, evincing nobility, loyalty, and greatness with every issue.

Once they identify with the K-strategy, that will affect their perceptions of themselves - and that will affect their decisions and behaviors in the future. Catch youth early enough and the truth is a powerful vaccine to the lies and dishonesty of leftism. Then every leftist lie becomes but a booster shot, further strengthening their immunity.

In short, the story of r/K Theory is not just an exposition on the truth of what is. It is also a force. If it can be spread widely enough among individuals that it has to be taught to everyone by our institutions, it will change the course of our history and our political battles.

But for that we will need the reader's help in telling others about it, because neither the media, nor the political establishment, nor academia are going to help spread this work. When you finish this book, your mind will be blown. From the explanatory and predictive power, to the amount of evidence supporting it, you will never see politics the same. Others in the heights of the political, academic, and media establishments have already seen this and had their minds blown as well. But despite how it blew their minds, you will never see it in conservative magazines until everyone already knows of it. You won't learn about it in political science courses. Nor will conservative radio broach it, until everyone already knows. Only the conservative grassroots, in its entirety, sharing this amongst themselves, can force it into those venues. Academia and the conservative establishment's refusal to even discuss r/K Theory, years after its introduction, despite its mind-blowing nature, itself speaks to this idea's immense power. Everyone in the know fears it.

Everyone in politics wants this idea to die, because this idea will take control of the political battle if it spreads. Only if the entire public hears of r/K Theory from friends and family will the establishment and academia break down and mention it, to avoid seeming out of touch and ignorant. This book is the first step in that process. You, helping to spread r/K Theory by telling others about it, will be the vitally important second step. You can spread r/K Theory, because without you, all of its power and mind-blowing greatness means nothing. It needs you.

Unfortunately, the next few chapters this book will be somewhat basic and repetitive, especially in light of your having read the overall theory of this book already. This is necessary, since this book must serve as the intellectual foundation of this concept. For that reason, it is first necessary to define ideology itself, as the literature defines it, define r/K Theory in the literature, compare them, and examine challenges to the idea that specialists in the fields might raise. If you have even a passing interest in politics, you may find yourself wondering, *"Why are we wasting time on this?"* You will be correct. None of this is necessary for the layman to waste time on, so if you do not specialize in Political Ideology or the study of Life History and Reproductive Strategies, you may safely skip ahead to chapter six, and you will not miss much.

This research has the power to indelibly alter our populace's view of our political debate. It is our fervent hope that by the end of this book, history, politics, and the structure of your government will appear much different to you. If so, for the good of our civilization, please help share this new perspective with others, by sharing this theory with them.

Knowledge is power, but only if it can become widely known.

Chapter Two

*Political Ideology Defined*_____

There has been considerable energy devoted to defining political ideology. Absent an understanding of the biological origins of ideology, researchers have generally accumulated observations and analyses of partisans on each side of the spectrum. This has been an attempt to characterize what positions ideologues take on issues, in the hopes some underlying theme might spontaneously emerge from the information, explaining the logical or psychological associations between various issue positions.

The accuracy of such studies has been frequently questioned by ideologues, who have often leveled accusations of unconscious bias at the researchers. Some have indicated that leftward inclinations on the part of researchers have led to conservatism being pathologized as some sort of disease of thought. As a result, the studies imply that conservatism should only be handled in an intellectual glovebox by appropriately vaccinated liberal intellectuals.

If we are to undertake this work, however, it pays to examine what these researchers have asserted. Even if biased in presentation, these analyses will offer an independent assertion of an issue position's association with an ideology. Indeed, even in cases where clearly biased, such as Altemeyer's work, the very fact that the (left-wing) researcher focuses on some issue as a delineation (for example, traditional marriage as defined by God vs. non-traditional, less restrictive sexual roles), indicates that an ideologue from the opposite point of view perceives such a perceptual difference as significant. Often they will have even amassed some quantity of data in support of such. That is significant in and of itself, regardless of any questions regarding the research. So if one wishes to examine ideology in any meaningful way, this prior art will have to serve our purposes here well enough.

In general, political ideology is perceived to exist on a spectrum. On the right of the spectrum is a group that today is referred to in America as conservative, and which advocates on behalf of the political ideology known as conservatism. On the left is a group which advocates for exactly the opposite social and political order. Within America members of this group are most often referred to as liberals and the ideology they espouse is called liberalism.

Throughout the world and in the United States particularly, each of these political movements would appear to have randomly aggregated many different positions on many different, seemingly unrelated issues, with each position almost completely opposite to the other philosophy's position. Conservatives have been noted as favoring private gun ownership, favoring war in response to threat, desiring low taxes and smaller government, desiring an environment where individuals accrue unequal rewards based on unequal ability, and they seek a more sexually restricted society revolving around the traditional monogamous heterosexual marriage and family.[2, 3, 4, 5] In issues of governmental authority, conservatives generally place emphasis on the freedom of the individual over the guaranteed well being of every individual citizen, they demand loyalty to a nation's authority, and in issues of personal behavior, sexuality, and morality, they emphasize the need for those in society to abide by certain behavioral rules.

Conversely, liberals tend to favor stricter restrictions on the bearing of arms, favor appeasement and negotiation in matters of conflict, favor higher taxes on the wealthy and more generous social programs to redistribute wealth, and favor a more sexually liberated society, where individuals sexually assort as they please, even in traditionally unusual sexual unions. In matters of governmental authority, they place emphasis on the need for government to provide for the safety and security of each citizen over the freedom of the individual, while in issues of personal behavior and morality they emphasize a freer, less restrictive society.

The panoply of issues which divide the two ideologies, though related by political inclination, have seemed unrelated psychologically, and unable to be characterized as deriving from any single base urge. A desire for freedom would predict a conservative's desire to support concealed carry of firearms for personal defense or their desire to limit governmental authority. Yet it would not predict their desire to see a more conformist, socially conservative society, whose behavior is restricted so as to abide by socially conservative mores and values with respect to sexuality, morality, and family structure. Nor would it account

16

for the conservative's desire that others abide by the group's authority, while engaging in ethnocentric competitions with opposing groups of individuals.

A desire for freedom would predict a liberal's desire to see citizens free to engage in all manner of sexual conduct between consenting adults and the assiduous safeguarding of all individuals against any deleterious effects from discrimination or competitive resource denial. Yet it would not predict the liberal's desire for higher personal income taxes for the wealthy, or restrictions on firearms ownership and carry. Religious affiliation also apparently fails to merit consideration as a psychological delineation, given the relatively common agnostic or atheistic conservative, or the religious liberal.

Each side of the political divide would seem to have its own unique perception of ideal human behavior, restricted in certain areas, liberated in others, and each exactly the opposite of the ideal espoused by its contrary ideology. To date, no single underlying motive force has been perceived which might account for the aggregation of these diverse positions on seemingly unrelated issues.

This theory will explain, from an impartial, non-partisan, biological perspective, why such a psychological bifurcation would inevitably develop within our society. It will also explain why each specific issue position should coalesce as it does with its complementary issue positions within each political ideology.

Next we will examine r/K selection theory in greater detail. Then we will show where these psychological drives exist in other species. We will then go on to explain how it would be inevitable that on attaining a sufficient level of evolutionary advancement, two political philosophies would inevitably develop within our species, and they would appear exactly as these two ideologies do.

This information will produce the inevitable conclusion that the psychology underlying each political ideology is an evolutionarily imbued behavioral program. Each program is designed to lead the individual who holds it to pursue a specific behavioral strategy that is designed to confer maximal survival advantage on them, in a specific environment.

17

Chapter Three

r/K Selection Theory

No individual can truly understand the intellectual battles that occur between political ideologies without understanding the study of r/K Selection Theory within Evolutionary Biology.

It has long been noted in the study of Evolutionary Biology that a species will adapt its reproductive strategy to the selective pressures placed on it by its environment. Out of the study of Evolutionary Biology, two main forms of reproductive strategies emerged, and the study of them has been termed r/K Selection Theory.[6, 7]

It must be noted that r/K Selection Theory has of late been supplanted by more case-specific theories within the study of reproductive strategies and life history traits (indeed the whole field of study of Life History traits has become an immensely complex discipline).[8] This has been due to the necessity of addressing differences between competing selective pressures, and their unique effects within each unique population and environment.

For example, diminished age at mortality, free resource availability, environmental instability, diminished population density, and the degree to which competitive stresses are absent within a species may all function as r-selective stresses. All such pressures will usually favor increasing reproductive rates. However, it is possible that unique factors may change this. If population densities are diminished due to predation, this will likely speak to an r-type strategy. However, if population densities are diminished due to resource shortage, this may speak to a more K-selective stress. If a species is preyed on by a predator whose predation is random in its application, this will likely produce an r-stress. However, if the predation favors some form of complex, energy-intensive adaptation, this may produce a K-strategy. Likewise, these pressures may all differently affect such specific factors of reproductive strategy as brood size, mating strategy, or sex-specific parental investments.

Additionally, other pressures may affect a specific species' tendency to adopt a purely r-type or K-type strategy further eroding the utility of a one size fits all theory which tries to pigeon-hole all reproductive strategies into the relatively simplistic r/K paradigm. So although r/K may not be a useful one-size-fits-all paradigm for every species, specific aspects of a reproductive strategy can still be characterized as r or K, based on their purpose.

Regardless, r/K Selection Theory is still a useful, well established heuristic, commonly used within the study of life history traits, reproductive strategies, and even in the field of human behavioral ecology.[9] It is for that reason that we use it here to describe the different behavioral strategies which are employed by humans in interpersonal interactions. Although its utility within biology may have grown limited, within our theory, the r/K paradigm is perfect for our purposes. This is because, as we will show, the two main ideologies each embody relatively pure forms of their respective r or K-selected reproductive strategy.

For the purposes of our thesis, we will now define the most relevant aspects of the theory here.

r/K selection theory draws its name from the terms r and K, which are variables used in many different algebraic formulas designed to characterize population dynamics (how population numbers will change over time). The variable r references maximal reproductive rate per individual, while the variable K represents the carrying capacity of the environment in these equations.

One example of this is the following equation, which attempts to mathematically describe how a population will balance its size based on maximal reproduction rates, and the limits of the environmental resources available to support a population.

$$\frac{dP}{dt} = rP \left(1 - \frac{P}{K}\right)$$

In this equation, P represents the population size, r represents the maximum reproductive rate per individual, and K represents the carrying capacity of the environment. The small "d"s can be read as referencing the change which will occur in the variable it precedes.

In other words, dP/dt is just the change in population per change in time. rP represents the maximal reproduction possible per individual (r) multiplied by the total number of individuals (P). That product will give you the maximum number of offspring produced by the population under ideal conditions.

(1-P/K) represents the real population number P, divided by the maximum population the environment can support, K, all subtracted from the number one. It is a factor designed to replicate how an environment of limited resources would act to kill off the excess organisms produced, beyond that which the environment can support.

As you can see, if the population is equal to the carrying capacity of the environment (P = K), the last part of the equation (1-P/K) will become (1-(1/1)) which equals zero. That zero, when multiplied by rP, will give a change in population of zero. Thus population growth will equal zero, regardless of how many offspring a species can produce. This is as would be expected of a population which did not have sufficient environmental resources to expand.

If there is room to grow into an environment, P will be less than K. That fraction, subtracted from the number one will produce a positive fraction. As a result, the population's maximal potential growth (rP) will be multiplied by a fractional sum greater than zero, and the resulting figure will represent the maximal growth rate of the population, moderated by a fraction representing the limits of its environment. In such a case, the population will gradually spread into its environment's full carrying capacity over time, until P is eventually equal to K.

Research has found that populations over a certain density often will tend to exhibit either a low (P/K) ratio (ie. exist well below the carrying capacity of their environment), combined with a high r (high maximal reproductive rate), or a low r (maximal reproductive rate, combined with a high (P/K) ratio (ie. exist at or near the carrying capacity of their environment, but reproduce slowly).

In other words, a population will either exist in numbers which are a fraction of what its environment could support, and it will multiply as rapidly as possible to try and fill the void, or a population will hover near the carrying capacity of its environment, and reproduce very slowly.

Each of these two strategies is recognized as a unique, evolved reproductive strategy. Each strategy is designed to help that species which adopts it, to best use the environmental resources available for reproduction, and best confront the unique environmental circumstances which face it. These two strategies have been labeled with the shorthand of r and K strategies, based on one's use of a large maximal reproductive rate (r), and the other's maintenance of a population at or near the carrying capacity of its environment (K). They are referred to respectively, as an r-selected Reproductive Strategy and a K-selected Reproductive Strategy, and those who follow them are referred to as r-strategists and K-strategists.

An r-selected species is one whose members have been selected for their exhibition of a large r, or high maximal reproductive rate. r-selected organisms will adopt a high r as a means of exploiting an environment which freely offers a surplus of resources to all individuals. This circumstance most commonly presents in response to a high relatively unselective mortality, such as aggressive predation. This predation reduces the population well below the carrying capacity of the environment. As a result of this mortality, the total resources available to the population will be split among fewer individuals, increasing the resources available to each.

Due to this surplus in per-capita resources, each individual will not need to fight or compete to acquire some of the copious resources. Here, an aggressive, competitive disposition becomes disadvantageous. Individuals, who fight and compete, will acquire the same level of resources as those who flee such dangers, since resources are everywhere. However the aggressive specimen will shoulder a risk which will over time, prove disadvantageous and cull his ranks. As a result, in this environment relative fitness is not a necessary requirement, nor is aggression or competitiveness advantageous. Here, Darwinian success will be based primarily on avoiding danger while out-reproducing peers with large numbers of offspring, each of which simply meets the base criteria of being able to reproduce quickly themselves.

As a species is exposed to these conditions, individuals will also be best served by mating as often as possible, with as many different mates as possible, beginning as early as possible in life. To mature later, and wait to reproduce, is to risk being killed before reproducing, and by extension, to fail from a Darwinian perspective. To mate rarely, or with a single mate, is to be out-reproduced by faster-multiplying peers, and simultaneously risk that one's few offspring themselves may fail to reproduce. (Promiscuity also offers advantages with regards to producing diverse offspring, referred to as risk-spreading/bet-hedging.) This environment will also favor lower-investment single-parenting, as a way of maximizing offspring production, by minimizing the rearing effort invested per-offspring.

Finally, since r-selected organisms tend to avoid direct competition for resources, any more advanced group competitions will tend to not arise within their populations. As a result, r-strategists generally will not exhibit any sort of group-centric, pack mentality or loyalty to in-group. Similarly, they will also not exhibit perceptions of in-group or out-group.

Under r-selection, those offspring who contribute to the next generation in the largest numbers will do so by exaggerating these qualities as much as possible. As time goes on, and a species is exposed to r-selection pressures, these traits will become ever more exaggerated, and ever more prevalent within the species.

Of greatest import to our treatise here, r-selected organisms will exhibit a psychology that is programmed with five primary traits. They will be driven to avoid all competitions and conflicts, and to be as comfortable as possible within an environment devoid of any intra-species competitive stresses. They will be programmed to mate promiscuously, as early in life as possible, as often as possible, and with as many mates as possible. The r-psychology will be programmed to embrace low-investment child-rearing, such as single parenting, and lack concern for the competitiveness of the children reared under such schemes. Such a psychology will also exhibit a simultaneous tolerance for early sexualization of offspring. Finally, it will also exhibit a reduced perception of in-group and out-group, as well as a reduced perception of any conflict between such groups.

A good example of this strategy in nature is the innate psychology exhibited by the rabbit, which exists in fields of grass it will never fully consume. Rabbits are docile, prone to flee from danger, they mate promiscuously, mothers raise offspring alone, they lack any sexual mores, and they exhibit no loyalty or interpersonal bonds with peers. A highly r-selected species, rabbits have evolved to exhibit all of the r-traits strongly, and exhibit little flexibility in their expression. As such, the rabbit is perfectly designed psychologically, to enter an environment of free resource availability and reproduce as quickly and efficiently as possible.

The K-selected species is one whose members have been culled by the limitations of the carrying capacity of their environment (K). If one's species exists at the carrying capacity of their environment, each new individual born will have to compete for a share of the limited resources to survive, killing off a less competitive specimen elsewhere within the species, even if only through a competitive denial of resources.

This selective pressure will produce a distinctly different reproductive strategy (and psychology) from the r-strategist, for whom resources are ever present, competition is disadvantageous, and fast reproduction is the path to competitive advantage.

The K-selected organism will eschew the strategy of mass producing offspring regardless of fitness. In K-selection, less fit offspring will be rapidly culled by the fierce competition for resources. In this environment, anyone who does not carefully focus on producing the fittest offspring possible will see their genes eventually die out.

Instead, K-selected organisms will favor a slower, more careful production of only the highest quality offspring possible, with the hopes that those few offspring will outcompete their peers, and in doing so, pass their genes forward to future generations.

Since to survive and reproduce, one must be capable of competing successfully, K-selected organisms will evolve a drive to compete aggressively with peers. They will also evolve to produce offspring that are as capable in competition as possible. To see one's genes persist for generations in K-selection, one must produce offspring which are as capable of carrying their genes forward, to future generations, as possible.

This produces a psychology which is fundamentally driven to engage others in aggressive, fitness-based competitions, and to seek to succeed in such competitions, acquiring the resources necessary to survive. Such a psychology will not tend to be programmed to concern itself unduly with the possibility of failures which occur in the competition. Rather, failure will be viewed (if it even is) as a consequence of life, and a motivator to try again.

In order to produce offspring that are as genetically fit and competitive as possible, K-selected organisms will seek to carefully assess mate-worthiness and fitness, and seek out mates that are as fit as possible. Having found the fittest mate possible, such a K-selected individual will seek to competitively monopolize their mate's fit genes through monogamy. Monogamous mating will prevent any other outside individuals from using a highly fit mate's genes to produce fitter offspring. Since the competition is to see one's offspring succeed, and carry the familial genes forward, monogamy is a potent advantage for one's offspring, if one finds a highly fit mate.

K-selected organisms will also seek to engage in high-investment child-rearing, where both parents help provision and raise offspring. In this way, K-selected organisms protect their immature offspring from the fiercely competitive environment, while carefully nurturing them, and helping them to develop their competitive abilities as much as possible. Here, single parenting may result in offspring enduring the disadvantages of malnutrition, poor development, and lack of protection.

Offspring will also be discouraged from early mating, so that they may attain their maximal level of fitness and mate-value, before seeking to acquire the fittest mate they can, for their own monogamous relationship. Since the goal is to produce as genetically competent an offspring as possible, those who wait to pair bond will see their genes housed in offspring with superior genes, from superior mates, and this trait will be favored. Bonding and mating with a less genetically competent mate, when immature and less maximally attractive, will only offer a detriment which could easily be avoided by waiting.

Finally, during K-selection group competition can emerge from the individual competitions for resources (probably due to specific environmental factors favoring it, such as resource densities, benefits of territoriality, etc.).

When it is able to arise, it will arise quite simply. As K-selected individual competitions rage, at some point, some individuals group together against lone individuals, only to see the strategy rewarded with success. As time goes on, ever more sociable organisms find themselves enjoying favor. In such cases, K-selection will also tend to produce individuals who will exhibit a pack mentality, consisting of loyalty to the interests of their in-group, and a hostility towards any out-groups. As a part of this, such individuals will come to view group members as extensions of themselves, given their shared fates. This will produce strong emotional attachments to peers, which one will not tend to see in r-selected species.

Inherent to this psychology will again, be five distinct traits. Among these will be an inherently competitive psychology, more tolerant of the competitive failures of others. K-selected organisms will tend to be averse to promiscuity, and supportive of monogamy. Such individuals will also exhibit a drive to see high-investment, two-parent rearing normalized, and avoid other low-investment forms of offspring-rearing, not solely focused on the success of offspring. K-selected organisms will also seek to prevent their offspring from mating too early, and risking violence in the mating market before they are mature enough to fend for themselves. Finally, in group-centric species, there will be a deep, innate drive to exhibit loyalty to in-group, and hostility to out-groups.

The best example of this psychology in nature is the wolf. Wolves are aggressive and competitive. They are highly sexually selective and monopolize mates. They invest heavily in offspring, discourage their young from mating until maximally mature, and compete in packs, where each individual exhibits a profound emotional attachment to its pack-mates. The idea of not exhibiting loyalty to in-group, not disregarding out-group interests, or the perception that all wolves are members of the same global wolf collective would be completely unimaginable to them. As such they are perfectly designed psychologically to compete for limited resources, in an environment in which someone will lose out. They are also perfectly designed to produce offspring capable of functioning in such an environment and carrying their genes forward to future generations as well.

This strategy is highly effective for the K-selected organism because in the competitive K-selected environment, ability will determine survivability and reproduction, and therefore, Darwinian success. In K-selection, a single, highly fit offspring will easily outcompete multiple inferior offspring from another family, through the competitive denial of the limited resources available. Over time, as K-selection kills back the less competitive competition, this is the psychology which will emerge spontaneously.

Interestingly, in each case, neither the rabbit nor the wolf has any logical reason to arrive at the perceptions they carry. To the rabbit, fighting is something which should not be done. To the wolf, if you need to fight, you do it - as violently and ruthlessly as possible. To the rabbit, mating promiscuously makes sense. To the wolf, there is a different way to do things, and those who do not abide by the rules will make everyone uncomfortable. Neither thinks about any of these drives, but rather just satisfies a behavioral drive which feels right, according to their psychology.

It will be the position of this text that in humans, r-type selection pressures will primarily result from a transient plethora of resources making competition relatively unnecessary, beyond demonstrating a simple ability to mate and produce young. Here, in the resource-rich environment of r-selection, Darwinian success is defined (however temporarily) by the simple ability to produce more offspring than one's peers.

This r-type adaptation may have acquired an early advantage from our migration outward. As individuals fled competitions in overpopulated territories behind them, they landed in new, unpopulated territories. These new territories were just like those that they had fled, except the new territory was filled with untapped resources and limited competition. This r-type migrator likely developed their psychology into an actual strategy, as the new territories became more populous, and more migration became necessary for the r-type trait's persistence.

For the purposes of this text, it will also be maintained that K-type selection pressures in humans result from simple resource scarcity, and the associated need for humans to compete with each other for limited resources. For this reason, we will ignore other factors which may affect this balance in nature, such as environmental instability, early age of mortality, etc. Although these may play some role in other species, here their role is minimal, and therefore, ancillary to our thesis.

As time went on, and resource availability fluctuated, both r and K would have enjoyed periodic advantages. The r-selection of discovering freely available seashells and seafood gave way to the K-selected clashes of overpopulation, just as the boom of agriculture gave way to the bane of climate change, bad weather, and famine. As these cycles played out, this may have produced an adaptability in some individuals. Those who could optimally exploit both excess and scarcity would prove optimally adapted to an environment which contained alternating periods of both. This adaptability allowed them to adapt their strategy to the environment, so as to seize maximal advantage at any given moment. We will discuss this in greater detail later in the text.

So in summation, nature postulates that there are two optimum psychologies which will naturally arise within dense populations. Each psychology will aggregate different behavioral drives, into a cohesive strategy, custom designed for its respective environment.

One strategy is averse to conflict and competition, promiscuous, prone to low-investment single-parent child-rearing, prone to perceive mating promiscuously as early as possible in life as normal, and lacking in any in-group-centric urges. The other strategy will be aggressive/competitive, monogamous, prone to two-parent rearing, prone to later age of sexualization of young, and in more advanced specimens, strongly group-centric and group-competitive.

The r or K-nature of individuals within a population will exist on a continuum, at each end of which will lay slightly more r and K oriented strategies. The variation in strategies will depend on how extreme and long-lasting the r or K-selecting conditions that the population was exposed to were, over time. Some species will overwhelmingly adopt r-type strategies, while others will overwhelmingly adopt more K-type natures, depending on environmental conditions. Other species may harbor a balance of each strategy, due to each finding a niche within the species which allows for its perpetuation.

The overall nature of the species will be determined by the balance of strategies exhibited by the individuals within it. As environmental conditions change, Darwinian selection can act on a population, and each strategy's prevalence may wax and wane in response. This will both, change the nature of the species, and help the species to adapt to its changing environment, by allowing it to effortlessly slip into a Darwinian reproductive strategy which is customized to its environment. Since most species have experienced fairly consistent environmental conditions over their histories, most do not exhibit much change in their natures over time. However in humans, this may work somewhat differently, as we will show.

Chapter Four

*A Further Note on r/K Theory*_____

Some will take issue with the characterizations of r/K Theory within this work, or its use to describe human reproductive behaviors. Some may try to make the case that r and K are separated by vast gulfs of behavioral differences and reproductive rates not seen in humans. Humans are all K, or r/K only applies to species, or in nature r and K traits can mix, are all common refrains. Others will assert that r/K, as previously characterized, is almost solely genetic in origin. Thus, presumably, they are asserting it would be impossible for any organism to eventually evolve an adaptability in strategy based on environmental conditions.

r and K have long been, both variable and relative. Among r-strategists one will find both mice and oysters. There are vast differences between the two in parental investment, numbers of offspring, and even direct, competitive aggression. Although it is tempting to use terms like differential or relative in this text to describe such relative variations, that would be confusing, and only render a fascinatingly simple insight obtuse to the layman. This is after all, a political book offering a window into Evolutionary Biology, and not vice versa. The field we are trying to change perceptions in is Political Science.

If one human strategy accepts single-parent rearing as normal, and one favors two-parent rearing in a family, if one favors abstinence until monogamy, and the other favors promiscuity, if one is conflict-prone, and one is conflict-averse, it is easier and clearer to simply describe them using the analogous terms r and K, while noting somewhere (here), that the difference is relative. These terms are used to simplify the description of aggregated behaviors and psychologies which served reproductive purposes in our species' evolutionary past. If viewed in that context, they will serve us well here.

In debating with others, it seems that some, of limited knowledge in the art, may try to imply that r/K Theory has somehow fallen out of favor of late, or even been rendered obsolete, and that impacts this work.

31

They may often cite the current research focus on the study of each species' specific life history traits and reproductive strategies.

First, to paraphrase Mark Twain, r/K's death has been greatly exaggerated. r/K was challenged decades ago, shortly after it was first proposed, as all new theories are likely to be. Of course you can find a citation from several decades ago saying it is not a legitimate area of inquiry, and should be abandoned.

r/K has survived the challenges quite well, and today is included in the most respected of current textbooks,[10] and taught in most, if not all, major university biology programs. I personally studied it decades after it was characterized, and there was no debate over it in class. It is even still actively published on and referenced in respected journals,[11] even in the field of human behavior. One study we cite from 2010[12] will note within it, that a gene associated with the formation of a liberal ideology in humans, produces behaviors which would offer advantage under conditions favoring an r-strategy. It is still used, because it is an efficient shorthand for describing the different purposes of reproductive strategies - ie. producing quality in offspring or producing quantity of offspring. r-strategists seek the latter, but sometimes nature will make the former necessary.

The intensity of interest in r/K has passed on as the concept has matured. Its broad generalizations about the purposes of various behaviors, has given way to characterizing the exact patterns of life history traits and reproductive strategies for individual species. Where r/K offered a broad brush to grossly describe what you would see as you examined most species, that focus has now shifted to settling down, and characterizing how each trait is adaptive in each individual circumstance. r/K is not gone however, or rejected. It is still taught to every student studying biology because of the solid foundational understanding of reproductive behavior that it offers. Just as "f = ma" in physics is not rendered incorrect by friction, so too is r/K not rendered incorrect by the fact some species have special environment circumstances which need to be described to gain a fuller picture of why they adopt the exact traits they adopt.

Nevertheless, whether one wishes to reference r/K when examining this work, or whether one wishes to characterize the specific differences in behavioral and environmental preferences between liberals

32

and conservatives as differences in life history traits and reproductive strategies, it is of no matter. The psychological differences, their reproductive significance, and their adaptation to specific environments, is what is truly of interest in this work, far more than any r/K theoretical framework used to present them. If one looks closely however, they will note that every r-trait and every K-trait have separated cleanly in humans, creating two ideological/behavioral poles in our populations. That, in and of itself, is noteworthy and makes the r/K heuristic particularly useful in describing this complex area to the novice in Evolutionary Biology. That this heuristic serves to preserve the copy fidelity of this r/K political meme, as it moves out into the population, only heightens its value in explaining these concepts.

Also, it is worth noting, many basic texts will portray the r-strategy as more of a defensive reproductive strategy. It is often said to be designed to counteract the high mortality foisted on any population which is confronted with an unstable environment. Under this theory, an organism, beset by high mortality, produces numerous offspring, in a defensive attempt to overcome the likelihood that many of their offspring will die. This is an incomplete portrayal.

It must be recognized that the r-strategy is actually a strategy designed to exploit a competition-free environment of relatively limitless resources. Such an environment commonly follows instability and mortality, but it can exist absent such harshness as well.

After a period of high mortality, one will find an environment where resources are more freely available to the remaining individuals. As a result, there is reduced competition necessary to acquire them, because the population will have dropped well below the carrying capacity of the environment. As a result, in such an environment, evolving some complex competitive advantage over peers is a waste of energy, as there is no competition for resources.

Within that uncompetitive environment, quantity of offspring will beat quality of offspring in the Darwinian battle to dominate a species numerically. Thus, it is vital to recognize that r-selection does not require instability or mortality. These are just the means by which nature provides periods of relatively limitless resources to individuals (within a world of inherently limited resources). It should be understood, the r-strategy is really an adaptation to exploit the absence of competition for resources that this instability and mortality produces. r-selection does not require mortality or instability in its environment to occur.

Many bacteria (Bacillus Calmette-Guérin comes to mind, as do many lab strains of E. coli), will devolve their genome to shed unneeded traits once they are placed within an environment of limitless resources. Once availed of free nutrients, any competitions to survive, or any related selective pressures, are removed. As a result, these domesticated bacteria will adapt to minimize all non-reproductive energy expenditures, so that they may focus all of their energy on reproducing faster.

In such a case, that bacterium is being exposed to r-selective pressures, not through placement in an unstable environment of high mortality, but rather through placement within an ideal environment of limitless resources and no competitive selective pressure. That is an environment one could accurately term as being exceedingly stable, and even devoid of significant mortality.

In such an environment, those few cells which evolve to minimize their non-reproductive energy expenditures, and focus all of their energy on reproduction, will reproduce faster than their peers and will gradually come to dominate the population. As a result one will see a shift in the reproductive strategy of the individuals within the population. They will adapt to maximize the maximal reproductive rate (r) of their line.

By contrast, the more complex, original, wild-type strain of Mycobacterium bovis (from which Bacillus Calmette-Guérin evolved) had developed a high degree of complexity within the hostile and unstable environment of a living host. This strain was confronted with a relentless immune assault It was forced to evolve complex adaptations to allow it to maintain its presence within the host, as well as a myriad of means by which to counter the immune attacks it faced.

Within the host, undoubtedly some individual bacteria attempted to seek reproductive shortcuts to speed their reproduction, at the expense of the complex adaptations which provided them with the ability to persist within a host. They were rapidly culled by the host environment. Those bacteria which persisted (and came to define the wild-type strain), were those microbes who outcompeted their peers in the competition to subvert host defenses, and maintain their presence within the host environment. Here, we see an unarguably harsh and unstable environment of mortality, and yet it yields an undeniable K-selection pressure, favoring advancement and adaptation over reproduction. Due to the presence of competition with peers (even if indirect), and a harsh environment with copious mortality, we see a bacteria shun enlarging its r in favor of producing a myriad of complex adaptations which take time and energy to produce and maintain.

It is for this reason that this work maintains that the main environmental selection pressure which produces r-selection is actually an absence of the need to compete with peers (either directly or indirectly), or demonstrate any form of relative fitness or ability to persist within its environment. This may occur under conditions of rampant, unselective mortality, or merely an environment of safety combined with copious quantities of freely available resources, and the associated absence of peer on peer competition which this produces.

Conversely, K-selection is not produced by environmental stability (though that can produce it, if the population grows until resources are limited). Rather K-selection is produced by the presence of a competitive stress which aggressively favors the survival and reproduction of only the more advanced and competitive individuals with more complex, energy-consuming adaptations. Only when an environment favors complex, energy-expending adaptations can the organism which exhibits them out-compete the more blindly fecund r-strategists within their ranks.

Such conditions may result from simple resource scarcity and the resultant peer competition, or an environment with a high amount of selective mortality favoring the reproduction of those individuals who are substantially fitter than their peers.

r-selection is literally about producing quantity over quality, in an environment where quality offers no advantage. In such an environment, the effort to produce quality is actually a disadvantage statistically, due to the absence of competitive stresses which would favor it, and the presence of the real numerical advantages of copious reproduction that will be seized by other individuals.

In response to such r-selecting circumstances, r-selection will gradually degrade all of a population's complex adaptations, so as to maximize r. In so doing, it will relentlessly devolve a species' greatness and abilities.

Here, within this work, this concept will be crucial to understanding politics, to understanding many events within our history, and most importantly, to understanding what this theory tells us about what the future holds for our species and our civilization.

Chapter Five

The Relationship Between Ideology and r/K Selection Theory

Clearly, if one performs a cursory examination of political ideologies and the psychological traits associated with r/K Selection Theory, one will be struck by the similarities. Some research has even touched on the similarities between the environments which ideologues are psychologically designed to confront, and the conditions which produce r and K-selection, though the authors did not seem to notice the specific connection to r/K Selection Theory.[13]

The r-selected organism is designed to function in an environment where merit-based competition is disadvantageous. Such an organism is psychologically designed to presume that resources will be freely available to all in unlimited quantities. They are also predisposed to accept promiscuity, will be more tolerant of children being exposed to sex at as early an age as possible, and they will either tolerate or embrace low-investment child-rearing, such as single parenting. Finally, since they exhibit a reduced drive to compete, r-selected organisms tend not to form groups for the purpose of group competition with others. As a result, r-selected organisms tend to lack any perception of in-group or out-group, and tend not to exhibit traits such as loyalty to in-group, or hostility to out-group. This is much more of an individualistic, hedonistic psychology.

Likewise, liberal policy is generally averse to all free, merit-based competitions among men, from capitalism to war. It operates with a presumption that resources are freely available in quantities that should allow all to enjoy a similar lifestyle equally, even using the catchphrases "Equality" and "Inequality."

Liberals seem to operate with an innate perception that scarcity of resources is not due to a lack of resources, but rather is due to over-consumption by "greedy," over-consuming individuals. Any implication that resources are naturally scarce, that interpersonal competitions for resources should be allowed, or that their outcomes should have reproductive repercussions is derided with the term "Social Darwinism." This is a subconscious reference to the liberal's abhorrence of the competitive, K-selected, Darwinian environment that naturally occurs within any population that has reached the carrying capacity of its environment.

Liberalism is also tolerant of promiscuity, and tolerant of early exposure of children to sexual behavior and information (even proposing early sexual education of children as young as five). Liberals are also embracing of such low-investment child-rearing strategies as single parenting, or other unconventional (ie. non-K-type) styles of parenting – even when they are not solely designed to produce competitive ability in the children being raised. For liberals, the emphasis is more on the right of individuals to be parents, rather than the rights of children to be raised in as optimal a fashion as possible. Liberals also tend to reject the concept of in-group or out-group, as well as the potential righteousness of any inter-group conflict that such perceptions might produce.

By contrast, the K-selected organism is designed for an environment where resources are scarce, and competition, often in groups, is merely a fact of life. For this reason, K-strategists tend to be aggressive and territorial. K-strategists favor monogamous relationships with mates, high-investment, two-parent child-rearing, and they favor children taking extended periods to mature, prior to entering the competition for mates and reproducing sexually. Those K-selected groups which tend to compete in groups will also tend to exhibit a group-centric, pack mentality, with strong emotional bonding between pack members. This will also produce loyalty to in-group, and an instinctual disregard for out-group interests.

Likewise, conservatism operates with an innate perception that resources are scarce, and that absent an effective demonstration of ability, determination, and effort, one should not expect to acquire sufficient resources to live comfortably, or reproduce. As a result, conservatism also accepts the necessity of Darwin-esque, fitness-based competitions among men. Conservatives support the concept of war's utility in conflict resolution. They support economic competitions such as capitalism. They support competitions between nations for regional hegemony, or economic dominance. They even support the ability of a citizen to engage a criminal in violent Darwinian competition with a firearm.

Conservatism also exhibits a relative intolerance for promiscuity, as well as an intolerance for the early sexualization of children, be it sex-education or simply the exposure of children to graphically sexual content in media and culture. They oppose the early onset of sexual precociousness in children, as well as any action supportive of early sexual behavior, such as the provisioning of birth-control to teenagers. Conservatives also detest low-investment styles of child-rearing, such as single-parenting, or other non-traditional rearing styles that are not designed expressly to produce highly competitive children. In many ways, the traditionalism of conservatism is really the desire to retain K-selected environmental conditions in a society which is progressing toward a more r-psychology (a phenomenon often due to a culture's success producing copious resource availability, which shunts the population's psychology towards r, as we will discuss later).

Conservatism seeks to see these behaviors replaced with a more K-type social attitude, shielding children from all sexualizing stimuli, and promoting abstinence until monogamy. Sexual behavior should solely be for the purpose of facilitating high-investment, two-parent child-rearing within a monogamous relationship. All child-rearing must be designed expressly to produce as chaste and competitive a child as possible, in an environment it terms as being infused with "Family Values."

Finally, conservatives also tend to exhibit high loyalty to in-group, and disregard for out-group interests, fostering a belligerence that seems confusing to the left. From issues of war, to international economic competition, to national sovereignty, conservatives approach the world with a jaundiced eye, always seeking to see "their own" win the competition with any outsiders.

Additionally, just as the r/K selection strategies exist on a continuum in nature, with extreme adherents on each end of the spectrum, and others spread out on the continuum somewhere in between, political ideology follows a similar pattern. Hardcore ideologues exist on both ends of the left-right political spectrum, with other individuals spread out between them as well. Just as with r/K, as you zoom out, you see two distinct primary patterns of behavior emerge, as most individuals coalesce around one ideology or the other.

Interestingly, in nature there is a third strategy of sorts, identified in r/K Theory. Though this involves delving into unsupported speculation, it is probably worth briefly examining here. r/K Theory is density dependent. That is, many of its traits require that individuals be packed closely enough together that they interact regularly (such as to either favor conflict and competition with each other, or favor avoidance of conflict and competition).

As population densities drop, and individuals encounter each other more rarely, r/K breaks down. If there are not enough resources in an area to support a densely packed group, individuals can end up roaming vast territories alone, and to them, no matter how scarce the resources, the idea of a group-centric aggression will seem illogical. If there are not enough resources to support a family within a territory, fathers may evolve to abandon mothers after mating, so as to not deplete foodstocks in the area around their offspring. They can still remain territorial, and aggressive and competitive, it is just that low population densities are known to unbind the traits of r and K, allowing them to mix more freely, as environmental conditions dictate.

It is possible that during our spread, r-strategists moved outward into similar resource-rich environments, like water spreading through the low points of a valley. As they built up in numbers, and K-Strategists began to emerge within their territory, a separate strategy may have moved outward (or up the valley wall, to use our stream analogy), colonizing harsher environments, where population densities were kept more sparse by the harshness and/or resource scarcity. Although this allowed these colonizers to escape the competition, it would also offer its own challenges.

If it occurred, this might have produced a strategy similar to the modern Libertarian, who seems to desire to live his life entirely free from the legal and social constraints normally demanded by both the left and right (both of which are means by which to compete within high population densities).

If the Libertarian psychology was designed to live in low population densities, where they ran into other's less frequently, then the idea of others, seeking behavioral or legal constraints levied on them, would seem odd and baffling. Likewise, they would have little urge to try and constrain the behaviors of others, either to force competition aversion, or make the group more cohesive and competitive. Similarly baffling to them would be the fact that others would not aspire to live the life they desire, viewing all external control and constraint by strangers as aberrant and foreign. This might also unhitch any sexual mores from their strategy, making them less prone to judge (ie. interact with) others.

It would not be surprising if many Libertarians today would relish moving to more rural areas with lower population densities, especially if that entailed fewer interactions with peers, such as governmental restrictions placed on their behavior by neighbors and countrymen. That is how in a state of nature, an imbued reproductive strategy can craft an individual's life path, and their strategy to survive and pass on their genes.

Of course, due to the nature of the low population densities they were designed for, such a Libertarian strategy would be a minority strategy within our species, numerically. This might make sense of the fact, that while Libertarianism always seems a perfect compromise in a world of left and right, it can never garner enough support to be a realistic political option. r and K are just too deeply embedded within the nature of most citizens within our populations for that battle to ever be abandoned.

Whether Libertarianism is a practical strategy today, or merely a vestigial psychology designed for environments we long ago conquered is unknown. But much like conservatism and liberalism, it is a psychology which would prove adaptive to certain environments in our past.

Returning to our narrative, the vast majority of policy positions of the two main political ideologies align closely with the psychological tendencies of the r-selected and K-selected Darwinian reproductive strategies. It should be noted that this theory is the only theory extant which would explain the nature of the unusual aggregation of specific moral and governmental policy positions inherent to the two main modern political ideologies. As a result, it is difficult to not view modern political ideology as merely an intellectual manifestation of the primitive urges which guide organisms to pursue either an r or K-selected reproductive strategy in nature.

As we continue, and examine how resource availability affects societal perceptions of the ideologies, this theory's apparent veracity will only grow.

Chapter Six

The Evolution of Competitiveness and Anticompetitiveness

As organisms find themselves forced to compete under conditions of K-selection, a quality we will refer to as K-selected competitiveness will emerge as a distinct trait within the species, as will its polar opposite, r-selected anticompetitiveness. Driven by each individual's drive to survive and procreate, it is here that these two strategies cease to be merely passively adaptive strategies by which to confront environmental circumstances, and become distinct traits, interacting with, and adapting to each other within populations.

Indeed, in many species, these two strategies would appear to exist in competition with each other. In this competition, each strategy is seeking to out-compete its opposite, to gain prominence within its population and species. In one such species, (to be described shortly), we show how a K-selected organism has evolved the competitive urge, to the point that it instinctually engages in a ritualized, fitness-based competition prior to reproduction. In other words, it is not just driven to compete to survive. It has evolved the urge to compete, for competition's sake alone.

Meanwhile, the r-selected anticompetitor in this species has evolved behavioral strategies to avoid this direct competition with the K-selected competitors. Their whole objective is to acquire mates without meeting the K-selected competitor in direct competition. To this end, they have developed instinctual deceptive behavioral ploys designed to facilitate mating, without engaging in any competitions which would test their relative fitness.

In this further evolution of the r and K-type psychologies, each psychology will see their distinct trait succeed, and advance within the population at the expense of the other trait. However, for all of their adaptations and tricks, it would appear that there is little that can alter the balance of strategies as much as a plethora of per-capita resources to attenuate competitive selection effects, or a sudden scarcity of resources

43

to enhance them. These strategies are more about persisting through conditions which do not favor their trait.

The assertion that r-selected anticompetitiveness and K-selected competitiveness (as well as the liberalism and conservatism which have evolved from them) exist as distinct traits, in Darwinian competition with each other is bound to be controversial. Inherent to this assertion is an assumption that all of the disparate behaviors inherent to these reproductive strategies, from interpersonal interactions to sexual predispositions and parenting styles, are joined into a single trait, or at least a closely grouped suite of traits which tend to travel closely together on the genome. This implies that there is perhaps some link between these differing behaviors and a single, heritable gene, or a suite of genes which likewise, travel together.

We will present evidence later that, in fact, there exists at least one gene in humans which is associated with optimism, competitiveness, aggression, promiscuity/monogamy, sex drive, high or low investment parenting strategy, and even loyalty, through its inter-relationship with an "ethnocentric" peptide. When this gene exists in a specific form it is associated with all of the K-selected versions of these traits together. When it is mutated and rendered less effective, it is associated with the exact opposite suite of behaviors.

Thus evidence indicates that the expression of the traits of K-type competitiveness and r-type anticompetitiveness are likely affected, at least in part, by allelic variation within at least one known gene. For this reason, the strategy of K-selected competitiveness and the strategy of r-selected anticompetitiveness should both be viewed as strategies for increasing the prevalence of their respective genetic alleles within a population.

K-selected competitiveness would appear to have evolved to exploit a more complex Darwinian strategy than it's opposite, r-selected anticompetitiveness. As a psychological trait controlling behavior, competitiveness can control its carrier's actions. We maintain that this trait uses this control to actively mold the genome of the individuals who carry it, so as to create a better specimen, more capable of carrying the competitive trait forth.

By driving individuals who carry the competitive trait to compete with each other in instinctual, merit-based competitions for fitness prior to mating, regardless of resource availability, competitiveness actually motivates the individuals who carry the trait to select the fittest carriers among them. These specimens are then utilized as the progenitors of the next generation. Through this process, the carriers of the competitive trait will gradually evolve to be fitter than those uncompetitive, less forcefully evolved individuals who lack the trait. The advantage this offers during times of plentiful resources is limited by comparison to the raw reproductive potential of the r-selected anticompetitor. However when resources grow scarce, and competing is necessary to survive, there will be a rapid shift in the balance of a population's strategies, as the K-selected competitors rapidly eliminate their competition through fitness-mediated denial of limited resources.

As time goes on, competitiveness would appear to become ritualized among those who carry the trait. This would often appear to occur in such a way as to maximize the effects of the competitive selections for fitness that it produces. This can be seen in examples ranging from a male peacock's bearing of an unwieldy, attention-grabbing tail to attract a female, to a Bighorn Sheep knocking heads with other Bighorns, to see who will prove to be the fittest specimen possible.

Since competitiveness will reduce the maximal reproductive rate of its carriers, it will come with a competitive disadvantage, relative to the r-type anticompetitive strategy, which can reproduce faster, but will produce less fit and capable specimens.

As long as a species' environment is such that there are not enough resources for all individuals to survive, competition with fitter K-type competitors will cull the inferior r-type anticompetitors preferentially, giving the advantage to the K-type competitor. If, however, a species' environment is prone to vacillate between resource scarcity and copious resource availability, r-selected individuals will be able to exploit the absence of competitive selection during times of plenty to reproduce quickly, and rise in numbers, relative to K-selected organisms. This will create a situation where the r-trait will generate massive diversity in traits during an r-period, only to see that diversity massively culled for adaptations during K-selection. Under such conditions, those r-strategists who best persist during the K-selection will likely have some adaptation which facilitated their persistence, and this will be added to the suite of anticompetitive traits. Such traits could range from outright deception to more complex emotional manipulation.

One of the more disturbing things that those who contemplate this will realize, is that because the r-conditions disfavor competition, it will likely not solely evolve r-individuals to avoid conflict and competition. Eventually an r-strategist will emerge who not only avoids conflict and competition, but who actively seeks to mire his peers in it, as he avoids it. By actively saddling his peers with the competitive disadvantage of conflict and competition, while avoiding it himself, he will enjoy great relative advantage, and become the de-facto model of the strategy.

We see this today, as we watch r-strategists insist on importing foreigners from less civilized parts of the world in ever greater numbers, and discourage their assimilation into our culture, as Americans. Even as radical Islamists call for jihad against the west, we are told that to bar entry to people from these regions and groups would be intolerant, and that would be deeply, morally wrong. We witnessed the same phenomenon in the fall of Rome, where the same foreign barbarians that Romans legionaries formerly fought off, were imported into the military, and eventually encouraged to occupy high office in the government.

We see this urge today in the constant attempt by r-strategists to encourage "diversity," even as they themselves seek out ever less diverse enclaves to inhabit themselves. We see it in the r-strategists who seek to own firearms themselves, or see themselves protected by armed guards, while also seeking to disarm their countrymen, and free criminals with lax sentencing. We see it in r-strategists who send our troops into battle for foreign interests, only to hamper their ability to fight with restrictive rules of engagement. We even see it in the form of r-strategists who seek to make America a multi-lingual country, where not everyone can even communicate with each other, in the same language.

No matter what the r-strategist will tell you, all of these are behavioral drives which will promote conflicts among the rest of the citizenry - conflicts which the r-strategist is designed, by their nature, to studiously avoid. It is evolutionary, and a predictable quality which you will see arise among the r-strategists, as a society descends into r.

As we examine this next chapter, we will see how an r-strategist within a primitive species can first begin to evolve to exploit a strategy using deception to get K-strategists fighting. It is a fascinating example.

46

Chapter Seven

Competitiveness and Anticompetitiveness
*The Cuttlefish Model*_____

On the ocean floor off Whyalla, on the western shores of Australia, thousands of Australian Giant Cuttlefish (Sepia apama) gather to mate every year between May and June. These fat, squid-like organisms mass by the thousands to reproduce. Large males, some as long as five feet, with long flowing tentacles, seek out the best caverns on the ocean floor to serve as egg chambers. Females, with short stubby tentacles, seek out such males, and pair with them to gain access to their egg chambers, knowing that the biggest and most impressive males hold the key to the most secure egg chambers.[14]

Over time, other large males arrive, and due to males outnumbering females by as much as 11:1, the males all begin to compete for the affections of the waiting females, in a fascinating mating ritual with several different phases. From displaying flashing and undulating patterns of color on their skin at each other, to charging each other threateningly, to actual wrestling matches, the males test each other repeatedly, to see which one will prove the fittest, and lay claim to the waiting female below.

This species was selected for this text because the Cuttlefish's skin is an amazingly complex organ, which required an amazingly intense evolutionary process to develop, much as human intelligence and physical development would also have required. For this reason, the mechanisms involved in Cuttlefish skin evolution can be viewed as being similar to the mechanisms involved in the evolution of the myriad of highly advanced, complex traits which make humans so amazing.

Within Cuttlefish skin, there is a deep layer of reflective cells. These cells, called iridophores and leucophores reflect ambient light up, through the skin cells above. Pigmented cells of various colors, called chromatophores, reside above this base reflective layer. Attached to muscles around their periphery, different cells are filled with pigments of different colors such as yellow, red, and brown. Each individual cell can be stretched flat by contracting the muscle fibers around it, so as to filter the light through its pigment. This will cause the area of the skin above the cell to adopt the color of whichever pigmented cell is stretched by the muscles surrounding it.

Alternately, these pigment cells can be allowed to contract back into small balls, removing the pigment from the light's path. Multiple cells can be stretched simultaneously, filtering the light through their combined pigments and producing almost any color imaginable, from blueish white, to bright orange, to jet black. The end result is a skin made up of millions of "pixels" of pigmented skin cells, any pixel of which can produce a myriad of colors, with each individual pixel's color and brightness under the neurological and muscular control of the Cuttlefish's brain.

The level of this control is truly astounding. In laboratories, Cuttlefish have been placed in an aquarium with a black and white checkerboard pattern on the floor, and they rapidly produce an almost matching checkerboard pattern on their skin, so when viewed from above, they appear translucent. It is unimaginable how complex their brain structures must be to control the neurons which innervate the 20-60 muscles attached to each of the pigment cells. Simply to perceive the surroundings through their eyes, and process it into raw data amenable to reproduction on their skin, would require immense brain power, but to control each of the 130,000 pigment cells (each with 20-60 individual muscles attached to them) per square inch of skin (on a five foot long cuttlefish, mind you), and to match what they see with their skin's pattern is unfathomable.

During the mating ritual they engage in, males flash aggressive "masculine" color patterns at each other, using vividly colored, undulating tiger-striped patterns that appear to ride over their skin, like waves traveling on the water's surface. Males have evolved to be intimidated by such patterns if they are impressive enough, and often this simple show is enough to settle the competition. When it is not, charging each other, or even physical wrestling matches are used to settle the issue of whom the female below will mate with.

To our human eye, this is merely a mating ritual. In other words it is something done to secure a mate. In truth, this ritual, as well as the fear, daring, and other emotions which drive it, is all part of a mechanism these organisms evolved. The purpose of this evolved mechanism was to increase the speed with which the members of their species evolved.

Cuttlefish depend on their skin to camouflage them. The world is a dangerous place for a Cuttlefish. They are preyed on by dolphins, seals, fish, and even other Cuttlefish, at times. Lacking a shell, or other protective mechanism, their best defense is to adopt the appearance of their surroundings, and render themselves invisible to their predators.

These Cuttlefish, by competing with each other and using these flashing patterns, are actually testing each other, and enhancing their species' development of this ability. These males are seeing who has the greatest degree of neurological control over their skin patterns, and the most ability to produce vivid and controlled patterns of color. They are seeing if any individual has a mutational defect which has rendered an iridophore, chromatophore, or a leukophore non-functional, and should therefore be prevented from breeding.

Of course, if one Cuttlefish has secured that golden ring of nature, a mutation which allows him to actually improve the ability of the species to control the colors on their skin, he will easily defeat the other males in this stage of competition. Males have evolved a fear of such vibrant displays, because such a fear aided the functionality of these competitions, and enhanced the evolutionary advancement which they produce. Cuttlefish skin is as amazingly evolved as it is, because males compete in every breeding cycle, to see whose skin is the most impressive, and those who lose such competitions are programmed to accept their fate, so that those who won might create the next generation in their magnificent image.

Having resolved who has the requisite chameleon-like skills, the remaining males then compete by charging each other, and testing their daring and courage. The final competition consists of fighting, testing each other's physical strength, muscular endurance, and vitality. The winner then acquires the right to pair with the waiting female, and pass his genes forward to future generations.

In short, the Cuttlefish's competitive mating battle is designed to improve the next generation's ability to deal with the rigors of a harsh underwater world, filled with predatory organisms which kill Cuttlefish.

These mating rituals evolved because over the eons, Cuttlefish that did not engage in them gradually failed to compete with the groups that did. The marvelous displays we see today, are what is left of the species after millions of years of natural selection preferentially killed those groups which failed to compete in such competitions and subsequently, failed to evolve fast enough. We shall refer to those K-selected individuals within the species who are driven to embrace such competitions as "competitors."

(Note, we will discuss later how the trait of competitiveness is not altruistic. For now, understand that where competitors compete in K-selected environments, although an individual may sacrifice his own personal reproductive advantage, the trait of competitiveness (and the genetic allele(s) underlying it) does not sacrifice its own survival or advantage. Rather, competitiveness selfishly arranges the parentage of future competitors, such that the carriers of the trait will be as fit as possible.)

Now here is where this subject becomes interesting. Occasionally, smaller, weaker Cuttlefish males, who would otherwise have no chance in battle among the larger stronger males, hover nearby as the battles rage. Normally, these small males would stand no chance in competition with the larger, stronger males who are fighting. However these smaller males have a different strategy.

They draw in their long flowing masculine tentacles, making them look short and stubby - like a female's. They then display the bland color pattern of a female on their skin, and glide in past the unsuspecting large males, who just assume this transvestite male is a female passing by. As the battles rage above, these cross dressing males mate with the female, all without fighting for her. They, in essence, pretend to be a female in order to avoid a conflict with the larger, more aggressive males - a conflict which they would likely lose. Clearly, this anti-competitive behavior, embracing of promiscuity, and rejecting of merit-based competitions, is an outgrowth of the more primitive r-selected psychology.

In this species, the K-selected males have evolved the trait of competitiveness to the point that they have ritualized its application in the search for a mate. Simultaneously, the r-selected males have evolved to exploit this ritualization by masquerading as females, breaking the K-selected competitor's rules of competition, and simply mating as often as possible with as many mates as possible.

As we will show, human liberals have been shown to be prone to rule violations, while conservatives were shown to be prone to strict rule adherence.[15] Here, in its purest form, is why rule adherence and rule breaking evolved as a delineation between the r and K-strategies.

Within the study of cuttlefish, these r-selected, transvestite males have been referred to as "sneakers," but we will call them "anticompetitors," as their goal is to subvert their species' evolutionary advancement through their subversion of the competitor's competitions.

This situation, where strong aggressive males do honest battle for females of high standing, while a smaller, weaker male affects a harmless, feminine personae in order to avoid his embarrassing defeat at the hands of a larger stronger male, may seem familiar to you. Clearly, the effete, competition averse, liberal intellectual, who seeks Darwinian success through deception, is a motif we have seen before.

It is an interesting evolutionary model. The progeny of the larger, stronger competitive males, through their father's success in competition, possess the obvious selective advantage of vitality, as well as enhanced camouflage ability, and even the daring of the courageous. Such progeny are strong, brave, and better suited to a life spent fighting for survival in a harsh state of nature. Females who fertilize their eggs with the sperm from such males will have more capable children, which are more likely to return to the reef, and carry those genes forward to the next generation.[16]

However, the smaller weaker anticompetitive male, though less well suited to actual survival, also possesses competitive advantages. He does not have to fight before mating, and he can impregnate more than one female. Though his progeny will not be as healthy, strong, or capable of camouflage, and likely will not survive in as great a number as the competitor male's, the few who do return to the reef will be able to easily acquire a female with very little risk, and thus his anticompetitive trait will persist within the population.

Again, the parallel between the highly-adapted K-type organism, which produces smaller numbers of highly fit offspring meant to confront a selective environment, and the competitor cuttlefish should be obvious. This is the reproductive strategy of quality over quantity, only it has been taken to the next evolutionary level.

Likewise, the parallel between the more-fecund and less-complexly adapted r-type organism and the anticompetitive cuttlefish should be obvious as well. Both exhibit inferior levels of adaptive fitness, both are less capable of functioning in a highly selective, fitness-favoring environment, and both attempt to make up for these shortcomings through the increased reproductive rates of promiscuity. This is a strategy of quantity over quality, only here it has been expressly evolved to not only function passively within an environment, but to actually compete with an opposing trait.

Similar divisions within populations, between those K-type psychologies which embrace competitive selections for fitness, and those r-type psychologies which avoid such competitions, can be found throughout other species in nature, from fish to monkeys.[17, 18, 19, 20, 21, 22, 23, 24, 25, 26]

Such strategies of competition avoidance have been shown to thwart sexual selection,[27] which has long been known to serve as a competitive selection designed to enhance the fitness of the species.[28]

Obviously, a reproductive strategy, designed to either embrace competition, monogamy, and concern with offspring competitiveness or to reject them all, is a compelling possible origin to the psychological bifurcation of our populations which has yielded the modern political debate. Here, we see further evolutions of both r and K-type psychologies existing, and competing, within the same species, side by side. As they compete, they develop actual behavioral strategies to try and overcome their opposing reproductive strategy. Clearly, the parallels between this model and our modern ideological divide are fascinating. As this text continues, they should only become more so.

Chapter Eight

Warfare and Group Competition

It has been said that war is merely politics, by other means. In truth, it is much more likely the reverse is true. Clearly, we had war, long before we had politics.

Being K-selected overall, our species has long engaged in all forms of group competitions, from the earliest battles between tribes for food and territory, to capitalist economic competitions, to simple sporting competitions among groups of individuals. The selection pressures offered by these competitions have molded our psychology and behaviors for eons. For this reason, a quick study of these group competitions is vital if one is to understand the final component of the evolution of our political ideologies.

Having been civilized for only a short period, evolutionarily speaking, primitive clan warfare would have been a prominent selection pressure molding our behavior, so it pays to examine how our more primitive r and K-selected ancestors would have responded to the first instance of a hostile group of individuals, seeking to seize survival advantage by force.

It is the K-selected psychology which would exhibit the truculence and competitiveness which would seem to drive group competitions among men. Indeed, those within our society who are accepting of war's utility as a tool in conflict resolution will tend to be conservatives,[29] likely a psychology descended from the K-selected, and competitive psychology.

These martially oriented conservatives will also tend to support individual competitions such as capitalism, tend to oppose early childhood sexual precociousness, and they will favor an environment of monogamy and high investment child-rearing, with an emphasis on "family values." This indicates that a predisposition toward engaging in group conflict arose from the K-strategy.

Conversely, it would seem that an r-selected individual, with their strategies' emphasis on reproduction as well as competition avoidance and mortality avoidance, would tend to eschew the mortality and competition of group warfare. Indeed, the most anti-war groups today are composed of leftward leaning liberals. Their members are unclear as to how anyone could possibly support the application of deadly martial force in national conflicts, or countenance killing another human being for one's group. To such liberals, exhibiting any type of ethnocentrism or group-centric truculence is seen as so illogical that its propriety is derided out of hand, as some sort of primitive evolutionary throwback and mark of diminished intellectual development. Just as with the conservatives above, those who tend toward such left-wing pacifism will also tend to be embracing of the r-strategy traits of supporting early onset promiscuity, being less supportive of free market economic principles, and favoring such low-investment child-rearing strategies as single parenting. All of these are r-selected psychological traits.

Obviously, not all liberals and conservatives are easily shoehorned into one group or the other. However r/K is not a clean divide in nature either. As with r/K however, as one zooms out from the individual, one does find two groups that individuals gravitate towards, with two different views on ethnocentric, group-conflict. In broad strokes, the marks of r and K are unmistakable.

As we will show later in our analysis of the personality traits of political ideology, many of the psychological and personality traits of liberals and conservatives are more easily understood when viewed as r and K-type adaptations to group competitions. For example, conservatives have been shown to exhibit greater loyalty to their group and less tolerance for out-group interests, while liberals have been shown to exhibit greater openness to satisfying out-group interests, while also exhibiting less loyalty to in-group.

These urges make little sense in the context of individual competitions, where everyone should be at everyone else's throats equally, and equally self absorbed. But if one realizes that the group competitor has one path to their K-type alleles' successes, then one will quickly realize that the group anticompetitor's drive is to thwart the competitor. In so doing, the anticompetitor can easily stifle the competitor's success, and even bring him and his alleles to death.

If viewed through a prism of group competition, two strategies, designed specifically to confront the dangers of group competitions such as warfare will appear to emerge, and each will appear to be a natural outgrowth of their more primitive r and K-type psychologies. Very shortly, we will detail these two strategies, before delving into the current scientific knowledge which would support the theory presented herein.

However first, we must address the elephant in the room, namely the current debate within Evolutionary Biology over group selection, and how it relates to this theory. The next chapter is important to avoid confusion regarding this theory. Absent a temporary digression into the group selection debate, this theory might risk being rejected by those skilled in the art, based on debates already hashed out, ad infinitum, within that community. For that reason, the coming chapter needed to be included here.

It will focus more on substantiating than explaining, and will probably be of little use to the average student of political science, who is merely interested in understanding the theory being presented herein. If one is not familiar with the work of John Maynard Smith or the current debate over group selection, this chapter will likely prove of little use in further understanding the essence of this work, and it may be safely passed over.

Chapter Nine

Altruism and Group Selection

There has been considerable debate over the nature and effect of group selection on the evolution of social traits within the field of Evolutionary Biology. A cursory examination of this debate is necessary for a proper and thorough understanding of this theory, so we will attempt to quickly present such a summary here.

This is presented here, since in the preceding chapters we presented a theory which entailed competitors enduring risk in competition, both for the good of their group of individual competitors and for the good of their competitive groups in group competitions. This is technically defined as altruism, or individuals accepting disadvantage for the good of their group.

To those unacquainted with the debate over altruism and group selection within Evolutionary Psychology, suffice it to say that group selection and altruism have been enormously controversial. Endless debates have raged over it, and they continue to this day, with many saying group selection effects do not have any significant role in the evolution of altruism. Some have speculated that political inclinations of the participants have affected the debate,[30, 31] though it would seem to many that the true origin of the debate's immortality is an endless war over trifles.

The debate began with Darwin's speculation that competitions between groups could yield advantage to a population whose individuals were imbued with the ability to function well as part of a civilized, cooperative group. As groups competed and groups died, these pro-social, altruistic traits would lend advantage to groups which possessed them, and doom those groups which did not possess them to extinction.

He hypothesized that this competition between groups might explain man's social nature, his tendency towards morality, and his embrace of societal organization.[32] In short, this theory postulated that man had evolved as a part of one group, competing with other groups, and man had won.

This theory of group selection experienced a resurgence in the last century. As the debate began, the complex suite of psychological traits required to function well within a civilization was condensed into a single trait for simplicity. It was referred to as altruism, and defined as a willing sacrifice of reproductive advantage by an individual, for the good of a group's success. Thus group selection theory was discussed as groups of men succeeding against other groups of men because individuals within the winning group exhibited the trait of altruism. This group grew, and produced a species composed of altruistic men.

A foundational error which was integrated into the early debate was that groups of individuals were viewed as similar to biological organisms, composed of individual cells. Those who were members of a group were viewed as stable parts of the group, much as cells of an organism are not routinely ejected from the organism arbitrarily. It was also assumed that individuals were not routinely absorbed into groups, just as individual foreign cells that an organism encounters in an environment do not find themselves spontaneously integrated into the organism. Thus the fundamental mistake which rendered the group selection debate meaningless was in assuming groups to exhibit an organic stasis in their membership, punctuated at most by occasional random re-assortment.[33]

As a result of this misconception, on one side of the debate individuals argued on behalf of group selection by maintaining that groups filled with altruists would grow faster, and outcompete groups composed of selfish individuals. As the selfish groups failed, what would be left were groups of altruists.

On the other side, the argument was made that even if a group made primarily of altruists eradicated all other selfish groups, within the altruistic group would inevitably be some selfish individuals. Those selfish individuals would reproduce faster than the altruists, and eventually take over the group, producing an overwhelming advantage to selfishness.[34]

Thus even if a group predominantly composed of altruists destroyed every other group of selfish individuals, the few selfish individuals within their group would proliferate faster than the altruists. Eventually, the group would become predominantly selfish, and collapse into an orgy of selfish hedonism. (By now the similarity between the fast

58

reproducing selfish individual, concerned only with reproduction, and the r-strategy, and the slower reproducing, rule-following altruist and the K-type strategy should be apparent.)

As time has gone on, it has been shown that altruism can enjoy an advantage within group selection of organically static groups, through a variety of mechanisms. For example, David Sloan Wilson proposed that trait groups would allow for group selection processes to confer advantage on altruists.[35]

Also, if one factors in what is referred to as the three R's, reputation, reciprocity, and retribution, altruism will also offer advantage in such groups.[36, 37] In essence, if one factors in that others will exchange altruistic acts, based on reputation and reciprocity, and that selfishness will be punished with retribution, the disadvantages conferred on selfishness will yield an overall advantage to altruism.

Of course, an even better, and likely more accurate case could be made that much of that debate is pointless, and bears little relation to how human group competitions actually function. Basically, it should be considered that human groups do not begin in existence. Rather, they form from scratch as like-minded individuals find each other and aggregate.

Obviously, as Lord of the Flies portrayed, humans are, by nature, far more fickle creatures, innately programmed to self assemble into groups, and once assembled, isolate and ostracize any individuals who do not "fit in." Nor is this fickle trait limited to its expression in childhood. Today our society feels no compunction with regards to locking excessively selfish people in cages, through decree of our judicial system, to remove them from our populations. Occasionally in history, humans have even ganged up on such individuals and killed them wantonly, as any posse of our past would demonstrate.

Conversely, humans are also capable of respecting select individuals from outside their group, and will welcome alliance with such individuals, if they exhibit qualities the group can agree are respectable and worthy.

In truth, much of life consists of solitary individuals setting out and entering the competitive world of adulthood all alone, and then seeking to be vetted for membership into a group of likeminded peers.

It may be a small business, or a multinational corporation. Young men examine the military, and choose a specific unit which they believe to be superior, and then seek membership in it. Young athletes idolize professional sports teams, and then seek to join them as adults, if merely as fans. Even Darwin undertook his travels, and accomplished his objectives following several periods of self-assortment into functional groups with strangers, as he organized his transportation, purchased his supplies, and submitted his manuscripts to others in the scientific community, seeking their imprimatur.

Of course, one can also be ejected from such groups, should one exhibit traits which fail to conform to the expected traits the group desires in its members. From a dishonorable discharge, to being fired, such groups will expel individuals quickly and easily, if they exhibit any selfishness which conflicts with the group's stated competitive objectives.

Such self-assembling of competitive groups within the world, and their policing of their members, and ejection of those who lose the favor of the group, would produce an environment where groups compete, and are selected through competitive selection processes. This would yield a moral, altruistic man, designed for group competition, with highly functional groups being rewarded for their functionality.

However in this self-assorting environment, where individuals formed into groups spontaneously through self assortment, it is the individual's full suite of psychological traits which are selected for. It is the individual who either succeeds wildly, through successfully self-assembling with others into a winning group of similar individuals, or fails completely, through failing to successfully self-assemble with other like-minded individuals into a successful group. Such failing individuals could fail any number of ways, from associating with a dysfunctional group, to not gaining entrance to a group, and being forced to compete alone, against committed groups of violent individuals. In each case, lacking a single facet of the group competitive psychology will doom one to Darwinian failure. Only those with the full complement of psychological traits necessary to assemble into a group, and function within it, will survive this selective pressure.

Individuals exhibiting the group-competitive psychology produced by this scheme will exhibit several facets to their psychology.

They would first need to accurately assess groups they encountered. Individuals who sought to associate with unfit, selfish, or unmotivated groups would enhance their risk of being culled, along with the entirety of their failure-prone group. This would produce a natural tendency to respect successful individuals and successful groups, combined with a wish to associate one's self with those successful groups of individuals.

Having selected a successful group, individuals would then need to exhibit beneficial and altruistic traits themselves, in an effort to lead the group to agree to select them for membership. From the sports team to the multinational corporation, to the small business, to the military, all competitive groups vet prospective members for indications of traits which will enhance the group's success, and look for warning signs that an individual may exhibit a psychology that is incompatible with successful group competition.

Since groups composed of altruists would tend to be more successful, individuals will seek to join with successful groups of altruists, so as to enjoy success themselves. Since such altruistic groups would see their success increase if all members exhibited altruism, such a group's members will evolve to limit admittance to their group, allowing entry only to those they deem sufficiently altruistic, and expelling anyone who exhibited selfish behavior.

This model offers an excellent means by which to preserve the concept of individual selection, while eliminating the practical weaknesses in traditional group selection theories. Additionally, it does this while simultaneously explaining the origin of research showing both, that group altruism and cooperativeness are variable traits produced by genetic influences,[38] and that in-group favoritism is a genetic trait, which leads an individual to process various salient cues, such as shared beliefs and ancestry, so as to produce better group cohesion and functionality.[39]

There can be only one reason individuals would evolve a variable ability to form into, and function well within, cooperative groups. Some individuals evolved a suite of psychological traits, driving them to join into groups of like-minded individuals, and work together with these groups to attain goals, while others evolved a more individualistic, personally selfish, Darwinian strategy.

61

Obviously, this exercise points out a flaw in the current arguments regarding group selection theories, which ignore this individualized aspect of group selection. There is another flaw however, which has mired the current debate over altruism, and group selection. This flaw is that such debate has been based on the concept of altruism as selflessness for the good of a group, with no personal advantage for the entity which exhibits it, beyond the advantage they reap from the group's success.

Suppose there are two traits in a population. We will call them r and K. The r trait tries to reproduce faster than the K-trait. The K-trait tries to make each of its offspring as fit as possible, using competitions to sort mates, pairing the fittest with the fittest, and removing the less fit.

When resource excess gives way to resource scarcity, the K's will have an innate survival advantage. Although the individuals who cede their personal mating opportunities to others, according to competitive rules, do endure a self-inflicted, altruistic disadvantage, this is not altruism from the perspective of the K-trait.

From the perspective of the K-trait, it has taken control of the minds of all of its carriers, and led them to engage in a ritual which will confer massive advantage on the trait, when resource availability falls. This trait actually leads its carriers to create the fittest vessel for carrying the trait forward, by imbuing carriers with a psychology intolerant of diminished fitness. This is actually incredibly selfish, from the perspective of the K-trait.

In short, I would view the willingness to accept defeat, based on honor, not as altruism for a group, but as a "fitness trait," designed to produce individuals who are capable of destroying any other individual who does not carry the trait. Given that resources inevitably diminish in availability, this trait is a long-view-strategy trait, enduring the mild disadvantage of temporarily diminished reproductive rates during resource excess, in order to acquire the potent advantage of extraordinarily high fitness levels when times inevitably turn bad.

Now imagine this fitness producing trait combined with the complete suite of group-competitive psychological traits. Add in affiliation drives, including a desire to display one's success in open individual competition, drives to join a successful group and surround oneself with peers of like mind. Add in policing drives, designed to police one's group, and expel those who are not altruistically committed to group success. On top of that, sprinkle in an aggressive intolerance for outsiders who do not exhibit the traits above.

In humans, these traits are all combined to create a maximally fit individual, prone to actively develop and evolve the vessel housing the competitive trait. It will also render the individual maximally capable of associating with a successful group, operating successfully within it so as to provide the group with advantage, and helping to police the group of any selfish individuals looking to exploit the group without sacrificing on its behalf.

As groups form, and individuals stratify into groups which vary by altruism of individuals, willingness to compete honestly and honor outcomes, ability, rate of policing, and discrimination between prospective members, those who best embody all of the traits within this model, form the most capable groups. If resources are sufficiently limited, it is the most functional groups which are left standing at the conclusion of the competition. Although inefficient, and prone to error, nature is in no rush. Over enough time, and with an entire planet of organisms throwing themselves into the evolutionary breach, we are the inevitable outcome.

This is congruent with Realistic Conflict Theory,[40] which explores how limited resources foster group conflict in humans. It also comports with evidence indicating that the trait of human cooperation enjoys great advantage in lethal group competitions[41] as well as the fact that altruism would appear to also have a genetic link which is related to pro-sociality in group interactions.[42] Additionally, our assertion that K-type traits are associated with altruistic cooperation is further supported by research showing that sexual selectiveness and monogamy (which are fundamental to the K-strategy) are associated with the type of altruistic cooperativeness which produces cooperative societies, and that promiscuity (an r-type trait) is associated with an absence of such cooperation.[43]

Indeed, the inevitable results of this process are what we see in modern humans, where group warfare and competition are a normal part of our history and psychology, and are well accepted as having molded our psychological evolution.[44]

There is even evidence that warfare's demand for effective interactions has produced the moral, altruistic, and social psychology we exhibit today. It is believed that this occurred through warfare's Darwinian favoritism of those who exhibited such a pro-social psychology, and its vicious punishment of those who did not.[45, 46, 47]

Thus in humans, group selection should be viewed as a process designed to confer competitive advantage to a specific evolution of the K-trait. As Darwin selects individuals who best embody this trait, the trait sees its advantage over its competition increase, as its next iteration emerges.

Of course, the r-trait is not going to passively sit by, and allow itself to be driven extinct. If the anticompetitor was to survive within a well vetted group of loyal K-strategists, the r-selected anticompetitor had to evolve to exploit the competitor's Greenbeard effect,[48] in such a way as to appear to be a contributing and loyal part of the group. (Indeed, today's liberal, "Dissent is Patriotic" movement, which repeats this mantra while opposing national success in international competitions with enemies, is a demonstration of this Greenbeard exploiting adaptation being expressed, while pursuing interests adverse to those of the group.)

This camouflaging adaptation however, would only offer the group anticompetitor the option to survive within the populace. If the r-selected anticompetitor was to gain an advantage in this environment, it had but one choice. Use the circumstances of the competitor's group competitions for personal survival advantage in some way.

Readers should note, before dismissing this assertion, that some research into the psychology of human altruism already indicates a substantial subgroup expressing a "traitorous" behavioral strategy is a natural outcome of a perceptible cooperative strategy among an in-group.[49]

If expectation, reputation, and tribe is accepted as the tag which renders the competitive altruist recognizable to other competitive altruists, this research indicates that a subgroup will inevitably evolve to betray their compatriots for personal advantage in competitions. If this loyalty-exploitative cohort must exist, its strategy would fit with both the r-selected organism's tendencies towards using deception in competition to avoid adverse outcomes, and the out-group supportive qualities noted

64

in research on liberals that has been aggregated by John Jost at NYU (to be discussed later in the analysis of personality traits of political ideologies).

If research indicates such a betraying strategy will arise, the only question becomes, where is it? Clearly, we maintain that the r-selected liberal ideologue is a prime candidate.

The psychological parallels between aggressive liberalism and a strategy of exploiting betrayal in group competition are difficult to ignore, if uncomfortable to confront. For the record, it should be noted, such behavior would not arise from a conscious desire to betray, so much as an innate perceptual framework which renders betrayal a perfectly logical and moral conclusion to reach. Nature would almost certainly produce the behavior absent a clear knowledge of its origins or purposes.

Treason as a Darwinian strategy will be even more likely to arise within the model of group competition presented here because within every group, the r-selected anticompetitor has one primary Darwinian threat, and that is the successful, K-selected, individual competitor within their population.

Thus, as in the Counterculture example of Hippies spitting on servicemen (to be presented later), the r-selected trait is in constant competition with their population's own K-selected trait carriers. It is not surprising that the r-selected trait should evolve a strategy expressly designed to confer advantage on themselves, while providing disadvantage to the K-selected competitors within their population.

This desire to manipulate the group's behavior for individual gain can play a number of ways. Perhaps a group of outsiders begins to threaten their population's K-selected competitor humans with either death, or the uniform oppression of an occupation. The r-selected contingent of the populace will be presented with a clear opportunity. By cooperating with the enemy, they can use a foreign force of K-competitors as a proxy, to eliminate the Darwinian threat posed to the anticompetitors by their own population's K-selected competitors.

We see this in our own politics, where the use of overwhelming force by our military is never allowed. Rather, the left insists that we expose our troop to risk, and potential defeat, rather than taking the gloves off, and eradicating our enemy by any means necessary. As one goes more leftward, one finds ever increasing sympathy for our enemies, and disregard for our own group's interests. There are even individuals who seek to release our terrorist enemies in Guantanamo into the US, and offer them reparations for their imprisonment.

Should the anticompetitor be able to bring about their society's defeat, they will have used the foreign competitors to deal a blow to their society's competitive population. It will be a blow which the r-selected anticompetitor could never have struck themselves, due to their innate martial and competitive inferiority.

Future chapters will cite examples of this r-type drive to bring about a defeat of their own group. We will also cite liberal psychological drives identified in the research literature which support this theory, from a tendency to sympathize with out-group interests, to diminished adherence to in-group authority during competition, to diminished levels of loyalty to in-group, to even the exhibition of less conscientiousness.[50], [51] All of these liberal traits are psychological motivators designed to provoke an r-type group-anticompetitive strategy, by which indigenous K-type competitors are eradicated from the populace, using defeat by foreign K-type competitors as proxies as a tool.

In closing, Maynard Smith was correct in his critiques of group selection theory. If every group existed as a closed population of individuals, then indeed, group selection models would favor the selfish over the altruists, and the r-selected humans over the K-selected.

However, if one factors in the easily observable fickle qualities of human social nature, allows for selection by the group as well as selection of the group, and considers the aggressive mortality possible under periods of extreme K-selection stresses such as group warfare (and the advantage a high degree of fitness might afford a trait which produced it), one will find a model for the evolution of both altruism and our political ideologies. It will prove wholly supportable, and will exactly mirror the very human natures we find among both, the most successful warriors and the most ardent leftists of today.

Chapter Ten

The Warrior

As we have discussed, war has been molding mankind's psychology for eons. It would have been inevitable, within a species where resources were scarce and competition was fierce, that some individuals would join together to outcompete other individuals.

From a trait perspective, the competitive trait gains its advantage through the eradication of non-carriers, and acquisition of their resources during periods of resource scarcity. Thus, individual competitors who evolved to join together in groups, and eradicate less competitive, more pacifistic non-carriers would quickly help the competitive trait to dominate the population during such times. Indeed, active eradication of an unusually fecund, competing phenotype could offer a radically effective strategy to overcome the r-selected anticompetitor's increased maximal reproductive capacity, even under conditions of r-selection.

Once that war-waging Rubicon was crossed, the group competitor would have quickly out-competed the individual competitors, especially under conditions of K-selection. Group-oriented K-strategists would have quickly become the predominant presentation of K-selected competitor within the species. Suddenly, a warrior species would have been born.

As the species became composed of many groups, all competing with each other, evolution would have played its hand. Over time, an endless stream of individuals would have spontaneously assembled into a nearly infinite variety of groups, competed, and either continued on to reproduce, or been eradicated through the rigors of such open competition. There would be collateral evolutionary damage, of course. Good specimens might die due to chance, and bad specimens might periodically persist through luck.

But as the statistical probabilities played out over the eons, what would inevitably emerge would be a population of individuals who were designed psychologically to spontaneously produce as capable and competitive a group as possible, and to actively seek out compatriots of similar dispositions, to form this group with.

As we have written, individual competitiveness, favoring competitions for competition's sake, is an evolutionary refinement of the simple contextual aggression of the K-selected psychology. Similarly, this adaptation to group-competition would produce a further refinement of the competitive, K-selected psychology. Here, we will seek to better characterize some of this psychology's behavioral traits, and the relationship it has assumed with respect to the subsequent evolution of the r-selected trait. For simplicity, we will refer to group-competitors as warriors.

Several facets of this group-competitive psychology will naturally tend to evolve, due to the advantages they will provide to groups whose members embody them. They are:

1.   Loyalty – This loyalty must be expressed by individuals in a selective fashion. Individuals who pledge loyalty to the selfish will be culled when their group is defeated, or when they are betrayed. Thus loyalty must be selectively extended, only to those who will extend it in return.

2.   Intolerance for disloyalty – As with retribution in games of Prisoner, a drive to see disloyalty punished harshly will be necessary. This drive is why traitors are allowed to be executed on the battlefield.

3.   Competitiveness – Warriors will be competitive, and want to see their group succeed, even at the expense of other groups.

4.   Intolerance and disregard for out-group interests – Warriors will not overly concern themselves with the success of groups other than their own. Under conditions of K-selection, the choices are live or die, and those who chose die do not pass their genes forward. Indeed, the warrior will view the success of their own group at the expense of outside groups as part of a natural, healthy process, not to be challenged or opposed.

5.   Support for leadership – As competitors, warriors will naturally fall into a hierarchy based on the outcomes of individual competitions within their group (a sort of spontaneous, merit/experience based hierarchy stratification). Having established such a hierarchy, warriors will demand adherence to, and support of the leadership while

in group competition. This urge will act in opposition to the individual competitor's desire to be free from authority's oppression in individual competitions with others, however. Thus in time of group conflict, warriors will seek subservience of all to their leadership. However, absent a group challenge, warriors will revert to their more basic, individually competitive psychology, demanding freedom from any subservience to, or oppression by, any external authority. This will be especially true of any authority which threatens to undermine honestly won outcomes of individual competitions.

6. Traditionalism – Traditionalism offers a reason to fight (to avoid changes to one's governing structure that might be imposed by an enemy). It also satisfies the warrior's drive towards adherence to our species' traditional K-selected, competitive, warrior behavioral standards. Since our species evolved this far due to an overwhelming adherence to K-selected, competitive psychological drives, traditionalism represents an adherence to these traditional, K-selected mores and virtues. This is likely also a natural aversion to every strongly K-selected society's inevitable, gradual descent into a more r-selected social structure, prone to failure and collapse (as will be discussed later).

7. Exhibition of pro-social, group unifying behaviors – It is the warrior who evolved pro-social behaviors as a means of promoting group integrity, and by extension, group success. Kindness, politeness, unifying patriotism, personal integrity, morality, altruism towards in-group, and demands to conform to group-unifying interpersonal behaviors all serve to tighten the bonds which are required for a group to compete successfully. From demanding patriotism from peers, to desiring a single culture and language, the warrior wants his in-group unified, and prepared to take on the world as a team. It is also worth noting that although K-selection is noted as favoring monogamy and mate guarding among more primitive organisms, group competition is believed to favor monogamy even more, through minimizing intra-group conflict, and fostering better cohesion among group members.[52]

8. Intolerance for deviations from the warrior ethos – Warriors will innately revile anyone who violates their behavioral drives, since such behavior will, in a very real sense, risk Darwinian cost to the warrior (through bringing about a defeat of his group which could kill him). Those groups of individual warriors who tolerate deviations from the warrior's programming would inevitably be culled in the violent,

war-torn, K-selected environment of mankind's past. Just as Maynard Smith hypothesized that an altruistic population would always cede its nature to that of the selfish within it, so too were those warriors who tolerated betrayal within their ranks prone to be lost beneath the seas of Darwinian selection.

In a highly competitive species, where the only means to have a chance to survive was to form groups and fight for resources, there would be an endless parade of individuals which would form groups, and thrust themselves into battle within their groups. Some would embody the full suite of warrior traits, and survive. Some would not.

As time passed and these weaker groups were eradicated, eventually Homo sapiens would come to predominantly produce individuals who spontaneously vetted peers for adherence to the K-selected, competitive warrior ideals while striving to proudly exhibit these traits themselves.

This psychology would become the warrior ethos, and as we will discuss, it would affect the very evolution of our neurobiology, as well as the abilities and tendencies it conferred on us. As we began to use our intellects to formulate structures of government, this subtle psychological programming would affect the fundamental precepts we used to guide our efforts. In so doing, it not only produced the very psychology which underlies modern conservatism, and defined every position on every issue within it, it also molded the very history of our civilizations, and our species.

Chapter Eleven

The Appeaser _____

The evolution of the modern K-selected psychology is easy to understand, because it merely took competitiveness, and added the group dynamic to it. The modern r-selected psychology however, is best understood through a more complex, multi-step evolutionary process.

Initially it was simply designed to exploit free resources, such as after a major random mortality event like a climactic disruption or pandemic. That would produce very low population densities. Then when the mortality abated, there would be rapid expansion into the newly created void in the carrying capacity of the environment. This would favor the most r-selected of r-strategists, who expanded fastest.

When such primitive r-humans multiplied, they would eventually overpopulate their range, until resource levels dropped and K-selection began. Then, the r-strategists who would survive would be those who migrated out, to uninhabited lands nearby with free resource availability once again. This could be seen in the initial migration of Homo sapiens, and its spread across the globe following a still debated near-extinction event and "genetic bottleneck" in our history, that some attribute to causes ranging from climatic conditions to plagues.

This spreading-out produces the second phase of the evolution of the leftist psychology. What had previously adapted to proliferate as quickly as possible in the presence of free resources, would now evolve to migrate to a new, unoccupied, fertile environment nearby, to escape the K-selected competition behind it. Once having migrated, they would face no competition, unlike in their over-populated homeland. As the K-selection behind them caught up, those most prone to migrate would just migrate again. Those who comprised this new, perpetually-mobile population of r-strategists would acquire and possess new traits designed to precipitate and facilitate this migratory strategy.

Once humans covered the globe, the third phase of r-strategist evolution began – the inter-population migration - migration not into uninhabited lands, but into foreign, inhabited lands with higher levels of resource availability. Here the human r-strategist was selected for urges and desires which facilitated their execution of the behaviors which comprised this even more complex strategy.

Much of the modern political leftist's urges, from novelty-seeking, to desire to be surrounded by out-groups, to willingness to engage in preemptive appeasement of foreigners, can be best understood in the context of these specific ingratiating, conflict-avoidant, pre-integrating, inter-population migratory urges.

If you are an r-strategist confronted with the onset of K-selection in your population, and you have to migrate to a new population with freer resource availability, you will need certain urges to drive the migrating behavior, and other urges to facilitate survival once you arrive in your new homeland. A comfort with, or even desire for the experience of living in a foreign culture would aid your motivation to initiate what would otherwise be a difficult emotional decision - to leave that with which you were familiar, and resign yourself to embracing that which is foreign. That is the likely evolutionary origin of the novelty-seeking urges that have been found to be integral to the leftist psychology. Human r-strategists, living in this new fully human-colonized world who exhibited this novelty-seeking urge would have a Darwinian advantage over other r-strategists, and as a result, this novelty-seeking urge was added to the suite of behaviors that comprised the human r-strategy.

Novelty-seeking urges, be it a desire to sample foreign cuisine, mate with different-appearing mates, live among different races, experience different architecture, or flora, or clothing, or language, or geography, or climate, or geographic location, all would render the r-strategist migrant more likely to make the jump and move to a new population early, as the initial waves of K-selection began behind them. Today, modern leftists exhibit this urge so thoroughly that they view those who have little desire to travel the world as somehow inferior. They see the less-traveled as lacking in an important intellectual curiosity and willingness to experience the unusual, which is in reality, just the leftist's migratory urges.

Similarly, lack of loyalty and emotional bonding to your own people, would also facilitate a migratory tendency. Those who disliked foreigners and felt closely-bonded to their neighbors would be much less likely to migrate out to live among strange foreigners. Indeed, a hostility

72

to one's own would actually drive the human r-strategist to be ready to migrate at the first subtle signs of impending K-selection.

Disdain for one's own combined with a psychology eager to please foreigners would also facilitate blending into a new land. On arriving, the r-strategist would instinctually ingratiate themselves with their host country by demonstrating their hostility to their old homeland. This would establish their non-threatening status to the residents of their new homeland. They would also demonstrate their willingness to sacrifice for their new foreign hosts through their own preemptive appeasement, as well as their vociferous demands that all other fellow migrants from their old homeland preemptively appease their new hosts as well. This would help them to avoid any conflict, and integrate them into their new homeland's citizenry. Should their new hosts end up in conflict with their fellow migrants, this would also make sure their new hosts did not associate them with the troublesome newcomers.

Just as a K-strategist feels an uncontrollable drive to loyalty as part of a strategy to see their group win, the migratory r-strategist feels an uncontrollable drive to demonstrate lack of loyalty to their group, as part of a last ditch strategy to be sure they survive, should their new hosts turn on their fellow migrants. You can see the selective pressures selecting for such urges, as well as the favor that having such a pre-integrated migrating psychology would offer an r-strategist.

Whether you look at the modern leftist's fairly aggressive drives to see physical and cultural diversity around them, their aggressive obsession with inter-racial dating acceptance, their innate drive to support the interests of foreigners while denigrating their own people's interests, their desires to experience new experiences such as culinary experiences, clothing, architecture, and even their desire for travel to foreign lands, all of those urges can only be understood if they are viewed as vestigial drives of an r-strategist migrant psychology, designed to land in a new society, already fully integrated into it.

If raw fecundity, migration to uninhabited lands, and inter-population migration are the first three iterations of the human r-strategy, there is a fourth phase of leftist r-strategist evolution. In this phase, r-strategist migrants who are existing in nations that are exhibiting high levels of resource availability for extended periods will find that actual migration from their perpetually wealthy first-world nations is disadvantageous, even as K-selection approaches. These wealthy first world r-strategists do not migrate, since even in a glut the Sudan can hardly be a more r-selecting environment than Paris, France, even if France is in the midst of a shortage.

Rather, these modern first world r-strategists express their migrant urges by importing the foreigners they are programmed to want to live among, and then betraying their own people to them. This "betrayal" is probably evolved from the "loyalty" of a psychology that is naturally pre-integrated with out-groups and foreigners.

This r-strategist iteration is designed to persist in the first world, where resources may never drop sufficiently enough to make migrating out advantageous, but where the r-strategist nevertheless finds themselves in some form of increasing competition with their fellow native K-strategists. I view this strategy, and those who exhibit it, as a sort of genetic Trojan Horse. This strategy hides its r-genes within the population while seeking to import foreigners (themselves r-strategist migrants) who will kill or oppress native K-strategists, all to facilitate the persistence and success of r-strategist genes within the territory.

This is the final evolution of the r-strategy, which we see as modern political leftism in the first world today. It is a strategy designed to compete with the K-strategists of their lands when the r-strategists grow ascendent enough during r-selection to exert their urges through the use of social pressures or legal/governmental systems.

This newer non-migratory r-strategy will not exist in equal measure everywhere in the world. Clearly this last iteration is an adaptation to conditions where K-selection threatens, but migration to other lands will not yield superior levels of resource availability, or its neurochemical proxy, the pleasure molecule dopamine. Thus in very poor areas such as in the third world, r-strategists may have stalled at the evolved stage of simply migrating out in search of free resources. There, the r-strategy of inviting in foreigners, to use as competitive proxies will not be as prominent a strategy.

However in richer European nations you will find this newer iteration. European r-strategists migrating to the Sudan when K-selection is imminent in Europe, will not enjoy sufficient Darwinian advantage. So there, they have evolved one final step - to express their migrant urges without migrating. In essence they reconstitute the foreign environment their migratory urges crave, right around them in their wealthy home nation, and then attempt to exploit the circumstances which that creates to defeat their own society's K-strategists, and further the interests of their r-strategy's genes.

This importation of the foreign may be a sub-par means of relieving the cognitive pressures produced in the leftist mind by approaching K-selection. The r-strategists are probably designed to experience stress, anxiety, anger, revulsion, disgust, depression, and disdain to motivate their migration in the face of rising K-selection at home. Having migrated, they would arrive in a land of superior resource availability, surrounded by foreigners they didn't hate, and they would feel relief from all of those emotions.

In this case, you have a migrant psychology which will feel those emotions, however they cannot migrate to relieve them. Like a brain experiencing an itch that can not be scratched, you would expect such a mindset to build up desperately high levels of the cognitive forces designed to provoke migration. Unable to be relieved by migration, those forces would eventually become intolerable.

In such individuals, they have evolved a workaround by importing foreigners. But it is a weak solution, so they will exhibit an ever greater need to import foreigners as shortage and K-selection intensifies. In addition, they will grow exponentially more afflicted with cognitive dysfunction on the face of any impediment to their importation of migrants. In essence, their brain will apply the requisite emotions in ever increasing amounts as K-selection closes in, but their inability to migrate leaves them trapped in an increasingly neurotic state.

You may even notice what some might term pathological levels of the depression, angst, stress, anger, contempt, hopelessness, and anxiety which would normally provoke migratory behavior. Those emotional imbalances are designed to only be assuaged by landing in a foreign land of superior resource availability and vastly reduced K-selected conflict stimuli. If that is not an option, the brain can easily spin out of control.

Thus, what would appear mental illness among the left, as K-selection takes hold in a society, may not be pathological. Rather, it may merely be a brain trying to apply a well developed set of emotional drives to motivate a programmed behavior that unusual circumstances

75

will not allow to be executed. In short, leftist insanity as K-selection closes in may be their brain doing exactly what it is programmed to do. It is just that the environment will not allow them to execute the behaviors their programming is attempting to drive, so they short-circuit.

There may be one other iteration of the r-strategy which will evolve in response to the emergence of the wealthy, non-migratory, first world r-strategist. Since r-strategists are opportunists, r-strategists who happen into a population composed of weak-willed, preemptively-appeasing, non-migratory, first world r-strategists, might find it advantageous to exploit the weakness of their hosts by using violence and aggression to demand free resource provisioning.

Being r-strategists, one could expect them to exhibit the entitled psychology of the r-strategist which assumes resources should always be free. Likewise they may assert that disparities in resource allotment are somehow contrary to the moral order of the world and in need of outside rectification. They will have less drive to compete for resources openly, and more expectation of free resource provisioning, meaning the likelihood of them becoming productive members of society is diminished, and the likelihood of them becoming dependent on state handouts or turning to the easy resource stream of crime will increase.

They will also probably exhibit more aggressive sexual drives and less sexual restraint, including less drive to monogamy and more drive toward promiscuity, rape, and even embrace of earlier age-at-first-intercourse (extending to pedophilia and homosexual pedophilia in the more extreme cases). They will have less rearing drive triggering care for the rearing of children and protection of them, more selfish attitudes, and just generally a less pro-social nature.

So far those are just general r-strategist traits. However in addition to this, they may exhibit an impulsive aggression, ostensibly similar to that of the K-strategist, but less willing to endure the sustained resistance of equals, or the disparate outcomes in resource allotment which would accompany true K-selection. The violence of these migratory r-strategists would be more opportunistic and targeted at the weak and unable. It might be seen as more akin to that of the common criminal than that of the soldier. (Although here we are referencing migratory r-strategists, it is also likely that criminals as a whole are exhibiting such an r-strategy, regardless of migratory status. It is also likely significant that first world non-migratory r-strategists who import violent foreigners will also have a soft spot for violent domestic criminals as well. At its core crime, migrant and indigenous, is a search for free, easy resources, often accompanied by lack of sexual restraint, reduced monogamy, low pro-sociality/loyalty, and weak rearing urges. Strangely, or not, all r-strategists seem united in promoting their r-strategist genes in the population, even regardless of differences in aggression and violence. In this regard, they all seem to recognize each other, regardless of ostensible differences which stand out to us.)

So in the modern first world, when global resource restriction begins after a period of r-selection, one should expect a rise in these types of aggressive r-strategist migrants, as the r-strategists of poorer third world nations, feeling the pinch first, will migrate out to wealthier nations.

So long as r-selection rules in these first world nations the aggressive migrating invaders will probably be tolerated on the whole, no matter how aggressive they are. Ironically, it will be the ostensibly pacifistic, native, first-world r-strategists who will aggressively embrace the foreigners despite their aggression, because as r-strategists they evolved to seek out, appease, and integrate with dangerous foreigners.

These aggressive migratory r-strategists will not last when real K-selection hits, and the K-strategy psychology rises to the fore in the population, triggering open violent opposition to them. At that point I would expect a new r-selected mass-migration out to begin. However until that time, the aggressive third-world r-strategist migrating to a first world nation may enjoy advantage where extremely wealthy, highly r-selected nations meet more primitive and violent r-strategists migrating in.

It is important to note, this aggressive migrant psychology is not a K-selected psychology, but rather just an r-strategy opportunistically seizing an easy, low-risk opportunity to avail themselves of free resources by using violence on an even weaker, less capable cadre of specimens – the wealthy, first world, non-migrating r-strategist.

It is counter-intuitive to view violence as a low-risk/free-resource producing endeavor. However where aggressive third world migrants, supported by the left wing media and governments, meet weak, elderly, infirm, and incapable, yet wealthy first world r-strategists, as well as politically correct courts that will not punish them, that is unquestionably the case - at least until true K-selection takes hold in the first world.

This book will use the term appeasement strategy to describe the first world, non-migrating evolution of the r-strategy, because this strategy will obviously present as a desire to needlessly appease an out-group, at the expense of the warriors within one's own in-group. Often this will occur while promoting circumstances likely to provoke conflict, such as increasing the proximity of diverse groups, stoking tensions, or through demanding concessions from their own group to any other groups with differing racial, religious, or class characteristics. It can even manifest in importing hostile out-groups, and insisting on their acceptance, despite human history clearly indicating that any such acceptance is likely to be temporary, and end in violence.

This is a complex strategy, with a very dark side from the perspective of K-strategists, since at its core, it seeks to *"genetically defeat"* us. It evolved from a mixture of the conflict-avoidance of anticompetitiveness, the migratory urges for novelty, combined with the r-type psychology's instinctual tendency toward betrayal of their own to save themselves. Here, they curry good will with potential enemies of their own, while engendering conditions prone to produce conflict. The psychology which underlies this strategy will be most advantageous to the r-selected individual if it possesses several facets, which are as follows.

1.   Underlying hostility to the native warrior – The warrior is the K-selected success, who will dominate an individually competitive K-selected population. His competitive trait is in direct competitive opposition to the anticompetitive trait in the r-type individuals. Those who embody the r-selected psychology will innately perceive the warrior as their competition, and will seek opportunities to control him, oppress him, and gain advantage over him, relentlessly. The most obvious manifestation of this will occur in the use of betrayal in group competition. This will manifest as a strategy designed to use foreigners as a proxy force to eliminate the K-selected warriors of the appeaser's own population. Other presentations of this hostility to the in-group's warriors may include a demand that warriors shoulder risk themselves in battle, to save the lives of foreigners - even foreigners who may be hostile to the appeaser's own in-group and its warriors. All of this will

arise from a sympathy with the interests of out-groups that will evolve to become so innate to this strategy that the r-selected appeaser cannot even perceive how it molds their perceptual framework or controls their decision-making process.

2.   Diminished or absent loyalty to group – Exploitation of a group competition for personal advantage may occur through several means, whether it be openly aiding an enemy to eradicate the K-selected competitors within your own population, or merely seeking to thwart the warrior's victory in war, to prevent them from assuming a higher social standing such as would occur on returning home after the defeat of a nation's enemies. All such strategies require a lack of loyalty to in-group, or a tendency to expand one's definition of in-group to include all individuals everywhere, thereby eliminating the notion of in-group loyalty entirely. This concept is as innate to r-selected liberals as the innate perception of competitions and in-groups is to the K-selected conservative.

3.   Conflict and Competition Avoidance – A psychological urge which is designed to forage on the copious resources present under conditions of r-selection, while avoiding all competition and conflict. Here, it will confer an advantage by delaying action in confronting an enemy. This will forestall the appeaser's worst possible outcome – successful K-selected warriors acting decisively, and returning as heroes to local high-value females, after quickly and effectively dispatching a hostile enemy force. This likely evolved out of an r-selected organism's maladaptation to a fiercely competitive, violent environment. If an environment shifts, and becomes K-selective, it will not bode well for the future of the r-selected trait - unless the appeasers can focus that violent environment on their K-selected competition while avoiding it themselves. And this is exactly what they have evolved to do.

4.   Openness to the interests of out-groups – An openness to the interests of out-groups will facilitate pursuing one's own interests, in contravention of the objectives of one's own in-group. Thus it is easier to aid an enemy to overthrow one's own government, if one is capable of viewing the enemy's cause as just. It is easier to support the killing of one's own warriors, if one innately believes that their own warriors are behaving immorally or wrongly. This trait will facilitate a pacifistic or treasonous strategy, designed to forestall the K-selected warrior's plans for success, as well as to facilitate the more obvious strategy of betrayal.

79

5.   Tendency to disregard leadership's authority – This again, allows for the appeaser to pursue their own personal advantage in the environment of group competition. If they can easily disregard their leadership during times of war, and ignore the will of their populace, which that leadership represents, it will prove easier to pursue their own personal interests, or even bring about circumstances which will cull their nation's K-selected warriors.

6.   Rejection of Traditionalism –Probably an out-growth of novelty-seeking, this facilitates selfishness in group competition. It leaves the appeaser detached from the past culture and history of their people, and capable of embracing any form of future, even one involving an adoption of a foreign enemy's culture, mores, and nature following a defeat.

7.   Rejection of pro-social, group unifying behaviors - Warriors demand individuals behave politely and considerately, in such a way as to foster tighter bonds within their in-group. The appeaser will oppose this through support for indecency, vulgarity, and intra-group conflict - though only so much as they can without alienating their population or risking retribution. The appeaser is subconsciously programmed to seek the defeat of their in-group. Fracturing the in-group into competing cliques, fostering dissension, and diminishing the loyalty individuals feel towards the group all serve to further these goals. From attacks on patriotism, to supporting a fractured multicultural society, to supporting multilingualism, to supporting indecency and impoliteness in culture, to demanding military casualties to protect hostile foreigners from harm - the ultimate goal of all of these actions is to foster a society's defeat by fracturing its people and eroding their bonds.

8.   Deceptive nature – As we have emphasized, the appeaser seeks to persist in an environment where the K-selected individuals are killed by group conflict. However they can only exist within a warrior society, as long as they can portray themselves as loyal citizens. r-strategists have evolved a range of techniques for doing this, from simply proclaiming their patriotism publicly ("dissent is patriotic"), to viciously attacking anyone who would challenge their patriotism as traitorous and opposed to values of the group, to seeking to live in populations which are as large as possible, as diverse as possible, and as fragmented as possible, so as to minimize the effects of reputation and retribution.

You could actually view this r-strategy's mode of operation as a greatness-reducing strategy by those who can't keep up. Suppose you are a mid-witted guy of average abilities who lucked out and became part of an 11 man team that features ten Donald Trump-level geniuses, and you. There are also 11 women available as mates. Ten of them look like supermodels, and one is a short, fat, diseased specimen. Normally, you would be stuck with the short, fat diseased specimen.

However, due to your group's success and free resource availability everyone becomes more r and tolerant of r-behavior. Due to the wealth and ease, they even become tolerant of the open treason we see typically from the *"Fake Americans"* and *"Fake Europeans"* who comprise the leftist migration-activists.

Look at how advantageous it would be to you if you could betray your team to a bunch of mentally retarded Somali Muslims. Imagine if you could take out those 10 Donald Trumps, and replace them with ten 90lb Somalis, each exhibiting the 69 IQ which is average for individuals within Somalia. Suddenly, even though your group is now officially mentally retarded by American standards, you personally, have ten ultra-fit supermodel-class women to choose from as mates, and your r-strategist genes dominate a population which is now filled with r-strategist migrant genes.

There may be some who would say the desire to be surrounded by the foreign is not necessarily designed to kill indigenous K-strategists competitively. I would point out that wherever we see a leftist r-strategist obsession with importing the foreign, be it the barbarians of ancient Rome, or the Islamists of modern Europe, the migrants imported are never those who would make the leftist's homeland more peaceful, more prosperous, or more successful. Leftists never become obsessed with importing Buddhists, or Christians, or Taoists, or European business geniuses. Whenever leftist r-strategists become obsessed with importing the foreign, the foreigners they want to import invariably are of one kind – they are the violent foreigners who kill, and who often are imported despite a known hostility to the r-strategist's nation and its people.

You can see this strategy express itself most clearly when the r-strategists' nations are engaged in aggressive conflicts with out-groups. There, a normally Fabian strategy of minor sabotage by importing small numbers of hostile migrants, becomes more clearly expressed as open support for the interests of enemies and blatant attempts to enact rules and policies designed to kill K-strategists engaged in the battle. In war, the r-strategist's behavior will stand in stark contrast to that of the K-selected group competitor who will strongly out-group the enemy, strongly bond with their own people, and relentlessly seek to protect their own K-strategist warriors at the expense of all outsiders.

The treason of the *"Fake American"* and *"Fake European"* non-migratory r-strategists is an integral part of their reproductive strategy. It is a competitive strategy to take out the K-strategist genes in their nations, and replace them with what they perceive as less fit r-selected foreigners. It is no coincidence this will free up superior mate access and superior levels of resource availability as it shift the relative proportions of r and K genes.

That is why the left focuses on importing low-IQ, savage, third-world foreigners who appear to be among the least likely to successfully integrate into a technologically-sophisticated first-world nation. Had they imported a similar number of high-IQ technologically-sophisticated, civilized foreigners who would resemble their countrymen and clearly integrate better, there would be no r-strategist advantage for them to exploit, as mates and resources became more competitive.

As we have discussed, even simple games designed to simulate cooperative behavior have shown that the use of treason by individuals as a competitive strategy is a natural outgrowth of group cooperation.[53] So it is not surprising to see this behavior occur in a cooperative, competitively altruistic, K-selected, group-competitive species such as humans – especially when one considers that had the r-psychology not found a way to gain the protection of a group, such a lone individual would have easily been culled in group competition.

You can even see a similar strategy in nature with the anticompetitor in the Australian Giant Cuttlefish. The appeasement strategist relies on deception to avoid the consequences of their violations of the warrior's standards of altruistic, group-centric behavior.

If an anticompetitive male Cuttlefish were to be recognized as a male while attempting to mate, he would quickly be attacked by the fitter, more violent competitors. Similarly, were the appeaser recognized as a descendent of the r-selected human, were they recognized as pursuing a selfish, inherently disloyal Darwinian strategy within a loyal,

82

warrior species, the r-strategist, leftist appeaser's duplicity would mark him for ostracization within the species, at best.

Here you can see how this suite of modern, first-world-leftist, r-strategist political instincts would evolve, in a stepwise fashion. It would begin with the basic r-selected reproductive strategy, progress to the migrant instinct to crave travel to the foreign, then move on to the non-migratory instinct to import the foreign, and end with a complete treasonous appeasement strategy that embraces all of the violent r-strategists, from violent foreign savages who rape and kill, to violent domestic criminals who they will try to free.

Notice how this would only thrive when free resources had corrupted the society's adherence to morals, and eroded the demands of loyalty from its own citizens. You will not see this as much once actual K-selection takes hold. Rather, its most aggressive, neurotic expression, by panicked leftists, will be a mark of peak r-selection and a harbinger of impending K-selection.

Every facet of the left's desires and perceptions is designed to facilitate this strategy. Research has shown that altruists (warriors) find it easier to police their ranks for the selfish non-altruist in small, cohesive, homogenous groups where everyone knows everyone. There both outsiders and the disloyal are easily recognized and ostracized.

It is no coincidence that liberals congregate in large, population-dense cities, promote multicultural diversity within the cities to splinter the populations, promote perceptions of differences and conflicts between different elements of their in-groups, oppose even the mandating of a common language for their people, and support the tossed salad model of immigration instead of the melting pot. They are programmed to desire that fractured, impersonal environment, because it is what they are designed to most effectively exploit.

Such fragmenting of a large population is exactly opposite to the conditions which foster effective policing of a small, single, homogenous in-group's ranks by competitive altruists, who demand loyalty to group before loyalty to self in group competition.

It is not a coincidence that in disputes between their in-groups and their out-groups, liberals will always side with their out-group, reflexively. They will also vigorously oppose any actions which would enrich in-group at the expense of out-group (for example, seizure of oil interests from radical Islamist enemy regimes in the mid-east after martial victories). They are programmed to want the out-group to win, because when implementing their strategy, that is how they gain advantage.

Despite every action being expressly designed to support hostile out-groups at the expense of their own loyal in-group, this will never be allowed to be characterized as disloyal or unpatriotic. Clearly selective pressures culled any prior r-strategists who failed to vociferously deny their own disloyalty or treasonous intent. Indeed, so innate are these urges to their very nature, that they cannot even fathom such acts could be viewed by anyone as disloyal. They will maintain their own patriotism, even as the r-selected liberal denigrates the very word *"patriot"* as somehow tainted by a lack of intellect, and views the very concept of nationalistic fervor and national symbols as dangerous, foolish, and viscerally repugnant.[54, 55, 56]

It is my personal belief that the r-strategist has no idea how any of their desires or behaviors could appear so aberrant, or even repulsive, when viewed from a neutral perspective. To them, every urge is rooted in logic, and every behavior is rooted in reason and morals, because they are unable to see beyond their own r-selected urges, to the consequences of their actions.

For them, importing millions of low-IQ, third world criminals and savages is common sense. It will not in any way turn their own nation toward the path of a savage, low-IQ, third-world nation. That threat may seem obvious to the K-strategist, but to the r-strategist, it cannot even be comprehended, because they lack the brain circuitry to see it. Their brain is adapted to blindly exploit the short term glut and seek to surround themselves with r-selected rabbits. It is not designed to plan for decades ahead.

The K-selected right, has the same issues of being driven by instinct over logic. However since K-selection is more inherent to our species, their K-strategist urges happen to be more amenable to the standards of our species. Also, since K-selection is designed to produce fitness and greatness, K-strategists can blindly follow their K-selected instincts to success, or even see where logic combined with a desire for success would support their instinctual adherence to the K-strategy. If you want a nation that is great, you exhibit a discriminating, selective mindset, you reward greatness where it arises, and you loyally protect your nation's interests against the interference of outsiders. The political right is blessed in that following logic is congruent with our instincts, as both are designed for creating greatness and happiness for our K-people.

As discussed, in humans the r and K-strategies play out slightly differently than than they do in nature. This book describes what is, and uses the terms r and K as memes to consolidate and confer the ideas of these strategies in our minds. In humans r and K have evolved more complexly in some ways, and failed to evolve in other ways, in response to new technologies like birth control and abortion. As a result r and K will not mean the same things in politics, as they do in biology.

In biology r means high offspring output by maximizing mating and minimizing rearing. In humans, r-selection means maximizing mating and minimizing rearing through birth control and abortion - often eliminating offspring output entirely. It is the same psychology, the same strategy, and the same urges, even if technology changes the outcome.

Nevertheless, there is no better way to describe these political psychologies than through the use of their evolutionary lineage, so the meme-terminology of r and K will continue to be used throughout this text, even if technology has untethered the biological programs from their biological purposes and outcomes.

These ancient r and K forces are the magnetic poles of politics. They create ideological field forces that permeate our populations and drive the massing of our two main political ideologies. They create the aggregations of individuals that seem to attract masses of similar psychologies into political groups. These political groups share similar psychological traits to those r and K-selected animals we see in nature. As this chapter shows, even where these human versions of the strategies have evolved considerably into much more complex strategies, the evolutions can best be understood through the prism of r/K Theory.

To some, the characterizations in this book will appear biased towards conservatism and the right. However the difficulty in presenting these concepts lies in the fact that humans are innately biased themselves, through their evolutionary history. Humans are overall, a K-selected species,[57] which further evolved to be individually competitive, and then further evolved to compete in group competitions. This fiercely competitive evolutionary history is what has produced the immense evolutionary advancement we see in our species, and even the sophistication and complexity of our cultures and civilizations.

This evolutionary history has also psychologically predisposed everyone, r and K-strategist alike, to recognize the superiority of the K-strategy. Within our species, the r-selected psychology is a minority and an outcast, embodying psychological traits which are directly opposed to the psychological traits that our species as a whole evolved to be guided by. Yet to confront this simple truth, is to exhibit bias – a K-selected bias imbued within us by our K-selected evolutionary history.

As examples of this innate bias, our species tends to hold monogamy as superior to promiscuity. It tends to hold competitiveness, ambition, and taking responsibility for outcomes as superior to entitlement, irresponsibility, and sloth. It tends to believe freedom in interactions and earned success is superior to uniform outcomes dictated arbitrarily by an outside party. We will view children raised by two monogamous parents, in an environment designed to defer their reproductive behaviors until maturity, far more positively than we would view an environment where children are raised by single parents, and exposed to stimuli designed to provoke sexual precociousness beginning as early in their life as possible. We will always favor those who are loyal to our nation, over those who sympathize with outsiders, and our populace will always innately respect the most K-selected, competitive warriors in our society, such as a military member or police officer, far more than we will respect the pacifist or the hippie.

This innate bias conferred on our species by our evolutionary history makes truly impartial characterizations of these urges difficult. If this work is correct (and the evidence to be presented shortly would indicate that it is), then any honest, accurate characterizations of these urges will be biased in favor of the K-selected competitive warrior, since that evolved psychology is the basis for the very standard by which we humans judge "good" and "bad."

Regardless of this difficulty, this text will describe these urges and their Darwinian purposes as clearly and as accurately as possible, and leave it to the reader to interpret the information in as unbiased a fashion as is possible.

Chapter Twelve

Issues and Political Philosophy in the Context of this Theory _____

For ages, the political left and right have battled over what would constitute the ideal social and governmental structure. Here we will discuss some of the current issues which the political left and right advocate on behalf of, and show how every conflict within an issue will have as its origin the inherent conflict between the r-selected, anticompetitive psychology, or the K-selected, competitive psychology. Every issue will come down to each side pursuing one the five main r/K traits, and seeking to create either an r or K-selective environment.

Economics

In issues of economics, conservatives favor a free market Capitalistic system, in which every individual engages in volitional interactions with others, as freely as possible, and then bears the outcomes of those interactions, whether good or bad. This produces an environment where businesses freely form and dissolve absent any external interference, their fates determined by the results of free, Darwinesque economic competitions.

In this scheme, individuals and business entities will enjoy varying levels of success. Some will exhibit high levels of ability, determination, and effort, and they will be rewarded with far more resources than are required for simple sustenance. Others will prove less fit and capable in these economic competitions, and they will endure the rigors of poverty. In acquiring excess resources, beyond what is necessary for mere survival, the successful individuals will gain substantial competitive advantage over their peers, and this will be reflected in superior rates of survival, superior choices of mates, and superior advantages for their offspring.

By contrast, the political left will prefer a far more controlled economic scheme. These left-leaning economic models will be designed to forestall all free competitions between individuals, avert or rectify any particular individual's failure in competition, and more evenly redistribute any resources and advantages that have been unevenly allocated in free competitions or interactions.

At the most extreme left, one finds Communism and Socialism. There, all advantages acquired by individuals through effort or merit are eliminated. Ideally, everyone will be provided with the exact same advantage. This creates a social environment approximating the r-selected environment, where resources are easily acquired without any need to compete with peers.

As in the case of the anticompetitive Cuttlefish, this thwarting of merit based competitions is also accompanied by the r-type Communist's pursuit of personal advantages (through corruption), wherever possible. This is as would be expected within a Darwinian strategy designed to provide personal, individual competitive advantage.

As one heads towards the moderated left, these models only moderate the limitations on freedom and competition, and the seizure and redistribution of resources. So within the moderate left, even when individuals succeed in limited free competition, the political liberal will still seek to use government to seize much of their earned resources, for redistribution to others who were not as successful. In doing this, they attenuate, to whatever degree is politically possible, the advantages acquired by the successful and ameliorate the disadvantages of those who have not succeeded in free competition with their peers.

Notice, the liberal does not seek to out-compete the successful, K-selected individual, and then reapportion their own earned income to the less fortunate. Rather, the political leftist seeks to use force of government to reapportion the success of the successful competitor. This ideology is a competitive strategy, designed to increase one's own relative success, through the diminution of another individual's superior level of success.

Liberals are not averse to competition with peers, they are merely averse to free, fair, rule governed competitions designed to favor merit and ability. Competition is just fine with them, as long as it is rigged in their favor, and does not reward ability, determination, or effort.

Social Policies

The political right will tend to pursue domestic social policies which parallel the K-selected environment, and the reproductive strategies it entails. In the view of conservatives, mating and reproduction should be monogamous, and should occur later in life, after competitive demonstrations of fitness. Child-rearing should be designed primarily to raise as competitive a child as possible. One father and one mother together, rearing a child to mate monogamously, and continue the cycle itself, is the ideal. Any unorthodox rearing styles, deviating from this ideal, which might potentially yield sub-par outcomes for the child are frowned upon. Programs or aspects of the social environment which may facilitate children pursuing a more r-selected model of early promiscuity and single parenting are also frowned upon.

Aspects of social policy which do not value children highly, or which even entail the killing of an unborn child before it is allowed to compete, such as abortion, will also be opposed. To a K-strategist, the only means by which one should ever fail in life is by failing in free competition with others.

Institutions such as marriage, which are designed to sanctify the K-selected model of two-parent, high-investment child-rearing will be viewed as unusually important, and efforts to diminish this importance will be fought vigorously.

Within this psychology, children are important, the proven traditional-model of family is necessary, and the rearing of children into highly fit, K-selected competitors, of impeccable morality and decency, is paramount.

The political left will tend to pursue a less K-selective social environment, more in line with r-selected values and mores. Mating and reproduction may be promiscuous, and unselective, and any cultural influence which promotes this (or which degrades more K-selected institutions and mores as antiquated) will be seen as modern and progressive, towards a better (more r-selected) society.

High-investment child rearing, by two monogamously paired parents will be seen as of little importance to a child's ultimate maturation. Programs which will facilitate or encourage children pursuing a more r-selected strategy of early promiscuity, sexual indiscriminateness, or single parenting, such as early graphical sexual education, generous single mother welfare, or provision of condoms or birth-control, will be favored. An educational environment which advances the concepts of sexual promiscuity, diminished confrontational interactions, less loyalty to in-group, less competitiveness, less patriotism, lower investment single-parenting (or other non-traditional models of family), diminished discrimination between good and bad, and less adherence to K-type behavioral rules will be favored.

Within liberalism, the value of children, and their ideal rearing environment, will be diminished considerably. This is consistent with r-type reproductive strategies which de-emphasize the importance accorded to rearing individual offspring. In the ideal r-strategy, parents surrender their children to a government, which educates the children to adhere to r-values, en masse.

From support for abortion, to less concern for the effects of unorthodox rearing styles, liberals will exhibit less concern for the ideal rearing of the young of the species. In the most r-selected species, even cannibalization of the young is accepted behavior, so it is not surprising to see the r-selected human denigrate the value of infants by implying they are not necessarily human beings (and by implication are thus able to be killed morally, at a weary parent's whim, for some period after birth).[58]

Additionally, whether supporting medical schemes which devalue older individuals and diminish their right to life, health, and medical treatment based on their age, or the liberal's support for abortion, the liberal would almost seem to support any form of unselective mortality which would diminish the population's ranks randomly, and thereby mimic an r-selected environment.

Personal Defense

Here, clearly the K-selected conservatives will embrace a more competitive, K-selective environment where citizens are free to carry firearms, and engage criminals in Darwinian struggles. This will foster an environment where individuals exhibit varying levels of competitive

90

ability. Some individuals will exhibit greater levels of fitness in this environment, and will be less prone to victimization. Others, who elect to not arm themselves, and who seek to follow a strategy of conflict avoidance and appeasement of criminal threats, will exhibit less fitness if confronted. They will endure an associated competitive disadvantage. This will create an environment of grossly obvious competitive disparity, where some individuals are well trained and well armed, while others are left helpless in the face of violence. To the K-selected psychology, such an environment is natural, while to the r-type psychology, nothing could be more repugnant and terrifying.

The r-type liberal will feel motivated to eliminate all fitness disparities by preventing anyone from possessing a means of engaging in self defense, such as concealed firearms, knives, truncheons, or other weapons. This will have the effect of preventing any segment of the populace from exhibiting a superior level of fitness, and enjoying a related competitive advantage. One will see this in any major city, where carrying firearms for self defense is forbidden. In such jurisdictions, BB-guns, many common pocket knives, and even non-lethal defense weapons such as pepper spray and stun-guns will also be forbidden.

This leftist strategy is similar to the strategy liberals employ in matters of capitalism and income redistribution. Here, those who would have exhibited inferior levels of fitness are able to raise their relative level of fitness by using government to force others to willingly diminish their levels of fitness. This has the additional advantage of potentially stoking confrontation between groups of K-selected police, and K-selected citizens who simply wish to defend themselves. No liberal will ever have the courage to visit a gun-owner's house, and demand their firearm. However, if you offer to send a cop to do it for them, they will rejoice at the possibilities.

Even if criminals continue to acquire weapons and victimize citizens, at least the liberal does not feel anyone else is more capable of dealing with the threat than they are. The liberal has thereby stopped anyone else from exhibiting a superior level of fitness, and enjoying the advantages thereof.

Interestingly, increased criminal victimization of the populace, absent any ability of highly fit individuals to defend themselves, would be a very r-type selection pressure, almost identical to the selective effects produced by the predation of prey species. It would diminish population numbers unselectively, absent the ability of some individuals to use K-type competitive aggression to gain competitive advantage.

It is very interesting that liberals are innately more comfortable in an environment of increased criminal predation, as long as there are no associated fitness-mediated disparities in the rates of predation. Offer to arm citizens, even show how it will diminish crime, and the liberal will still choose the higher crime-rate of disarmament. There is nothing as unacceptable to the liberal as a selective pressure which offers advantage to fitter, more K-selected individuals. We will discuss this psychological quality more later.

Foreign Policy

Issues of foreign policy will mimic issues of domestic policy, though here the primary focus will be on the warrior/appeaser paradigm.

The conservative seeks group competitions between nations at every opportunity. They will innately perceive profound differences between in-groups and out-groups. This will facilitate conflict, and these conflicts will play out at every level, from the economic, to the martial.

Conservatives will demand loyalty to their in-group, and once conflict begins, they will also demand subservience to leadership, so long as the leadership appears to be attempting to win the conflict or competition, and acting with their group's best interests at heart.

Liberals, by contrast will not be able to find comfort in such a competitive environment. Once exposed to it, the liberal will begin to adopt positions designed to gain advantage within such a competitive environment, without actually enduring risk, or partaking of the competition. Liberals will seek to first stifle the competition, in an effort to prevent the onset of the competitive, K-selected environment. This is the origin of liberal pacifism, and it is why no matter how noxious, the enemy, no matter the sins he has committed, the liberal will tend to oppose any call to war.

If that attempt fails, liberals will seek to ally with the out-group while denigrating their in-group's ability to win the competition. This drive will be present in all liberals, though the degree to which it is openly exhibited will depend on the intensity of the liberal's partisanship. Extreme liberals will travel to the enemy's lands, and openly support him. Moderates will seek to stymie the war effort more covertly from home, while still maintaining their ties with their own people, by couching such efforts as reasonable or compassionate.

These urges can be modified by practicality, as every r-selected individual will support their own interests first and foremost. However every r-type psychology will tend towards this model of behavior, when confronted with group selection processes.

By pursuing a strategy of allying with the out-group while covertly betraying their in-group, the r-selected appeaser will not just diminish the success of their in-group's K-selected warriors. In our evolutionary history, the r-selected appeaser could actually defeat their in-group's warriors outright, through the use of a proxy force composed of their out-group's competitive warriors.

We will show cases in history later, where this behavioral drive is quite apparent in the most ardent of leftists during the most group-selective environments. We will show that the existence of this strategy is completely inarguable. The behavioral tendency towards disloyalty underlying it is also documented by such researchers as John Jost (himself a liberal), who points out that diminished levels of loyalty to in-group, as well as a desire to rebel against their own, are a hallmark of the liberal psychology.

Thus to a liberal, disparities in national economic fitness will require that their own nation sacrifice resources to more primitive and violent nations. During wars, the liberal's own nation must endure disadvantages, to appease hostile outsiders. Such disadvantages will range from enduring military casualties, so as to avoid killing foreigners who oppose their nation, to providing resources to individuals who hate their nation simply to avoid appearing greedy, to accepting defeat before stooping to ruthless eradication of their nation's enemies. Treaties will be opportunities to generate good will with enemies and competitors by sacrificing national interests to these outsiders, and economic agreements will be designed to appease those who least favor their nation, in the hopes of generating good will for the leftist.

This strategy, executed most effectively, does demand that individuals pursuing it maintain a plausible deniability as to their motives, so as to prevent an expulsion from their in-group. This will come naturally to the r-type psychology because the motivational force producing these behaviors is not consciously treasonous to the liberal. Rather, the r-type psychology engenders a perceptual framework which leads honest individuals to be predisposed to seeing their own people as evil, wrong, or unfair, while seeing enemies as inherently more noble, justified, and moral. This leads the liberal to honestly sympathize with their enemies over their in-group out of an honest moral conviction, based on their altered perceptions.

However, from the betrayal of our allies, such as Israel, to the demands that our society endure civilian casualties rather than perform the torture of terrorists, to limitations on other forms of extreme violence on our enemies to safeguard our own, the r-selected, anticompetitive liberal appeaser's subconscious, unwitting goal is to simultaneously gain the favor of our enemies while limiting our own ability to successfully win the conflicts we engage in.

It is the firm position of this text that this is an evolved psychological adaptation to group competition, and it underlies what researcher John Jost spoke of as the conservative's "underlying psychological need" for "loyalty" to their group, and the liberal's "underlying psychological need" for "rebellion" against their group.[59]

Governmental Size and Scope

There will always be a debate over governmental size and scope, due to the differing views each psychology will hold over the role government plays in the lives of citizens.

In the view of K-selected conservatives, all citizens seek to compete in freedom in our competitive, K-selected environment, and they are willing to endure the consequence of bad decisions. In this environment, citizens are as free as possible to interact with each other. As each individual offers value and services to other citizens, this will produce an individual competition to accrue resources, based on one's ability, effort, and determination. As a result, each citizen will end up

94

indirectly competing in rule governed, competitive measures of relative fitness and ability. Ideally, in the view of K-type conservatives, this will occur absent any meddling by outside parties, and the outcomes will be accurate measures of the relative fitness and ability of the entities competing.

Due to this view, in the eyes of a K-type conservative, the role of government is to foster as efficient a competitive environment as possible. Under this model, government should perform services designed to facilitate free interactions, such as protecting each individual's freedom to interact with others as they see fit, enforcing rules of fairness and morality in interactions, providing a means by which to exchange value (currency), facilitating business through aiding transportation and financial infrastructure, and safeguarding the earned property of individuals from seizure by others, either through laws against theft, or oversight of financial institutions. The purpose of all of this is to promote institutional stability and trust, so free competition may flourish.

This will result in a generalized perception that government should be minimal in its size and scope, and merely facilitate, rather than interfere, in personal interactions between citizens.

To those on the leftward side of the political spectrum, however, every citizen desires to live in the r-selected environment - with freely available resources and absent any competition between individuals or disparities in competitive outcomes. To these individuals, this state of affairs is forestalled by a few greedy individuals who horde wealth unfairly. To the liberal, government is a tool by which to enforce a safe and secure r-selected environment on a populace. This leftist will believe that unless so controlled, a population would revert to primitive and evil urges to strive and compete with each other. These primitive urges to compete, uncontrolled, would rapidly spiral out of control, resulting in disparate apportionment of resources among individuals, and the creation of winners and losers in the society.

Thus, as one heads increasingly towards the left of the political spectrum, the job of government is to stifle all competition, and reapportion any resources which accrue disproportionately. In its most pure form, this urge will present as an effort to provide equal levels of resources to everyone, regardless of ability or effort, exactly as one would see resources apportioned in the r-selected environment. The farther leftward one travels on the spectrum, the more one will see these desires manifest. Of course, even the moderate leftist still seeks the redistribution of wealth and suppression of free competition, to ameliorate such disparities in ability. They merely temper their urges out of practicality.

The K-selected urge for freedom and free competition exists in the majority of our citizens. Since r-selected liberalism requires a government that is capable of oppressing the natural urges of all of those citizens, the leftist will see a need for a government which is as large, powerful, and controlling of all individuals as possible. The more leftward their political leanings, the larger they will seek to see the government grow, and the more power and regulatory authority they will seek to bestow on it. That, of course is exactly where leftism, unrestrained, leads.

Environmentalism

Environmentalism is an area where the liberal clearly strives to produce an r-selected environment. Consumption of all available environmental resources, to the point of inducing scarcity, is one of the hallmarks of the K-selected environment.

Here, the r-selected, anticompetitive liberal seems to perceive, on a very primal level, that high levels of consumption by individuals can bring about a more K-selected environment, and that this Malthusian outcome would be a bad thing for the liberal. As a result, liberals tend to be in support of sustainable environmental initiatives, such as recycling, energy conservation, and other forms of diminished personal consumption, all of which would forestall the onset of the restricted environmental resources which will foster a more fiercely competitive, K-selected environment.

By contrast, conservatives exhibit far less concern regarding the effects of their own personal consumption, and do not exhibit the aggressive phobia of resource scarcity or environmental exhaustion that one sees in liberals. Nor does the conservative fear environmental change. Rather, the conservative views any adverse environmental circumstance merely as a challenge to demonstrate their worthiness, similar to how the K-selected organism would view any adverse environmental conditions they encountered.

National Sovereignty

Liberals will oppose national sovereignty, and support ceding authority over their nation's affairs to outside bodies such as the United Nations, the World Court, or some form of international treaty obligation. This is an urge likely borne of a desire to avoid group conflict and competition. It is also a desire to cede authority to an outside force which will uniformly control and oppress everyone, and a desire to perpetuate a more pacifistic, r-selected environment within the international arena.

By contrast, conservatives will strongly oppose any infringement on national sovereignty, and will fully support engaging in the conflicts and international competitions such a strategy may lead to. To the K-type warrior psychology, one acts autonomously with principle, and lets the chips fall where they may, based on merit based assessments of relative ability, effort, and determination.

The difference between the desire to act autonomously and endure any outcome, or to see everyone's innate urges controlled and oppressed by authority in return for some measure of security, is the fundamental difference between both of our political ideologies. If one understands the r and K-type origins of these two psychologies, it is not hard to see why this is.

Discriminations Between Good and Bad

Under the tenets of this theory, liberalism descended from the r-selected psychology. Designed to maximize reproductive rates, the liberal psychology is designed to focus behavior primarily on mating and reproduction, while simultaneously avoiding any direct, open conflict or competition with peers. We maintain that this history has produced within the liberal an aversion to moral judgment and discrimination between good and bad (an aversion which we will show later has a very clear neurological root).

This aversion to a judgmental environment exists partly because liberal urges inherently clash with our species' K-selected moral drives. As a result, any such discrimination between good and bad will force the liberal to confront the fact that they espouse mores and values which run counter to our species' normative K-type mores and values.

Liberals will also be averse to the judgmental environment because retribution by groups (in the form of discrimination) is the primary means by which altruistic groups punish non-altruists. Discrimination against those who would support an enemy in time of war is a very real threat to liberal competitive advantage, as well as to the persistence of the r-selected, anticompetitive trait within the population.

Most importantly, such discriminations can form the basis of conflict and competition. As a result of the liberal being programmed to avoid both competition and conflict, they are inherently designed to avoid making such judgments, and to try and dissuade others from doing so as well.

By contrast, the conservative, having descended from the K-selected psychology, will find themselves strongly driven by the moral urges that are normative to our species. As a result, they will be more inclined to render judgments of other individuals based on their adherence to such K-mores, and more likely to spot deviations from such mores and values in others.

Additionally, the K-selected psychology is programmed to engage in conflict and competition. As a result, the rendering of such verdicts can initiate the very conflicts and competitions that K-type conservatives are programmed to engage in.

Finally, retribution offers a vital advantage to the altruist in group competition. As a result, the altruistic competitive warrior trait will be immensely advantaged in an environment where those who are not selflessly loyal to group and its success are judged, and either discriminated against within the group, punished outright, or expelled entirely.

Thus, this theory would predict that the liberal would be instinctually averse to a society rendering judgments and engendering conflict, while the conservative would be driven to constantly render judgments between good and bad, draw distinctions between liked and disliked, differentiate between in-group and out-group, and discriminate against members of their own group who have violated our species' traditionally K-type moral virtues.

The r-selected psychology needs an environment where any disparity in individual ability is meaningless, where the population makes no fitness affecting judgments between good and bad, where no individual can be discriminated against by the group for any reason, and where the measure of success is merely the degree to which one can mate promiscuously, and abandon one's offspring without consequence.

In light of this, the liberal drive to eradicate all forms of discrimination between good and bad would have the effect of being beneficial to a selfish Darwinian strategy, less concerned with group success than personal success. Conversely, the conservative drive to discriminate between good and bad, and punish those deemed bad would tend to be the mark of a more altruistic strategy. And indeed, that is exactly the case made within this work.

Political Correctness

The drive towards political correctness is another example of how the liberal seeks to recreate the anticompetitive environment of the r-selected organism.

An outgrowth of the drive to eliminate discrimination, political correctness is an overt attempt to create an environment where any stimulus indicating potential conflict and competition, is eliminated. This is done by forcing all individuals to assiduously avoid any form of personal interaction which could be construed as offensive, and which might therefore provoke conflict.

If no one says anything which could possibly be considered offensive, and no individual acknowledges any competition between any groups, then there will be no aggressive stimuli that could provoke conflict. As liberals become accustomed to this hyper-pacifistic environment, any violation of this unwritten behavioral rule will be perceived as an exceedingly unpleasant behavioral faux pas.

K-selected competitor men, by contrast, will tend to be more "macho" and brash in their personal countenances, instinctually rejecting the tenets of political correctness. These more confrontational behavioral traits will be commonly found among aggressive K-type males throughout the species. Brashness provokes conflict, and drives those who fear it either into passive submission, or away from the group. Those who regularly engage in K-selected endeavors, such as warfare, will often be found to be brash and confrontational, by the standards of the politically correct, r-selected liberal.

Among warriors, friendly insults and jibes build rapport, through individuals demonstrating their comfort in a confrontational, K-selected group, and their refusal to take umbrage at anything said by an ally. Such insults, however, will make more r-selected individuals uncomfortable, as they might herald the onset of a more competitive, and selective environment.

Tendencies towards brashness will be portrayed as anti-intellectual by r-strategists, while tendencies towards political correctness will be portrayed as weak and cowardly by K-selected humans. In reality, each is merely an attempt to recreate the environment one's Darwinian strategy was evolved for, as the r and K-type traits seek to enhance the chances of their advance into the species' genome.

Public Health Policy

Death is an ever present consequence to our choices in life. If you smoke, eat fatty foods, over indulge in sugar, or just do something dangerous like skydiving, death may result.

This creates a competitive environment, where some people will make good choices, some will make bad choices, and as a result some will die, and some will prosper.

The K-selected environment is inherently competitive, and as a result, K-selected competitors have a comfort within that competitive environment of free choice. K-selected individuals are also more tolerant of competitive mortality within their population, since rapid population growth is not an imperative to the K-strategy (K-selected individuals will have greater issues with any unselective mortality, or mortality targeted randomly against their in-group).

As with K-selected individuals, conservatives are also tolerant of mortality arising from competitive selections. For example, if individuals choose to not wear motorcycle helmets, and die in accidents, the K-selected psychology will not see that as a pressing problem in need of a governmental intervention. Similarly, conservatives will not see deaths from obesity, smoking, or firearms violence as requiring increased control of the populace to remedy. From eating fatty foods, to not carrying health insurance, to smoking, conservatives seek to allow all people to weigh the individual aspects of their circumstances, and then do as they wish. If there are adverse outcomes to these decisions, it is the conservative's position that one should bear the burden of the responsibilities for the decisions made, and that this is fair, just, and respectful of everyone's freedom.

By contrast, r-selected organisms have evolved specifically to feel averse to any competitive environment. Indeed, when competitive selections begin within a previously r-selected environment, it does not bode well for the future of the r-selected organisms within that population. Just as the K-selected organism is tolerant of competitive mortality, the r-selected organism is intolerant of any mortality within their environment, if it results from competitive selection due to personal decisions. For the r-strategist, if individuals choose to eat fatty foods, and subsequently die of obesity, that is a problem which must be remedied with an application of government control of the populace to force dietary changes on everyone.

For this reason, the K-selected individual will always exhibit a comfort within a competitive environment, where individuals are free to do as they like, and their decisions and actions regarding their personal health have consequences. Likewise, the r-selected organism will seek an environment absent any competition, where everyone is forced, by any means necessary, to avoid any adverse health outcome that is a result of competitive failure.

Within the debate over public health policy, we see this dichotomy manifest, just as one would expect, were they to assume

101

liberalism and conservatism are outgrowths of the more primitive r and K-selected strategies.

Immigration

Within the immigration debate, we see two positions. One holds that America has plentiful resources, and there is no reason to prevent fellow citizens of the world from coming here, and helping themselves to our bounty. To this psychology, resources will always be freely available, conflict or denial of resources to anyone else is wrong, and there is no real out-group or in-group to either show loyalty to, or withhold loyalty from.

Additionally, in seeking to give the foreigners the right to elect leaders who will dictate policy to our native citizens, this strategy also sets the stage for conflict between individuals who are conflict-predisposed, in the future. If r and K are traits, then the r-strategy is setting the stage for K-trait carriers (both domestic and foreign) to become embroiled in a depopulating fight, which the r-strategists will try to avoid and hide from, instinctually. This would be a brilliant competitive strategy for a conflict-averse trait to engage in.

The other psychology sees American prosperity as limited in nature. It perceives foreigners as an out-group, to whom we owe nothing - and who should be fought if they feel otherwise. Any out-group we allow to immigrate is seen as potentially consuming limited domestic resources which should be reserved solely for our in-group, out of loyalty. This psychology is innately programmed to see a world of limited resources, and group competition.

One psychology sees a world of limitless resources, where competition is wrong and immoral. The other sees a world of limited resources, and groups which need to be fought off to secure them. If conditions turn K-selective, there is no doubt which psychology would quickly dominate the scene.

Conclusions

In closing, every issue of politics will come down to issues of embracing or rejecting free competition, (and the strategies best suited to each, either group or individual), or adoption of r or K-selected mating strategies. In all of these issues, the positions of the conservative and liberal political ideologies will be able to be predicted by examining the issue in light of r/K selection theory, and the pursuit of success of the group in group selection processes, or the pursuit of failure of the group (either through outright defeat, or failure to dominate) in group selection processes.

r-selected psychologies will always tend towards using governmental control of the populace to suppress our innate drives to strive and compete, while seeking to curry favor with enemies in group competition. By contrast, K-type psychologies will tend towards minimally intrusive forms of government, since their goal is to allow the citizenry to abide by their natural urges to strive and compete with each other. In matters of group competitions, K-type psychologies will favor the ruthless pursuit of group success over enemies, while r-selected psychologies will pursue a much more murky strategy.

If this is understood, politics ceases to be a debate over logic and morality, and becomes more of a competition, to see which strategy should determine the future of our nation and the course of our species. It is an assumption of this work that as this theory inevitably works its way through the sciences, it will fundamentally alter the nature of our political debates.

What effects this will have on our debates, remains to be seen.

Chapter Thirteen

The Scientific Evidence

In the coming pages we will examine further evidence which supports the theory we have presented thus far, and which will hopefully illuminate the mechanisms within individuals by which nature has imbued these strategies.

Drawn from a wide range of disciplines, this evidence will offer a compelling case that two psychologies exist within our species. These two psychologies revolve around issues of individual and group competition, they are produced primarily by two different brain structures, they are associated with a variation in a specific gene, their expression is associated with early life rearing experiences, they begin to manifest very early in life, and they may be profoundly affected by the neurochemical affects of resource availability, or lack thereof. Combined with an understanding of the material previously presented on r/K Selection Theory, the conclusions are inescapable.

Hopefully, the reader will find the following information compelling, but not fail to see the need for further research on this topic, as a means of more fully understanding ourselves, and our species.

Finally, biology is not destiny, any more than ignorance is actually bliss. Every individual acquires information, and makes decisions themselves. What will be described here are cognitive filters, which skew the perceptions of information, and mold the nature of decisions.

Every action we take creates the person we are. Every piece of data we acquire adapts our own informational filters and alters our decision-making processes, affecting those actions. Used properly, to better help us understand ourselves and the decisions we come to, this information can aid us to make better individual decisions, improve the effects they will have on our civilization, as well as help us control how those decisions mold the very nature of who we are.

It is my hope that everyone who reads this material and examines the mechanisms of ideology will recognize this, and open themselves to the concept that right or wrong, their decisions may be affected by the following mechanisms. Only in accepting that possibility, can they truly unhitch themselves from their instincts, and enjoy free will.

Knowledge is power, and it can be useful in leading people to do good. Open yourself to your own innate urge to be free, and make your own destiny by your own hand. Perceive the beauty of loyalty, and the joy of the common cause. Then recognize that others will wish to be afforded the same luxury of determining their own fate, within a loyal nation.

Chapter Fourteen

Liberal vs. Conservative Brain Structures

Dr. Ryota Kanai of the Institute for Cognitive Neuroscience, University College, London led a team which did some fascinating research into the brain structures of political ideologues. In their 2011 study,[60] Dr Kanai's team examined MRIs of the brains of ideologues on the left and right, and found that there were two main structural differences between the brains of liberals and the brains of conservatives. This research further supported earlier work examining differences between the cognitive processes of partisans.[61]

In short, Dr. Kanai and his team found that liberals possess a smaller right amygdala volume and a larger anterior cingulate cortex (ACC) than their conservative counterparts. This is consistent with other work which has linked amygdala function with political affiliation.[62]

The amygdala is a brain structure most commonly described as being responsible for the generation of fear. This definition is incomplete, however. The amygdala is primarily responsible for assigning emotional significance to encountered perceptions.[63] What that means, is that the amygdala essentially scans all incoming information and flags the information that it deems as important. Likely due to this, it is also strongly associated with the ability to perceive threat, and it is this which leads many to say that it is responsible for the production of fear.

The amygdala, in this light, is best viewed as akin to the character of Captain Kirk, on the old Star-Trek TV Series, with the entire brain viewed as the Starship Enterprise. Captain Kirk sits on the bridge of the Enterprise, with all the big TV screens before him, flooding his awareness with quick flashes of data. Like the amygdala, Captain Kirk cursorily examines the wide range of data, and chooses what to flag as significant, and focus upon, usually based upon the threat a stimulus poses. Then he will focus the Enterprise's (brain's) relevant resources on the flagged subject. Imagine on one screen, a ghost starship, floating lifeless and fully infested with tribbles, glides by and off into space, while on another screen, a heavily armed Klingon attack ship approaches rapidly, while charging their ship's weapons to fire. A well developed amygdala will scan those threats, and quickly determine what is most important, just as Captain Kirk would. Immediately the ship would be focused on the Klingon threat.

Like the amygdala, Captain Kirk does not personally do all the functions performed in the course of the Enterprise's (brain's) operations. He has medical specialists, communications specialists, engineering specialists, security teams, and even a logic specialist, in the form of Spock. They all report their observations to him, advise him of their analyses of them, and he decides what must be focused upon, and what decision will maximally reduce the potential for future negativity to the ship and its crew. Likewise, the amygdala is widely wired in to vast areas of the brain. Imagine realizing that you forgot to take care of some job at work, and combine it with having overheard another employee say that layoffs begin next week and those who under-produce will be the first to go. As the logical realization hits that not doing that job could cost you your employment, your amygdala will flag all of that as significant, even though it didn't do the auditory processing of sound waves to words, or the processing of words to thoughts, or thoughts to logical outcomes. All of the data was reported to the amygdala. When you quickly finish that job the next day, it will be because the Captain Kirk of your brain issued orders to do it immediately, and the rest of your brain followed those orders, to minimize the aversive stimulus that your amygdala would have inflicted, had they not.

Like the amygdala, a Starship Captain's ability is based on skill and experience. If your Captain is well-trained, and highly experienced, then when a Klingon-attack vessel approaches, like Kirk, he calmly sits back, and barks orders to the various parts of the ship, to defend and counter the Klingon attack.

Just like a poorly developed amygdala, shielded from consequence and never developed, if a Captain isn't well trained, you end up with Nathan Lane's character from Birdcage on the bridge of the Enterprise, jumping up and down on his seat, neurotically waving his arms and frantically crying for somebody to do something to save him. Using his ACC mediated cognitive model, he will focus unduly on each trauma the ship endures, panic immeasurably, and fail to predict how

108

best to avoid future traumas. That emotional freakout, and the fear of it, is what will motivate all sorts of strange policy proposals, from asking terrorists, who just killed thousands of our countrymen what it was that we did to make them angry, to banning children from having pop-tarts at lunch that have been bitten into the shape of a gun.

To describe amygdala function in a more simple and technical manner, when one encounters a perception of their environment, and that perception is followed by a negative event, the amygdala will record that the perception preceded a negative event, and attach emotional significance to it. This will mark that specific perception for future recognition. Should the perception be encountered in the future, the amygdala will immediately recognize it, even before it is consciously registered, and warn the brain that a negative event is likely to follow, so that one may prepare for it.

The most commonly described example would be an event which preceded an attack by a predator. Suppose, for example, one heard grass rustle a short distance away, a stick broke, and then a lion jumped out and attempted to attack you. If you escaped, your amygdala would assign significance to the sound of grass rustling, followed by a breaking stick. The next time you heard grass rustling, followed by a breaking stick, you would immediately experience panic, and prepare for a lion attack mentally, without the intervention of logical thought.

Due to the amygdala's interconnectedness with other structures within the brain, this response operates on a very primal, physical level. One individual, known to one of the authors, fell through the ice on a pond. He was entertaining a friend's dare to go out on the ice, when it suddenly broke apart beneath him. Immediately preceding the plunge, he reported that he remembered the feel of the ice cracking subtly under his feet for a second or so, before it gave way.

For years afterward, he would watch his step carefully in the spring. Small, thin puddles on asphalt, frozen solid during the night, would find themselves in sunlight in the morning. The sunlight would warm the black asphalt, and melt the ice where it met the ground. The melted ice would drain into the asphalt, while a thin sheet of solid ice above remained frozen, due to the cold air temperatures. As a result, the top of the puddle would be a frozen sheet of ice, unsupported by any ice beneath. When stepped upon, these four or five inch diameter puddles would produce a crushing sensation under the feet.

This individual would carefully watch his step in the spring, never stepping on these puddles. Even the small cracking of this unsupported sheet of ice under his feet, would send a physical wave of fearful shock up the center of his abdomen. His amygdala was warning him of that stimulus's significance by simulating the sensation of his sudden plunge into ice cold water. So deep was his amygdala's response to that single negative incident, that years later he found it easier to watch where he stepped, than to intellectually disregard the stimulus as a neurological false alarm.

The amygdala also assigns significance to less fear-related stimuli. In several studies, the amygdala has been found to be involved in the reading of emotion in facial expressions, the judgment of threats presented by others, and the analysis of the intentions of others.[64, 65, 66, 67] The amygdala is therefore crucial to the perception of threat presented by other individuals, likely through attaching significance to, and drawing attention to, subtle indicators of threat in other's countenances.

Reduced amygdala function is assumed to reflect diminished development, and reduced functionality.[68] Interestingly humans exhibit a fair degree of variability in amygdala volume, even accounting for differences in measuring criteria.[69]

In an experiment, monkeys with damage specifically to their amygdalae, were found to be unable to read social cues, or respond to threat stimuli. As a result, they were described in the research as, *"retarded in their ability to foresee and avoid dangerous confrontations."*[70] To anyone who is not a leftist, the similarity is obvious.

Some have reported that the inability of those with amygdala deficiency to judge other's intentions is a result of a strong tendency of such individuals to avoid eye contact. In avoiding eye contact, such individuals subconsciously deprive themselves of perceiving emotional cues which manifest in the area surrounding the eyes of peers.

Oddly enough, such individuals only avoid examining the area surrounding the eyes on images which contain a recognizable face. In images of inverted faces, such individuals examine the eye area freely, and do not exhibit any tendency to avert their eyes.[71] Of course such instinctual aversion to eye contact would correlate with the hypothesis that liberalism is an anticompetitive strategy designed to help less physically competent specimens seek Darwinian success while avoiding any direct competition or conflict with peers. The avoidance of eye contact would be a highly effective means of avoiding conflict.

The thesis that diminished amygdala development represents a diminished ability to perceive and gauge threat, and that this is a neurological correlate of liberalism, is also consistent with the fact that conservatism predominates among members of the military,[72, 73] a vocation which requires the perception and prioritization of threat, as well as the rapid confrontation of it - an occupation this theorem would predict would be likely to exhibit the increased amygdala development of K-selected conservatism.

The real significance of this is that the amygdala is a structure designed to help us perceive, remember, and respond to the realities of our environment – particularly the negative ones. If K-selection is an environment of potential negative outcomes, which must be navigated and avoided, it would be expected that a K-selected amygdala would be unusually well developed. It would have to acquire a large degree of experience perceiving impending negative outcomes, flagging them for significance, recalling where they were seen in the past, and then guiding an individual to pursue a path which negates any possibility of enduring the negative outcome. That would all require amygdala development.

By contrast, in the r-selected environment, negative outcomes are rare and easily avoidable by fleeing the conflict. There are rarely two bad choices, such as fight or starve. Nor does it require complex planning, such as strategy and tactics, where experience would play a critical role. Those are the realm of K. In such a pleasure-producing environment of free resource availability as r, one would expect to see the amygdala atrophy, since it would rarely be called on to help one navigate a dangerous, complex, competitive environment.

There is further research into amygdala function which would support the notion that liberalism is associated with the r-type psychology of diminished competitiveness, early mating, promiscuity, and low investment parenting.

The amygdala has been found to be responsible for the expression of aggression, or lack thereof. In one early experiment,[74] the temporal lobe of the brain (which contains the amygdala) was removed in monkeys. One of the two monkeys so treated was described thusly:

"Prior to the operations he was very wild and even fierce, assaulting any person who teased or tried to handle him. Now he voluntarily approaches all persons indifferently, allows himself to be handled, or even to be teased or slapped, without making any attempt at retaliation or endeavouring to escape...."

"Every object with which he comes in contact, even those with which he was previously most familiar, appears strange and is investigated with curiosity. Everything he endeavours to feel, taste, and smell, and to carefully examine from every point of view.... His food is devoured greedily, the head being dipped into the dish, instead of the food being conveyed to the mouth by the hands in the way usual with Monkeys. He appears no longer to discriminate between the different kinds of food ; e.g., he no longer picks out the currants from a dish of food, but devours everything just as it happens to come..."

"About this time a strange Monkey, wild and savage, was put into the common cage. Our Monkey immediately began to investigate the new comer in the way described, but his attentions were repulsed, and a fight resulted, in which he was being considerably worsted. The animals were, however, separated and tied up away from one another, but our Monkey soon managed to free himself, and at once proceeded, without any signs of fear or suspicion, again to investigate the stranger, having apparently already entirely forgotten the result of his former investigation.

Of the other monkey who had her amygdala removed, the researcher wrote :

"But the creature shows the same change of disposition that was manifest in Monkey No. 6 [the previous case above]. She appears to have lost, in great measure, intelligence and memory. She investigates all objects, even the most familiar, as if they were entirely unknown, tasting, smelling, and feeling all over everything she comes across. She is tame, and exhibits no fear of mankind, but shows uncontrollable passion on the approach of other Monkeys, so that it is now necessary to shut her up in a cage by herself. Like Monkey No. 6, she now invariably

devours her food by putting her head down to the platter, instead of employing the hands to convey it to her mouth. Moreover, her appetite is insatiable, and she crams until her cheekpouches can hold no more."

It is interesting that both monkeys displayed a combination of docility, intense curiosity and analysis of even that which they were already familiar with, desire to explore the novel, and a voracious appetite.

Combined, these traits would produce an individual which avoided confrontations, searched out that which was novel, investigated everything they came in contact with, and was desperately driven to consume whatever resources could be acquired whenever they became available, regardless of palatability.

This would result in a psychology programmed to avoid confrontation, migrate to new environments, and be intellectually willing to explore creative new sources of resources (which would aid in conflict avoidance), rather than continue to aggressively battle for the same resources everyone else is seeking.

This willingness to explore new sources of resources would also correlate with research showing that the specific allele of the DRD4 gene (the 7R allele) which is associated with a predisposition to ideological conditioning towards liberalism[75] (and which will be discussed later), is associated with novelty seeking,[76, 77, 78, 79] and is highly elevated within migratory populations.[80]

Thus, the liberal's desire to explore an issue from every possible angle may likely be derived from a deeper, base urge to seek out and explore the novel, so as to identify means by which to avoid confrontation. Such a novelty seeking, exploratory urge, would be designed to aid an r-selected individual identify new and unique resource streams in an environment they are already familiar with, or to seek out a newer, less crowded environment. All of these traits would be immensely advantageous to an anticompetitive, r-selected psychology that was suddenly confronted with a resource depleted, K-selected environment.

Kluver Bucy Syndrome is a psychological illness in humans produced by deficient amygdala function.[81] It is associated with docility (an absence of aggression) and hyper-sexuality (frequent mating with inappropriate objects or partners), demonstrating a linkage between the amygdala and tendencies towards promiscuity, as well as conflict-aversive behavior, such as docility.

Amygdala lesions that diminish function are also associated with diminished investments in child rearing.[82] Together, tendencies towards docility, promiscuity, and low investment parenting are three of the four individual elements of the r-selected psychology in humans. Among the individual r-traits, only early childhood mating is missing, and it could be argued that those who exhibit hyper-sexuality would also likely exhibit an earlier age at first intercourse than peers. After that, all that is missing from a group-competitive perspective is diminished in-group loyalty. As we are about to show, even that r-selected behavioral trait is facilitated by deficient amygdala function.

Since the amygdala is involved in perceiving the emotional states of others, as well as providing a behavior-controlling, aversive stimulus, this would indicate that an amygdala deficiency would impair the production of empathy, by impairing the perception of empathy-eliciting cues. Indeed, diminished amygdala activation is highly associated with a lack of empathy expression,[83] and volume deficits have been associated with such unempathetic psychologies as Antisocial Personality Disorder[84] and other forms of psychopathy, most likely due to the resultant deficiency in aversive stimulus failing to motivate one to constrain behavior within appropriate societal norms.[85] Thus deficient amygdala function does appear to be involved in the exhibition of more selfish, less altruistic behavioral drives, partly due to a diminution of perceptions which produce empathy, and partly due to a lack of behavioral constraint by aversive stimuli. Indeed, deficient morality and moral judgment,[86] deficient moral emotions,[87] deficiencies in guilt,[88] and deficient empathy,[89] all are associated with reduced amygdala function, reduced activity levels or reduced volume. Psychopathy specifically, is associated with reduced overall amygdala volume,[90] with slightly greater reduction in the right amygdala.[91] This reduction in volume is assumed to signal a deficit in functionality of the structure.

Callousness and Unemotional traits (CU traits) are an important core feature of the psychopath.[92, 93] These traits entail a lack of empathy, and are correlate with diminished amygdala functioning in functional neuroimaging tests.[94, 95, 96] If one accepts previous evidence that the amygdala is required to "flag" the signals of emotions in other people,[97] those with deficient amygdala function likely find themselves simply unable to discern subtle emotional cues indicating distress in peers.

Other research shows that reduced amygdala responsiveness underlies the reduced cooperation seen in psychopathy.[98] Research has also found that those who better read emotional cues in peers (and therefore likely exhibit larger amygdala development, and therefore likely tend conservative) exhibit more pro-social behaviors.[99] Given the 260+ million who have been murdered by leftist revolutions throughout history,[100] this should make any citizen look twice before supporting a leftist, and should bring into question the genuineness (or practical utility) of any leftist claim of empathy.

Liberals would also seemingly display impaired fearfulness in the approach behavior they demonstrate towards threats, be they terrorists or criminals. No matter the obvious danger, or the conservative calls to confront it and dispatch it, liberals insist that any perceived threat is a result of irrational fear, and should be disregarded. Similarly, in monkeys with amygdala damage, the absence of any fearful stimulus produces the docility and pacifism which marks the r-strategy. Impaired fearfulness is also a trait commonly associated with personality disorders such as psychopathy,[101] with some theorizing that the absence of this fear stimulus is what unburdens the psychopathic conscience, and facilitates the psychopath's immorality and rule-breaking,[102] (a trait John Jost has strongly assimilated with those who hold a liberal ideology).

We maintain that one aspect of the r-strategy is a reduced drive to engage in group-centric pro-social and cooperative behaviors. Here we see that psychopathic individuals with deficiency in the same structure which liberals appear to exhibit deficiency in, exhibit this trait. It is also worth noting that psychopathic personality traits have been explicitly linked to an r-type reproductive strategy (described as "an exploitive cheater strategy"),[103] prone to pursue high numbers of short term mating opportunities, while eschewing longer term relationships.[104]

When examining the amygdala's role in political ideology, it is important to understand this structure's purpose and operation. The amygdala provides what is called an aversive stimulus. This is an uncomfortable neurological sensation designed to both draw attention to what precipitates it, and motivate one to take actions which will shut it off by addressing the precipitating stimulus.

In essence, the amygdala motivates a normal person to alter their environment, in such a way that the amygdala no longer perceives the offending stimulus. Once the environment has been altered to remove the offending stimulus, the amygdala will lift the aversive stimulus, and allow you to proceed. To use the individual who fell through the ice as an example, once his amygdala was trained to cue in on breaking ice, and associate it will the agony of dropping into cold water, it motivated him (with aversive stimulus) to never let ice break beneath him again.

Activation of this aversive stimulus is conditioned, through being exposed to an event, and then suffering a negative outcome immediately following it. The more sudden and negative (read traumatic) the outcome, the more the amygdala will flag the preceding piece of information as significant. If it is ever encountered again, you will pay attention to it, and prepare to deal with the negative event which follows it, because your amygdala will apply a psychologically uncomfortable aversive stimulus until you do.

In small quantities, the aversive stimulus the amygdala provides can simply flag incoming information, marking it as significant and drawing attention to it. For example, in looking at another person's face, there is a tremendous amount of information being presented to your brain. If you notice that an individual makes a small sneer expression, and then becomes angry, your amygdala will flag the sneering facial expression with a subtle emotional sensation of what followed. Should you encounter it again, within the flood of information one receives in examining another person's face, your amygdala will draw your attention to it, through a light application of aversive stimulus. In response, you will notice the expression, and consider whether you need to take any action, though you will not experience anything explicitly uncomfortable.

In larger amounts however, aversive stimulus will provoke a psychologically uncomfortable state, akin to panic or anguish. Thus it can regulate behavior, provoking behaviors which are not immediately satisfying, or which are even uncomfortable to perform. The amygdala will accomplish this by making failure to perform them more uncomfortable than simply performing them, through the application of aversive stimulus. Through this controlling mechanism, the amygdala can provoke such non-hedonistic behaviors as strenuous high investment child rearing, personally costly moral acts, costly acts of loyalty, and other unrewarding behaviors which require the motivation of an inner force. There is also evidence that the amygdala may learn to provide aversive stimulus at the thought of not attaining a reward, and thus motivate hard work and effort expenditure in pursuit of success.[105]

This behavior-controlling aversive stimulus which the amygdala provides, can also make otherwise pleasurable, hedonistic activities unpleasant, thus dissuading one from simply following their more base urges to acquire pleasure. From dissuading selfishness and disloyalty, to making one empathetically prevent potential harm to others, many of the behaviors we engage in which are not personally advantageous (and are even altruistic) have their root in the amygdala.

As this book maintains, it is the K-selected group-competitor who is motivated by Darwin to be the altruist within our species, and here we see one mechanism by which this is made so. A more highly developed amygdala is able to more widely apply aversive stimuli to force the group competitor to abide by costly, altruistic rules under a wider variety of circumstances. Failing to place the interests of the group first in K-selected group competition will precipitate the aversive stimulus that arises, when defeat is imminent. By contrast, a less developed, r-selected amygdala would be expected to blindly pursue any personal advantage in an environment of r-selection, regardless of perceptions around them.

It is also interesting that the amygdala is designed to be developed through the experience of adverse outcomes. An individual living within a K-selected environment would be exposed to frequent adverse outcomes, as they learned how to pursue competitive success, and how to avoid competitive failure. Such an individual would be expected to show greater development of this structure, and indeed, would require it to survive. Only a well developed amydgala would be able to guide an individual's behavior, by flagging potential adversity before it was experienced, and driving a person to avoid it through the application of aversive stimulus.

By contrast, an individual living in an r-selected environment would be expected to encounter adversity less, and thus experience less development of this structure. As this structure remained undeveloped, one would expect the individual to be less able to recognize adversity, or route any fear from perceived adversity into productive actions designed to avoid the adversity. If one's undeveloped amygdala was unable to route the fear of a competitive environment into productive, adversity-avoiding action, it is easy to see how one might find eliminating the competitive environment altogether an effective amygdala-assuaging goal to pursue.

It is interesting, that not only is the brain structure designed to function within the environment. The environment is also designed to provoke the brain structure's development. The significance of this will become clearer later, as we discuss how societal chaos can produce a psychology which will then create a successful society, and how a successful society can then produce a psychology which will produce societal chaos.

The other difference is brain structures Kanai identified was that liberals exhibit a larger Anterior Cingulate Cortex (ACC). The ACC is involved in a wide variety of neurological tasks, though it is often described as a neural alarm system. In this role, it signals when something is wrong, or some perceived stimulus requires more detailed analysis. If the amygdala identifies a reason to panic, the ACC is the button it pushes which triggers the panic.

The ACC has been noted as being activated very strongly during periods of physical pain,[106] and is shown to be very strongly activated during the psychological stress of social exclusion[107, 108, 109] (perhaps explaining the liberal's preoccupation with social discrimination in society, or their inability to perceive their own in-group).

It is also activated by perceptions of unfairness,[110] a stimulus very similar to social exclusion, at least to those of narcissistic tendencies who are socially excluded.

The ACC has also been noted as being highly active during the production of envy, when viewing others with access to superior quantities of "self-relevant resources."[111] If an r-selected individual, growing up within a competitive, K-selected species often experienced such an envious emotion when out-competed as a child, that could explain how the structure would come to be highly developed in an adult liberal. If this envy was elicited often during critical developmental windows in childhood, it could profoundly alter the development of this structure, increasing the ability to perceive envious stimuli and increasing the sensations of envy evoked in adulthood.

118

It is interesting that liberals exhibit a larger "envy center" within the brain, given frequent left-wing calls to "tax the rich," or engage in other forms of what is referred to as "class warfare" and income redistribution from successful to unsuccessful.

More easily engendering a state of envy would also increase the willingness of such an individual to violate rules, and pursue a more direct, less honor-driven path to competitive success. That individuals, unsuccessful in the competitive environment of childhood play, would tend to be socially excluded, might explain this neurological linkage between envy and the psychological pain of social exclusion.

Additionally, one who had well developed their ACC (which appears to create a perception of social exclusion) in childhood, might tend to carry an underlying, constant, subtle perception of being socially excluded from their in-group as an adult, thereby diminishing their drive to exhibit loyalty to their in-group - a psychological trait of liberals that is well documented by John Jost.

Thus the r-selected liberal may carry a subtle sensation of being socially excluded as well as exhibit a heightened predisposition towards envy. Combined with less aversive stimulus to constrain behavior, this all would produce a more desperate psychology, willing to do what is necessary to win personally, regardless of such notions as loyalty to group, honor among peers, fairness in competition, or justness of action. You would have an individual who perceived their group as hostile to them, felt envious towards other successful members of the group, and who was not behaviorally constrained by the neurological structure which promotes rule adherence. This is a neurological recipe for an individual who would be driven to ally with an out-group, against their in-group, for personal advantage, or exploit societal fissures for personal gain.

ACC activation is also seen during the exhibition of empathy, probably due to it simulating the pain of others[112] Interestingly, given the ACC's role in fostering feelings of empathy, and the amygdala's role in detecting empathetic cues, and then forcing one to behave in an empathetic fashion, this may point to neither political psychology as being optimally designed for the performance of unbridled, true, selfless empathy. This would be consistent with the premise that all Darwinian strategies are designed to be selfish, to some degree or another.

Conservatives will perceive the emotions and pain in others better, allowing a better perception of the appropriate time to be empathetic. Due to their larger amygdalae, conservatives will also have a better psychological force motivating them to act on empathetic feelings, through empathetic behaviors. However their smaller ACC will lead them to feel less empathic sensations of psychic pain.

This will produce an individual capable of perceiving when to be empathetic, capable of enduring discomfort while performing the sacrifice of altruism, but less motivated by the emotional stimulus of empathic pain. This would be consistent with a psychology prone to compete with others, and view those who lose the competition as receiving of a fate that is fair, and necessary, in some fashion. Since under this theory, the primary drive among conservatives towards altruism will be specifically-directed loyalty to peers, and not aimless empathy for everyone, this information is consistent with this theory.

Liberals, due to diminished amygdala volume, could be expected to be less capable of correctly flagging cues and perceiving when to feel empathy. They will also have less psychological force motivating the personal sacrifices consistent with true empathetic behavior. Thus liberals may support higher taxes in principle, yet seek to lower their own personal taxes, regardless of their stated stance. A combination of strong feelings of empathy for anyone, regardless of merit, combined with a lack of aversive stimulus driving them to sacrifice personally, would produce this conflict between ideals and behavior.

Envy, combined with an overdeveloped empathy that is only triggered by extreme stimuli, would also produce an individual overwhelmed by the sight of the very poor, but unable to sacrifice themselves personally to assuage their empathetic drive. Simultaneously, they would be envious of the rich, whom they wish were not so wealthy. Clearly, heavily taxing the rich to give money to the poor would be a perfect solution to assuage such a mixture of behavioral urges.

This is consistent with the observations that liberals engage in less charity,[113] yet demand higher taxation on others so as to serve empathetic ends. As our society grows increasingly r-selected, it is no wonder that half of our nation pays no federal income taxes, while we are continuing to hear calls to raise the taxes on those remaining productive citizens who do pay.

Deficits in both the amygdala and ACC would appear to be involved in Antisocial Personality Disorders,[114] where the individual neither feels empathy nor abides by common social rules. In this case, the amygdala deficit is hypothesized to diminish the ability to perceive distress in others, as well as diminish conditioning to abide by social rules. Meanwhile diminished ACC volume likely impairs such an individual's ability to feel empathy. The result is an individual who cannot perceive distress in others, couldn't feel empathy if he did, and whose behavior is unrestrained by any aversive stimulus anyway. Combined, this produces a pronounced personality disorder, distinct from the more nuanced (and accepted) competitive Darwinian strategies one sees within both common political ideologies.

Given that altruism requires a certain willingness to endure personal harm, it is interesting that volumetric measurements of the Anterior Cingulate Cortex are also positively correlated with personal harm avoidance. Thus a larger ACC might further deter liberals from both displaying altruistic, pro-social tendencies, and embracing the risk of harm inherent to free competition with peers.[115]

Neither strategy will be purely psychopathic, however. In the conservative, heightened awareness of other's emotional states combined with the behavior-constraining aversive stimulus produced by the amygdala, will serve to prevent psychopathy. In the liberal, enlargement of the ACC will increase feelings of empathy, likely also avoiding this condition through the introduction of a conflicting urge to balance their lack of aversive stimulus.

It is important to note that both conservative and liberal psychologies will maintain an element of personal competitiveness, however. The conservative will feel less empathy, while the liberal will perceive its necessity less, and exhibit less willingness to sacrifice on its behalf, due to feeling less aversive stimulus when contemplating it, and more ACC-mediated neural alarm when contemplating enduring it. That both psychologies would maintain elements of personal competitiveness is what one would expect of individuals created in the Darwinian environment, and designed to pursue specific competitive Darwinian strategies which would advance their own interests.

Finally, note how a working knowledge of this information is capable of explaining a wide range of political behaviors and inclinations. For example, conservatives find one of the more vexing aspects of liberal policy to be the refusal to perform simple discriminations between good and bad in individuals. Liberals support criminals through support for lax sentencing. Liberals support terrorists through limitations on their detention and rendition. Liberal's oppose Airport Security performing targeted screening based on perceptions of threat. liberal's seek to eradicate human judgment from punishment through the imposition of zero tolerance laws.

The liberal opposes the use of human judgment to access threats and make discriminations, maintaining that such judgment is inherently flawed, and that such a flawed mechanism is highly prone to produce injustice. As a result, liberals propose hard and fast rules designed to supplant human judgment by being applied uniformly, regardless of individual circumstance.

It is possible that liberals are correct in their assertions, at least from their perspective. If the liberal actually lacks sufficient development of a brain structure (the amygdala) that is necessary to perceive and judge threat, then it is possible that when the liberal contemplates looking at others and judging threat, they see a mechanism which is, in their personal experience, wholly flawed.

Thus unable to imagine what it would be like to perceive threat, the liberal assumes everyone lacks such an ability. Therefore conservative assertions of the threats posed by others must be wholly illogical and flawed as well. To the liberal, the main difference between the ideologies is the conservative's inability to perceive their own cognitive limitations, and their cruel willingness to punish others based on flawed and erroneous fantasies of omniscience resulting from intellectual inferiority. Liberals reject such assessments simply because they are unable to perceive the threats others present themselves.

Perhaps, if everyone lacked an amygdala, then frisking old grandmothers at the airport, or creating litmus tests for punishments (to be applied absent any personal judgment of the accused), or replacing all personal discretion of Police Officers with procedures, would be the most logical courses of action. If threats could not be accurately judged or discriminations made, then such random searches or litmus-test applied rules would be preferable to a flawed system of inaccurate targeting, prone to randomly punish innocent people.

122

In summation, the amygdala is involved in the triggering of aggression/competitiveness, sexual libido, and investments in child rearing, as well as driving altruistic behaviors, such as loyalty to in-group. That it is associated with the genesis of all of the behavioral characteristics found in both r/K selection strategies and political ideology is strongly suggestive that political ideologies are related to these more primitive reproductive strategies.

That the amygdala's level of development within humans is associated with adoption of one ideology or the other, is further evidence that our political ideologies and r/K selection strategies are at least associated, if not exactly the same animal, simply viewed from different perspectives.

A final note of caution is in order. The brain is an amazingly complex organ. The amygdala, for example, has discrete regions, with many different purposes, and many connections to other areas of the brain which are responsible for a vast array of processing functions. Although we have presented a very simplified argument here, which accurately summarizes the current understanding of the neurological basis of political ideologies, this is merely a starting point for future research, based on the best understandings to date.

In the future, it is reasonable to expect that the general picture presented here will come into considerably clearer focus, especially as functional neuroimaging comes into its own as a research tool, and is applied to this issue. All readers should eagerly anticipate the revelations that this will bring.

Chapter Fifteen

The Temporal Theory of Ideological Cognitive Models_____

There is another facet to ideology which emerges as one views the neurostructural underpinnings. The ACC's neural alarm functions are deployed in response to stimuli indicating that unpleasantness is present, in the moment, whether that pain be present physical pain, ostracization, or unfairness. In contrast, the amygdala issues calls for neural alarms in response to stimuli indicating that unpleasantness is forthcoming in the future, based on unemotional perceptions of present conditions, extrapolated out logically to their expected outcomes.

When viewed in this sense, ideologies become about temporal focus. Those reliant upon their ACC's are likely more focused upon present, in-the-moment unpleasantness, and less focused on later outcomes arising from in-the-moment conditions. This will drive one to reduce in-the-moment pain, even at the expense of inflicting future pain (which their weakened amygdala is less capable of perceiving). Meanwhile those who are more amygdala-reliant will be more focused upon future unpleasantness, and perhaps more willing to endure present unpleasantness, in order to minimize later unpleasantness.

This leads to a perception of ideologies as being akin to the psychologies of the grasshopper and the ant. One psychology lives their life constantly avoiding present unpleasantness and maximizing present pleasure, regardless of the cost to anyone, even themselves. They live in the moment, while the other psychology will spend their present time enduring whatever they must, to make the future optimally pleasant, and see their own, specifically, succeed in life.

You see this throughout politics. Liberals focus unduly on the plight of people presently poor, leading to desires to raid government coffers, and institute economic measures which, while designed to

125

address that present unpleasantness most effectively, create much greater unpleasantness later on – unpleasantness they seem to be totally unable to register cognitively. Conservatives are more willing to endure that present unpleasantness, because as they contemplate the Liberal's proposed solutions, their amygdalae flag all sorts of negative future outcomes forthcoming, should they accede to measures such as massive deficit spending, massive increases in taxation, enlargements of governmental size, scope, and authority, and any punishment of success and rewarding of sloth in the populace.

Unfortunately, this would indicate that there can be little agreement among ideologues, and that those on opposite ends of the political spectrum should ideally be separated in some fashion, if we are to maximize the political happiness for all. Conservatives, in structuring matters so as to minimize later unpleasantness (and the consequent amygdala-stimulation produced) will maximally antagonize Liberal ACCs, by demanding that present unpleasantness be endured. Liberals, by contrast, in demanding that later unpleasantness be created, so as to minimize present unpleasantness, will maximally antagonize forward-looking Conservative amygdalae, as they set the governing institutions they have influence over, on declining trajectories, heading towards the maximal unpleasantness of economic and societal collapse later on.

Viewed in the context of r/K Theory however, each psychology will make perfect sense. r-strategists are about exploiting the bloom now, while it lasts, however best they can, with little regard for later, and little regard for their offspring, others, or even themselves. That rabbit who minimizes his reproductive output in some fashion, as he prepares for later or sacrifices for a friend, will end up numerically outcompeted by other rabbits, in a perpetually r-environment. That environment will inherently favor those who seize food and mating opportunities now, and constantly operate with an innate assumption that there will never be consequence, because those opportunities will always be there later. Thus over the eons, Darwin has imbued liberal r-strategists with this psychology.

Likewise, that K-strategist who seizes hedonistic bliss now, at the expense of his group and his preparations for later, will find himself eventually culled from the population, by an environmental selective pressure which only favors those who endure what they must in the moment, for their team and their own, in a never-failing quest to always succeed in the end, when it matters. As a result, when nature imbues a K-strategy, inherent to it will be a desire to always temper present-moment hedonism with an eye to the future and all potential costs.

Of course one can argue that one psychology is better suited to producing a long-lasting government which endures the test of time, and that the other is likely to eventually produce the societal collapse and economic ruin of any society which embraces it. With even a cursory examination of history, that assessment is obviously correct. However until political ideologies are widely seen as outgrowths of r and K Selection Strategies, those of us on the inside will have great difficulty turning the tides of r-strategy produced by resource production and availability.

This again demonstrates how understanding ideology in the context of r/K Theory, and its neurostructural underpinnings, can facilitate a much fuller understanding of our ideological battles, and the ancient purposes that these psychologies are attempting to serve , as they mold the nature of our governance. At the grand, population-level, none of these changes to society that we witness occur accidentally. At that level, they all can be best understood logically through their ancient evolutionary and reproductive purposes.

Chapter Sixteen

*The Genetic Aspects of Political Ideology*_____

Environmental conditioning toward a liberal political ideology has been noted to be facilitated by a specific variation in the gene for the D4 dopamine receptor (DRD4-7r),[116] which controls dopamine activity in the brain.[117]

Widely known as a neurochemical reward, proper dopamine function is necessary for proper functioning of the prefrontal cortex (PFC).[118] The PFC is responsible for both perceiving the nature of one's environment and organizing behavior in the pursuit of success.[119]

The PFC is also associated with suppressing amygdala activation,[120] probably in response to perceiving positive circumstances in the environment, indicating that goal attainment is likely. In this model, stimuli which indicate success is likely will stimulate a normal PFC. The PFC will then suppress the amygdala from producing negative emotional sensations that might dissuade one from continuing their activities. Unencumbered by aversive stimulus from the amygdala, one will experience an absence of anxiety and depression, and feel free to strive for success.

Given this, it is likely safe to assume that dysfunction in the dopaminergic system (such as might arise from inheriting a less effective receptor gene, like the 7r allele) would affect the PFC's engendering of optimism. This failure to engender optimism would then produce tendencies towards anxiety and depression, and a resultant aversion to striving. Clearly, K-type competitors are programmed to strive in competitions, despite risk, while r-type psychologies exhibit a clear aversion to fair, fitness-mediated competitions between peers.

Allelic variations in the gene for the D4 dopamine receptor are associated with anxiety, depression, and neuroticism.[121] Proper dopamine function has also been shown to have a critical role in the production of incentive salience (the desire to pursue a reward).[122, 123] Combined with the necessity of dopamine signaling, at proper levels, for proper function of the PFC, and the PFC's role in suppressing the amygdala, one can see how a slight variation in the product of the D4 dopamine receptor gene that reduced its function, such as is produced by the 7r allele associated with liberalism, could have a role in altering competitive drive. DRD4 is a single gene which is capable of altering perceptions of optimism/pessimism, anxiety/depression, and the desire for a reward> As we will show, it also affects other aspects of the r-selected psychology.

Allelic variation in the DRD4 gene is responsible for derangements in libido,[124] earlier age at first intercourse,[125] and promiscuity and infidelity[126] (a study where the paper even discussed how the 7r DRD4 allele associated with a liberal predisposition, would enjoy favor in r-selected environments, due to its promotion of promiscuity). Liberals have been shown to exhibit increased depression,[127, 128, 129] as well as increased libido,[130] resulting in their support for a less sexually restricted society.[131]

Thus, within the D4 dopamine receptor gene, we see a single gene in which long form allelic variation is responsible for the four behaviors inherent to the r-strategy. The allele associated produces lack of competitive drive, promiscuity/infidelity, earlier age at first intercourse, and low investment parenting (for now this may be inferred from infidelity's tendency to produce single parenting). Indeed, at least one researcher has even stated that this "political" gene may produce an r-selected reproductive strategy in humans.

Variations in the DRD4 gene would serve as a simple means by which to encode within the genome a predisposition towards one of two Darwinian strategies. One strategy will pessimistically avoid the fear of a competition that they feel destined to lose. The other strategy will optimistically embrace the thrill of a competition that they feel destined to win. One strategy will depressively see defeat at hand, while the other will optimistically see victory within reach. One strategy will desperately increase their sex drive and mate at every opportunity with anyone they come across, while the other will patiently wait, to find the best possible mate with whom to have children, and rear them carefully.

It should not escape the readers notice that if the PFC's function is diminished, and it is unable to curtail amygdala activity, a child may find themselves learning to reflexively avoid any circumstances which could result in amygdala stimulation (such as free competition and the risk of defeat it offers). One might also find such children developing cognitive tricks to diminish amygdala activity, through intellectually altering their perceptions of their environment and themselves. They might even learn to remove amygdala stimulating environmental cues through denial of the threat they present, rather than taking affirmative action to alter their environment.

Together, this defensive shielding of the amygdala from stimulation would produce a much less developed structure, which would be easily overwhelmed with the slightest stimulus, such as an intrusion of a reality they might not want to face, and cannot ignore. This would lead to an adult liberal who viewed the behavior of a conservative confronting threats, as being motivated by irrational fears, which need not be confronted.[132]

Just as issues of sexual behavior are interlinked with other issues of political ideology, this political gene has been shown to be associated with sexual drive in humans. Likewise, sexual behavior is associated with the drive to embrace or reject intra-species competition in nature, through the adoption of an r-selected or K-selected psychology.[133]

Current research into social behaviors and cognition in humans show them to be a product of multiple genetic influences,[134, 135] and clearly this should apply to the adoption of a political ideology as well. Additionally, adoption of, and adherence to political ideologies, have long been believed to be affected by experience. However the evidence does indicate that DRD4 allelic variation plays some role in the adoption of political ideology in humans, and clearly it offers several possible biological avenues by which to exert such an effect.

That said, the role that genetics on political ideology is an extraordinarily complex area of study. Many neurotransmitters play many different roles within the body and mind. A single neurotransmitter will have several different receptors, each exerting differing effects on different structures and tissues within the body, and even within different areas of the brain. That this one gene appears to play a role in adoption of r/K strategies will not exclude others from also exerting effects.

131

Indeed, neurotransmitters do not even appear to be the sole means by which to alter reproductive strategy in humans. Interestingly, it has been found that a competitive environment increases testosterone levels.[136] It has long been known that competing and winning (which would produce an acute release of dopamine-facilitated pleasure), will produce a surge in testosterone for an extended period following the victory. This is interesting given that we assert our society is temporarily transitioning to a more "r" model, with less competitive stimuli.

This would lead one to expect that testosterone levels would decrease in our population, and indeed, scientist have noted drops in serum testosterone in men,[137] leading some to postulate that the manliness of men is threatened by some heretofore unknown factor.[138] Given testosterone's role in producing aggression and competitiveness, this would offer yet another means by which humans adapt their behavior and their reproductive strategy to resource availability and perceptions of competitive stimuli.

The main purpose of this exercise however, is to point out that all of the behaviors of the r-selected psychology (and of liberalism) can travel together very closely on the genome, in effect often existing as a single, heritable predisposition. Furthermore, these r-selected alleles could easily be in direct competition with competing K-predispositioning alleles, associated with conservatism.

Nevertheless, it is worth noting that here in the DRD4 gene we seem to see a gene which is associated with the behavior behind reproductive strategies, and which at least one researcher has postulated can produce an actual r-selected mating strategy. This evidence also demonstrates the potential of this work to unite the political and governmental aspects of political ideology with the sexual and social aspects, all within a theory which explains not only how all of these disparate issues are linked, but exactly why evolution has chosen to link them in the first place.

Chapter Seventeen

A Further Note on Dopamine and Oxytocin ___

As originally envisioned, this work viewed ideology as produced by genetic effects, epigenetic effects, early rearing and social conditioning, and finally by a logical filter which operated subject to the first three effects. Then Reactionary Blogger Dennis Mangan posted the transcript of a speech he gave,[139] and it brought to mind a critical facet to this work, without which it would have been woefully incomplete.

In the speech, he discusses a phenomenon called Supernormal Stimuli, and points out that high levels of chronic dopamine exposure will desensitize an individual to dopamine exposure in the future, through a phenomenon known as the down-regulation of receptor transcription.

This phenomenon is most commonly seen in individuals who abuse anabolic steroids. Steroids, just as dopamine does, bind to a receptor on a cell's surface. The receptor is like a switch, which sends a signal along a wire, to the inside of a cell. Once inside the cell, the signal activates whatever internal process the dopamine or steroid elicits, while the dopamine or steroid molecule remains outside the cell. Old receptors on the membrane surface are constantly being degraded and consumed by the cell, which replaces them with freshly produced receptors, keeping the system highly functional.

In many cases, cells exhibit a feedback mechanism, whereby the quantity of "replacement" receptors produced is tied to the level of signal produced by the receptors. In the case of anabolic steroid abuse, if the cell senses a high level of anabolic steroid signal inside the cell, that high signal inside the cell also slows the production of new receptors. As old receptors are consumed, they are not replaced as quickly, leaving fewer receptor "switches" on the cell's surface, to transmit signals to the cell's interior, where they have their effect. As a result, fewer receptors will mean less of a signal reaching the inside of the cell.

This feedback mechanism is designed to moderate critical signal levels, and prevent any signal from going too far outside its standard healthy levels. In the case of anabolic steroids, as a user floods their system with testosterone (an anabolic steroid), the testosterone binds to the numerous receptors on a muscle cell's surface. The numerous receptors, all transmitting a signal to the inside of the cell, create a massive signal inside the cell that triggers massive amounts of muscle growth. However, this massive signal also shuts off the production of "replacement" receptors.

As a result, when the receptors on the cell's surface are degraded and consumed, they are not replaced. Gradually, the density of receptors on the cell's surface will dwindle, and this will diminish the level of anabolic steroid signal inside the cell, irrespective of how much testosterone is outside the cell. Since there are fewer receptors to transmit the steroid molecules' signals from outside the cell to inside, the cell receives less signals inside, where they have their effect, and the cell behaves as if there is less steroid in the blood.

When the signal reaches a lower level, receptor production will resume, but to a lower level than would exist, absent steroid use. As a result, individuals on anabolic steroids are forced to cycle their dosages between high dosages and low dosages, since if they took steroids at a consistently high level all the time, the steroids would eventually lose their effects.

In nature, this feedback mechanism likely had many functions, among them balancing out any endocrine problem that produced abnormally aberrant signal levels. This would allow an organism with some problem relating to signal production to still balance out the level of signaling, and continue to function.

This mechanism would operate similarly with dopamine. Flood an individual's brain consistently with the pleasure molecule dopamine (such as by placing them in an environment of constant free resource availability, and/or copious sexual activity), and the cell surface receptor density of dopamine receptors would plummet, reducing the amount of dopamine signals inside the cell that would elicit its pleasurable effects.

If one wanted to imagine a real world example of such a phenomenon, one might look to the drug addict. Cocaine is a dopamine mimic (or agonist). If one takes copious quantities of cocaine, one will desensitize the brain to dopamine by affecting receptor densities. Now, when this individual goes off cocaine, they will seemingly have lower than normal levels of dopamine signaling, because they will have made their brain less sensitive to dopamine.

Without the cocaine, they will have a less pleasurable mood at rest, than they had before the cocaine. If they take the cocaine regularly, they will find that they need to be on some level of cocaine all the time, just to feel normal. Of course, as an addict, this will manifest as an addiction. They will gradually find themselves ever more driven to seek out the dopamine rush they were partaking of.

If they were in a state of nature, and the drug they were on was real dopamine, elicited by consuming food freely, or mating more promiscuously, they will begin to become addicted to those behaviors (something which is actually adaptive under conditions of r-selection). If mating opportunities are everywhere, and food is freely available, that is r-selection. There is a reproductive strategy that is ideally suited to function within those conditions.

Interestingly, we discussed the linkage between the DRD4-7r gene and the predisposition to a liberal ideology. It is believed by researchers that the 7r allele codes for a dopamine receptor which is a poor transmitter of the dopamine signal, producing a weaker signal inside the cell, per activation.

This would produce an individual whose baseline dopamine receptor function was similar to that of an individual with more functional receptors, who had used cocaine, or some other dopamine agonist. In short, by having a less capable dopamine receptor system, the 7r carrier actually begins with a cell structure which exhibits a sort of pre-addicted receptor structure. They will require a higher baseline level of dopamine signaling to function properly. Indeed, DRD4-7r has a long linkage with addiction and substance abuse.

In summation, this insight by Dennis Mangan regarding Supernormal Stimuli and the role of dopamine receptor down-regulation, explains how a society availed of free resource availability, and plentiful, pleasurable, dopamine eliciting stimuli (from food, to sex, to video games, to smart phones, to social media, to 3D movies like Avatar), would quickly become driven to become addicted to pleasure, averse to hardship, and toil, and prone to the early and frequent mating strategy inherent to the r-selected Reproductive Strategy.

This cognitive difference, due to dopamine function, is highlighted by a study[140] examining the brain function of those with high baseline dopamine signaling (such as high receptor densities and a fully functional receptor would facilitate on a continual basis), or low baseline dopamine signaling (such as low receptor densities or a less functional allele like DRD4-7r, would facilitate).

In the study, individuals with increased dopamine activity better tolerated hardships, such as cheating by opponents, in the midst of competitions, were more rule oriented in competing, and made more use of brain structures associated with reward and motivation. They tended to continue adhering to the rules of their competition, while trying harder to win within the rules.

By contrast, those with lower dopamine function tended to exhibit greater rule breaking, even acting out aggressively when confronted with hardship in the midst of competition. The areas of the brain they used most were areas associated with self-awareness, and social behavior - as in, "Can I get away with this?" Much of liberal behavioral strategy is about using social manipulation to break rules, and avoid direct, rule-based competitions with peers. Don't compete directly in a capitalistic environment with someone. Rather, manipulate the social environment so government agents will oppress the other person, so they can't do as well. Don't develop the ability to defend yourself. Rather have government disarm everyone else, so you aren't as weak by comparison. Don't go to a gun owner's house and take their guns yourself. Rather, manipulate the political system so a police officer will go in your stead, and endure the risk you fear enduring, and compete on your behalf.

Indeed, reduced dopamine receptor sensitivity, produced by free resource availability, would explain yet another mechanism by which the r-strategy of liberalism could be produced by a nation's success. It would also offer a very fast way to adapt one's strategy to free resource availability on the fly, further refining the predispositions produced by genetic effects, epigenetic effects, and early rearing experiences. It would offer a much faster mechanism by which to hack the brain, and produce an immediate shift towards the r-strategy. It might even play a role in seasonal variations in mating behavior and resource consumption.

This does beg the question, however, what about lower rearing investment, monogamy, reduced nationalistic drive, and reduced loyalty to in-group? How would these behaviors tie in with reduced dopamine sensitivity and signal strength, be it genetic in origin, epigenetic in origin, or feedback inhibited?

Here you will need to examine what is sometimes called the trust-hormone, oxytocin. Liberal researchers had a brief love affair with oxytocin, because it exhibited several properties which might have made it a candidate for a modern day Soma, to pacify the masses. It briefly held the promise of turning everyone into good little automatons, who would exhibit high levels of trust and altruism for everyone, and stop being so covetous and prone to group conflict.

Oxytocin began to gain notice because it was found that if you gave an individual a dose of oxytocin, they would be more trusting of others,[141] and more generous.[142] Oxytocin also had other beneficial aspects. A tremendous body of work[143] demonstrates that it is released by mothers, and triggers bonding to their offspring,[144] presumably producing a higher maternal investment. Although human evidence is lacking, its release is also associated with paternal investment in some mammals.[145] Its release has also been associated with the behaviors and bonding between mates which produces monogamy.[146, 147, 148]

Recently, however, discussion of it has carried a wary tone, describing, *"The Two Faces of Oxytocin."*[149] Another researcher cautioned, *"Oxytocin is developing a reputation of being the sort of thing you'd want to dump in someone's coffee in the morning to make them soft and nice and fuzzy and good to you... That's just not the case. oxytocin is much more complex than that."*[150]

The shift occurred because it has been noted that oxytocin does enhance all of these positive behaviors, but it does it in relation to one's in-group, as a part of facilitating ethnocentrism, and increasing loyalty to one's own.[151]

This is all interesting because the function of oxytocin is closely related to dopamine activity.[152] In rats, a pulse of dopamine signaling triggers the release of oxytocin in their brains.[153] It would stand to reason that one who carried a less effective dopamine receptor polymorphism, such as the 7r allele, or whose receptors had been diminished in number through sustained exposure to dopamine-eliciting stimuli, would release less baseline oxytocin, and thus exhibit a more r-strategy with regards to parental investment, monogamy, and loyalty to in-group/ethnocentrism. Picture a junkie, whose only concern is his next fix, and to whom parental investment, personal loyalty, and honor are not overriding concerns.

Thus, when stressed, such as would be produced by the resource limitation of K-selection, humans may be programmed to group up, and ally against outsiders, both with friends, and family, to seek out powerful waves of dopamine from success in competition. These waves of dopamine likely produce pulses of oxytocin, which facilitate bonding and loyalty to the group, and more success.

By contrast, when resources flow freely, and dopamine is everywhere, humans may be programmed to not place as much emphasis on personal bonds, or group affiliations, as a way of minimizing the likelihood of conflict.

This perspective gives important insight into the mechanisms by which a population's ideology might shift. It also adds a critical element to this body of work, supporting the concept of political ideology as a reproductive strategy.

Chapter Eighteen

Social Science, Rearing, and r/K Psychologies _____

One interesting observation about r/K strategies is that many organisms appear to be able to partially mold their psychological reproductive strategy during childhood. During early developmental periods, such organisms perform subconscious assessments of their childhood environment. These assessments produce reflexive changes in their biochemistry, which then produce changes in their neurological development. These changes then more permanently alter their psychology (and their reproductive strategy) as adults.

Put simply, such organisms are subconsciously extrapolating out the likely resource availability and environmental harshness they will encounter as adults, and adopting the best reproductive strategy possible to confront their specific environment. On maturation, they will then exhibit a customized version of their innate r or K-selected psychology, as a result of these early environmental assessments.[154]

Thus in many organisms, the adoption of an r or K psychology is not wholly a product of genetic selection, nor is the psychological trait itself solely imbued in the sequence of the genome. Rather, over time, the genome has developed the ability to modulate the expression of the strategy individuals are genetically imbued with, should an early assessment of the environment indicate that such a change in tack would be advantageous.

This would mean that such an individual may be genetically programmed with genes prone to produce an r or K-selected psychology, however their early rearing experiences can override their genes to some degree, producing biochemical cues which will lead them to modify the developmental path that their genetic predispositions would place them upon.

Of course, as the environment selected for the exhibition of a specific reproductive strategy, one would inevitably see a rise in genetic predispositions towards that reproductive strategy designed to confront the environment they are faced with. Regardless, evidence does indicate that environmental cues presented in childhood do affect the degree to which one exhibits an r or K-type strategy at adulthood.

It is noteworthy that the primary cues which trigger this r/K divergence of psychology in mammals are believed to be presented to the individual within the rearing environment. In rodents, the nature of maternal care is a specific motive force producing the divergence of relative r/K psychologies in offspring.[155] In these models, maternal care is presumed to be determined by the environment the mother is confronted with. A mother constantly stressed by fierce predation, will experience increased stress, and thereby offer a lower standard of care to her offspring, and they will then tend to develop more r-selected reproductive strategies, within the bounds of genetic predispositions. If a mother provides strong and consistent maternal nurturing (higher investment parenting), the same genetic lines of rodents will trend towards more K-selected psychological tendencies.

Evidence generally indicates that the divergence towards an r-type strategy in rats is due to a stress mediated, epigenetic effect,[156] designed to produce a longer lasting, stress-mediated epigenetic modulation of the expression of genes in the individual. In other words, exposed to a stressful early life period, portions of the individual's DNA will experience temporary modifications, which will not alter the code of the DNA (ie. what it produces), but which will affect how capably the cell can read certain parts of it, and execute their instructions (ie. how much it produces). This effect on the expression of these genes will last for an extended period, likely lasting at least into adulthood.

The main points to be considered here are that many organisms can read their early childhood environment, adjusting their r/K status accordingly in response, and that early life stress is established as producing an r-type shift in psychology.[157]

Having established that some mammals can adapt their r/K psychological strategies in response to stress, it pays to examine whether any evidence exists which would indicate that this occurs in humans.

There has been considerable examination of the phenomenon of father-absent parenting and the resulting stressful home life this produces. Research has focused specifically on the effect these conditions have on the psychologies of children reared under them.[158, 159, 160, 161, 162, 163, 164, 165]

In their seminal paper on the topic, Jay Belsky, Lawrence Steinburg, and Patricia Draper proposed a theory that the psychological traits produced in offspring by father-absent parenting could be viewed in terms of an evolved survival strategy.[166]

Under their theory, the father absent environment and maternal harshness could be viewed as some of the stimuli which a human child's developing brain would encounter. These stimuli would be interpreted as indicating that the environment the child would encounter as an adult would be one that their parents were having difficulty in. Maternal stress and father absence might indicate that either the child's father had been killed, or more likely, their father had followed an r-strategy and abandoned them, due to the environment favoring such a strategy.

The stress hormones produced in a child by these stimuli, would biochemically activate a developmental pathway which would mold the child's brain structure. This developmental pathway would produce a distinct behavioral strategy encompassing a tendency towards sexual indiscriminateness and promiscuity, an aversion to monogamous relationships, a denigration of males and masculinity, a hostility to authority, antisocial behavior, and a male tendency to depersonalize women.[167, 168, 169]

It was hypothesized in their original work that, as with the r-type strategy in nature, this developmental pathway would include a mechanism by which the age of sexual maturation would occur earlier in life. Subsequent studies have borne this out, leading to an overall acceptance of this research within the Social Science community. In short, it would seem that if one's parents adopt an r-selected, low investment, single-parenting style, then their child will be more likely to adopt one at maturity, as well.

Thus today, it is generally accepted that both father absent parenting and maternal harshness are associated with increased rates of antisocial behavior in children (involving both rule violations in social interactions/competition, and diminished loyalty/altruism/empathy), as well as earlier onset in sexual activity, increased promiscuity, and a psychology that is more prone to lower-investment parenting. Together, this all produces a more selfish, r-type psychology in adulthood.

Interestingly, it is reported that children in families in which one parent is deceased do not show the same degree of r-type behavioral issues as those in whom the parents have willingly gone their separate ways after conception.[170], [171] This would lend support to the belief that the stress of the single parent environment alone does not have as much effect on the child's later psychology as either their inherited predispositions, or an environment of early psychosocial stress, such as that created by a single parent which exhibits a more selfish, r-type psychology themselves.

Finally, it is likely that not all individuals are equally susceptible to the effects of early rearing experiences.[172], [173], [174], [175] Some of early symptoms in children of these environmentally mediated r-type psychological changes are most exacerbated in children who exhibit the liberal-associated DRD4 7r allele.[176], [177] It is also interesting to note that among those who have the 7r allele of the DRD4 gene, not all become liberals, indicating a moderating environmental stimulus, as is seen here in the study of rearing strategies and r/K psychologies.[178] This link between childhood stress-mediated r-type development and the DRD4 7r gene further emphasizes the link between liberalism, and the r-selected psychology from which it evolved. Thus, if a child is genetically susceptible to an r-type psychology father absence will only exacerbate the condition, and this stimulus may also affect political predispositions in a similar fashion.

The presence of two distinct psychologies in children is further supported by research conducted by child psychology researcher Carol Dweck, at Stanford University. Dr. Dweck has identified two distinct psychologies, which children will adopt at a very early age, and which will govern the children's approach to challenges and activities.[179]

One psychology exhibits optimism, views defeat as a natural part of the process of self-improvement, and holds a perception that they can develop their abilities to whatever level they desire. Viewed within our evolutionary paradigm, this psychology is willing to risk defeat in a challenge such as free competition. It will not allow a potential defeat to deter their pursuit of future success in competition. These children possess an imbued perception that their abilities will grow even after defeat, and that their failures will ultimately increase their abilities, leading to future success. Thus they will throw themselves headlong into challenges, repeatedly, with an optimistic view that defeat is

142

meaningless, and they will succeed eventually, even if only by gaining experience.

The other psychology identified by Dweck is the exact opposite. Children who possess it do not have confidence in their own capability to develop abilities through repeatedly pursuing challenges and hard work, and they are strongly averse to failure. Viewed from an evolutionary perspective, this psychology will avoid challenges which would either require an investment of effort or a risk of defeat. Instead, they will opt to quickly seize opportunities for easy, certain success, wherever such opportunities might present themselves.

Obviously, here again are two psychologies. One welcomes challenge, accepts competitive risk, and tolerates personal defeat, while the other views their abilities as limited, is risk averse, is strongly averse to failure, and thus will tend towards a strategy of opportunistic advantage taking. Note, those afflicted with depression also exhibit hypersensitivity to any sense of failure or loss[180, 181] as does the less challenge embracing psychology identified by Dweck. The importance of this will become clearer as we discuss the relationship between depression to anticompetitiveness and liberalism later.

To be clear, the presence of various environmental factors within a child's early environment do not determine a child's fate, or political destiny with absolute certainty. Although these stresses are associated with the psychologies they have been linked to, there is always the human element.

Some children, presented with the harshest circumstances, will never break, and will grow up to embrace all of the K-selected virtues of humanity. Others, wholly absent any such stresses, will all too readily collapse and embrace the opportunistic advantage taking and rule-breaking selfishness of the r-selected psychology. Regardless of whether there is a good parent, a genetic strength, or just an indomitable spirit, there will always be an element of mystery to the individual human's motivations and psychology.

Our point in this chapter is not that we can identify a predictable pathway by which political ideology is adopted. Nor are we seeking to maintain that one's ideology can be easily characterized by past experiences alone. Rather we are primarily seeking to link the adoption of political ideology with both the r/K reproductive strategies and their related life history traits.

Chapter Nineteen

*Depression, Infection, and Anticompetitiveness*_____

Ideological liberals appear to exhibit increased rates of depressed mood compared to conservatives.[182, 183, 184] Here, we will offer evidence supporting the hypothesis that depression may be an evolutionary adaptation designed to provoke an anticompetitive, r-type psychology.

The evidence we will present will support the thesis that depression creates psychological changes that are designed to diminish incentive salience (also known as the desire for a reward), and that it does this preferentially in individuals who are best served by avoiding competition.

One premise of this text is that the r-selected psychologies will have evolved to be competition-averse, simply due to the fact that r-selecting environments will contain copious resources, making competition for them unnecessary.

The possible relation of a depressed mood to the r-selected, anticompetitive psychology merits a quick examination of some other research relating to depression, in the context of this theory.

To be clear, it is not the position of this book that Clinical Depression is synonymous with the r-strategy. It is clearly not. Although it is possible that Clinical Depression is some type of dysregulated form of the mild, normal form of depression which we maintain produces an r-strategy, that is far beyond our scope here, and we are not asserting such.

Rather, we are merely positing that the r-selected liberal likely possesses a depressed mood relative to their peers which fundamentally alters their world view (though they are likely not aware of this), and that this mood tendency has a clear evolutionary purpose within this theory.

Some evolutionary psychologists posit that depression may be an evolved response designed to solve problems that were frequently encountered in our ancestral environment.[185]

One current theory is the Behavioral Shutdown Model,[186] which posits that depression evolved to prevent an individual from going forward into a situation which would produce Darwinian disadvantage. Under this model, behavioral shutdown is triggered if an individual will not get a positive Darwinian return on energy expended in pursuit of a specific course of action.[187]

As discussed, early rearing experiences likely play a key role in the development of an anticompetitive psychology. Psychosocial stress, such as ostracization, competitive failure, or simply repetitively engendering envy would condition depressive neurological tendencies, and thereby mold a developing brain to experience a more depressive mood, and pursue a more anticompetitive psychology as an adult.

Were one of our ancient ancestors to have experienced such developmental cues as a child, indicating that they would be uncompetitive with peers as an adult, they would have developed a Pavlovian predisposition towards a depressed mood when confronted with competition in adulthood.

This mechanism would have allowed a child to determine their likelihood of exhibiting competitive ability during the protected safety of childhood play. As an adult, when the consequences for failure would have been much more severe, this imbued conditioning towards depression would have served as a means of curtailing any drive to engage in open competition with peers, and potentially suffer Darwinian defeat.

Obviously, this mechanism would operate within parameters set by genetic predisposition, itself a result of ancestral experiences in testing competitive drive against genetically transmitted physical ability.

Some cognitive researchers liken the depressed to investors who lack resources, and thus pursue a risk aversive investment strategy.[188] Here researchers liken personal interactions with the world in the context of an economic competition to acquire resources. On the one side are individuals willing to risk capital in pursuit of gains. On the other side are individuals who will not risk capital, but rather will seek out easy opportunities for certain gain, absent risk or challenge.

This theory may speak to one's mood existing as an approach to Darwinian competitions, making such metaphors particularly apropos. In this case, the r-strategist lacks the resources to compete in a higher risk, K-selected environment. As a result, they adopt a risk-averse strategy of avoiding competition, while looking for the easy win (or free resources).

Rank Theory posits that depression may be an evolved means by which those of lower rank are psychologically guided to avoid openly striving for dominance with powerful superiors in their social hierarchy who are capable of defeating them.[189, 190, 191, 192] Under this theory, when powerful superiors are likely to defeat an individual, that individual will adopt a strategy of diminished striving, through the subconsciously forced adoption of a depressive psychology. Here, an uncompetitive individual will exhibit an aversion towards competition, as a Darwinian survival strategy – a model of behavior which this text asserts would be typical for an r-selected reproductive strategy.

Chronic inflammation is associated with a depressed mood,[193] as is diminished social functioning,[194] as well as diminished socio-economic position.[195] In all three cases, individuals exhibit diminished competitiveness and fitness, either due to diminished physical vitality, diminished ability to gain high social standing, or diminished earning potential. It is not impossible that humans, presented with such conditions of impending defeat, would have evolved a psychological drive to pursue a risk averse, anticompetitive strategy. It is even more likely that humans which exhibited such frailties, and who would have been likely to fare poorly in competition, would have evolved to seek a competitive advantage that did not involve openly competing with peers. It is a premise of this text that, as in the transvestite cuttlefish, the advantage more advanced r-strategists evolved was a psychological ability to break rules, cheat in any competitions, and perform opportunistic advantage taking.

When confronted with the prospect of direct competition with peers, competitiveness would not prove advantageous for such individuals. A mildly depressive state might be a means by which to engender this r-psychology.

Interestingly, neuroimaging studies of patients with depression have shown atypical function in both the prefrontal cortex, as well as the amygdala-hippocampal complex,[196, 197] both of which this theory predicts would play a role in adoption of an anticompetitive psychology through the imposition of fear, anxiety, and a failure to perceive environmental conditions positively.

Finally, although depression is often seen as a result of environmental perceptions or disease pathology, it has been established that genetic predisposition plays a significant role in its etiology.[198] One of the genes which is associated with increased depression is an allele of the DRD4 dopamine receptor gene,[199] a gene which is also associated with conditioning of a liberal political ideology,[200] sexual promiscuity,[201] and the adoption of r-type behavioral patterns in humans.

Together, this evidence is consistent with the theory of political liberalism as an evolved anticompetitive Darwinian psychology, mediated by a depressive mood, and designed to produce an aversion to the risk associated with rule-governed competitive tests of fitness.

Chapter Twenty

*Further Support of the Dopamine/Amygdala Ideological Nexus*_____

Toxoplasma gondii is a protozoan parasite capable of infecting several different species of mammals. Concentrating its cysts within the brain, it alters neurological functioning, producing distinct changes in the psychology of its hosts. Infection is associated with changes in a range of behavioral drives in both rat and human infections.[202] Of interest here, is that the psychological changes induced by T. gondii infection are similar to the psychological drives motivating the liberal ideology, and the r-selected reproductive strategy. Even more interesting, is how they are engendered.

T. gondii is probably best known for its ability to make one of its natural hosts, the rat, approach predators such as cats, as if they pose no threat. In doing so, the parasite coerces the rat to carry it to its second host, the cat. The cat will then eat the rat, ingest the cysts, and become infected itself. The cat will, in turn, spread the parasite in feces which will infect other rats, who will carry the parasite to other cats, continuing the host-vector cycle.[203]

On infecting humans, T. gondii does produce many diverse psychological traits,[204] many of which are similar to the psychological drives motivating both liberalism, and the r-selected reproductive strategy.

T. gondii infection has been shown to be associated in men with tendencies to envy success and break rules,[205] while infected women exhibit greater levels of promiscuity.[206] Additionally, population-wide studies find that populations with increased levels of T. gondii infections also tend to exhibit increased levels of personal guilt-proneness (tend to be more apprehensive, self-doubting, worried, guilt-prone, insecure, and self-blaming), as well as exhibit increased tendencies towards uncertainty avoidance, producing what one researcher termed a desire for a *"rule oriented society geared to reduce uncertainty"*.[207]

Uncertainty avoidance can a confusing term, as related to political ideology, even as described by Hofstede and McCrae.[208] Under their definition, it encompasses both the desire for increased governmental laws designed to limit unstructured interactions among individuals, such as liberalism desires,[209] as well as intolerance for novel ideas, such as exhibited by conservatism.[210] What is described here, in T. gondii however, is a desire to restrict individual interactions through rules, so as to eliminate uncertainty in freely competitive outcomes. This work maintains that this desire to increase governmental scope and authority, so as to limit the disparity in freely obtained competitive outcomes between individuals, is a trait common to liberalism, and is borne of the competition aversion of the r-selected reproductive strategy.

Here in T. gondii, we do see many behavioral traits which would appear to correlate with both liberalism and the r-selected organism. The tendency towards promiscuity and away from monogamy has been well documented as a delineation between political ideologies,[211] as well as a trait of the r-selected reproductive strategy.[212]

Envy of established success implies a desire to change an outcome at the conclusion of a competition which was lost. As we have discussed, liberals show increased volume of their ACC, a structure strongly associated with the production of envy. Envy can function as a powerful motivator to upset established competitive outcomes, in violation of the rules governing such outcomes. Those who can lose, and possess no envy, would be much better suited to accepting established outcomes of competitions, in accordance with the rules governing such outcomes.

Note that the willingness to violate rules is a fundamental personality trait of the modern liberal, while a desire to abide by rules within society has been found to be a fundamental trait of the conservative,[213] and here we see the same rule-violating trait identified in those infected with T. gondii.

Finally, those infected with T. gondii seek the imposition of rules on others, designed to eliminate personal individual risk, such as those risks which free competition will produce. Whether one is talking about the political left's aversion to free market capitalism, or the r-selected organism's aversion to risk in competing, this desire for a secure guarantee against failure is a hallmark of the r-psychology, and the desire to use government to this end is a clear mark of the liberal philosophy.

As in liberalism, this desire to see one's fellow citizens limited in their behavior by rules is combined with the personality trait of personal rule breaking. The net effect of this is a subversive competitive strategy entailing oppression of one's peers by governmental rules and authority. This is combined with personal opportunistic advantage taking, performed freely, absent the constraints of the rules one has imposed on others.

This is a strategy in direct opposition to the K-selected competitor's drive to engage in free, open competitions, designed to honestly confer advantage on the more fit individual, regardless of the outcome. Despite all of the selfless rhetoric of liberals, just as conservatism is personally competitive, so is liberalism. It is the psychology of a personally ambitious, selfish, competitive (even if subversively so), Darwinian strategy. The only difference between the two lies in the willingness to see differences in fitness, ability, and determination honestly rewarded.

Since the mechanism by which T. gondii alters human personality has been roughly characterized, a brief study of it may shed further light on the underlying neurobiological mechanisms behind the adoption of either the K-selected or r-selected psychologies.

Current research indicates that T. gondii's mode of action is to alter dopamine signaling,[214] while concentrating its infective cysts in the amygdala[215] and, to a lesser degree, the cortex.[216]

The prefrontal cortex (PFC), and particularly the left prefrontal cortex, is involved in engendering a state of optimism, by perceiving good in the environment.[217] Studies of depression have found that one coincident occurrence during depression is a power failure in the left PFC.[218]

T. gondii does produce a depressed mood,[219, 220, 221] less able to perceive good or engender optimism. As we have discussed, such a mood would diminish one's willingness to face a challenge such as competition, and embrace the uncertainty in outcome it offers. Clearly, an optimistic individual, prone to see success, will engage in competition far more often than a depressed pessimist, prone to only see potential failure.

Also, T. gondii affects the activity of the neurotransmitter dopamine,[222] which is responsible for the healthy functioning of the prefrontal cortex,[223] as well as incentive salience, or "want" for a reward.[224, 225]

As discussed, there is ample evidence that depression and depressed mood occurs at a higher rate among liberals compared to conservatives, and mutations in the DRD4 dopamine receptor gene are associated with both political liberalism and depression. Together, all of this offers potent evidence of a genetic and neurochemical nexus between a Darwinian strategy of depressed competition avoidance, and a countervailing optimistic psychological state which would embrace competition.

Rodents are designed to fear the cat, however as their amygdala function is altered by the infectious cysts of T gondii,[226] they cease to perceive the threat presented by the cat, and will approach it willingly.[227] As with the studies of monkeys and amygdala damage, this further supports the contention that the liberal's preference for negotiation and appeasement over conflict when confronted by threat, is related to anomalies in amygdala function which alter threat perception. Here, the cat, whose only desire is to kill and eat the rat, is transformed into a friend, waiting to be approached, entirely through small alterations in the function of the amygdala.

If one's amygdala is incapable of perceiving threat, even the most menacing and evil enemies, wholly bent on killing you, will seem wholly trustworthy and deserving of unreserved friendship and trust. Compounding this problem would be a lifetime spent observing one's own deficiencies in threat perception, which would produce an unwillingness to trust one's own instincts. This would naturally lead to an unwillingness to believe that others could perform accurate threat assessments, as well. As a result, such an individual would be prone to reject, out of hand, the threat assessments of conservatives, due to an honest ignorance of the cognitive and perceptual capabilities generated by a fully functioning amygdala.

As we have discussed, the concept of diminished amygdala function as responsible for diminished liberal threat perception is supported by research showing that humans with amygdala lesions will show diminished ability to judge the trustworthiness of individuals, and will tend to judge those who mean them harm as approachable.[228, 229, 230, 231] It is further supported by the evidence that liberals exhibit diminished amygdala volume, as would be expected of atrophy or developmental failure.

In closing, both the liberal, and the individual infected with T. gondii exhibit increased levels of depression, altered dopamine signaling activity, a willingness to approach and trust threats, a desire to live in a strict rule-governed society to perform competitive risk avoidance, an envy which might offer the justification to not abide by rules of competition, a tendency towards rule breaking, and a tendency towards promiscuity. Additionally, we can show where similar brain structure anomalies and neurotransmitter functional derangements are present in both cases.

This work is not making the case that T. gondii causes liberalism. We are merely asserting that an infection which alters dopamine signaling and amygdala function may also induce some behavioral characteristics of liberalism. For this reason, this analysis is presented here to help elucidate the mechanism by which evolution created the ideological divide within our species.

Chapter Twenty One

*Liberals, Homosexuality, and the r-selected Reversal in Sex-Specific Traits*___

In r-selected species that have parental responsibilities, there is often a reversal of sexual dimorphism, and sex-specific behavioral drives, compared to the K-selected organism. In K-selected species, males are expendable, and tend to endure risk and danger to provision and protect their family and offspring. Meanwhile nurturing and feminine females, who are bonded to their male partner, will tend to guide offspring away from the dangers that the male confronts for the family.

In r-selected species, males abandon females after mating, so the responsibility to provision and protect young will fall to the female. As a consequence, such independent females will evolve to be more aggressive and traditionally (from a K-selected perspective) masculine, so as to be better able to provision and protect the offspring they raise alone. The flight-prone males, by contrast, evolve to exhibit the diminutive size and fleeing-behavior traditionally ascribed to K-selected females. Referred to as a reversal of sexual dimorphism and sex-specific behaviors, this polarity reversal in sexual traits produces individuals perfectly adapted to the changing roles of genders in the r-selective environment, where females take on the roles of provision and protection, and males avoid responsibility assiduously.

If human r/K strategies are adaptable to resource availability, this would lead to a prediction of a possible reversal of sexual dimorphism and behavioral drives in males and females, as a civilization experiences copious resource availability, and its inhabitants transition to an r-strategy. Men would become increasingly feminine and competition-averse, while females would transition from the sweet, feminine K-selected model, to an aggressive/competitive/domineering, masculine model.

Interestingly, this would be accompanied by a reversal of the physical traits that individuals of each sex would seek out in mates. If an environment is r-selective, one would expect females to begin to prefer males who exhibit superior adaptive traits to the r-selective environment. This would mean females would begin to express a sexual preference for more feminine traits when assessing potential (male) partners.

Likewise, males would begin to favor more (traditionally, K-selected) masculine physical traits in their potential mates, so as to find mothers who would best be able to provision and protect the offspring the male would produce with her, and then abandon her with.

This would raise the question, might homosexuality in humans, where females prefer feminine physical traits to the point of preferring female partners, and males prefer masculine traits to the point of preferring male partners, have any relation to the r/K adaptability in our species? There is certainly enough interesting evidence to raise the question.

To begin with, male homosexuals do show reduced physical aggression,[232] as well as increased promiscuity and reduced relationship duration[233], [234]. Liberal males also exhibit a more traditionally feminine physicality, with diminished physical development and upper body strength, implying a reproductive strategy focused less on competitive ability.[235], [236]

Then there is what is called the Balancing Selection Hypothesis of Homosexuality. The concept states that homosexuality may be the result of a gene. The gene would produce reproductive behaviors in some heterosexual carriers which would increase the numbers of offspring they produce. This increased reproduction balances out the fact that the homosexual carriers do not reproduce. A quote from one study says:

"Our analysis showed that both mothers and maternal aunts of homosexual men show increased fecundity compared with corresponding maternal female relatives of heterosexual men... analysis...showed that mothers and maternal aunts of homosexual men (i) had fewer gynecological disorders; (ii) had fewer complicated pregnancies; (iii) had less interest in having children; (iv) placed less emphasis on romantic love within couples; (v) placed less importance on their social life; (vi) showed reduced family stability; (vii) were more extraverted; and (viii) had divorced or separated from their spouses more frequently."[237]

What is of interest here, is that there may be a gene which produces women who are more fecund, want to deal with children less, exhibit diminished emotional bonding with mates, and are more prone to divorce or separate. At the same time it makes men prefer more masculine qualities in female mates, as well as be less aggressive, and more promiscuous.

One study implicated the long form DRD4-7r polymorphism that is associated with development of a liberal ideology, with a predisposition towards homosexuality. In the research, the author wrote:

"About half of the subjects with the long gene (ed note: the DRD4 7r allele) *had ever had a male sexual partner..."* (among self-identified male heterosexuals).[238]

He went on to note that this gene appeared to be promoting not homosexuality per se, but rather, merely an increased drive to experience sexual novelty. (Risk spreading/bet hedging through mating with genetically diverse partners, to produce genetic diversity in offspring, is also a commonly seen mating strategy among r-strategists. Where raw offspring fitness is not as high a priority, producing diversity in offspring can be an advantage with little risk.)

As we maintain with r/K variability in mammals, homosexuality also shows evidence of an epigenetic role in its biological genesis, such as might arise from maternal stress. Studies have either offered potential linkages between homosexuality and epigenetic alterations to DNA,[239] or they have linked homosexuality to X chromosome inactivation,[240] itself a common byproduct of methylation,[241] a mechanism common to epigenetic effects.

Finally, homosexuality does show indications that it can be induced by high sustained exposure to dopamine, at least in the fruit fly.[242] High dopamine exposure would approximate the r-selective environment of free resource availability, while reducing the density of cell surface receptors, likely approximating the diminished signaling effects of inheriting a less effective, long form receptor gene such as the DRD4-7r polymorphism. Although data in humans is sparse, there is at least one anecdotal case of a heterosexual father of two who took a dopamine agonist (mimicking compound) for a medical condition, and after an extended period ended up pursuing gay sex compulsively, until his medication was changed.[243]

It is also interesting to examine the link between political affiliation and amygdala development. Interestingly enough, one study of the neurobiology underlying homosexuality stated:

"Homosexual subjects also showed sex-atypical amygdala connections. In (Homosexual Males), as in (Heterosexual Women), the connections were more widespread from the left amygdala... The results cannot be primarily ascribed to learned effects, and they suggest a linkage to neurobiological entities."[244]

Similarly, Kanai's study of the brain structures of ideologues found that, *"We found that ... greater conservatism was associated with increased volume of the right amygdala. These results were replicated in an independent sample of additional participants."*[245]

So here, homosexual males exhibited greater relative numbers of connections to the left side of the amygdala, while political liberals exhibited greater relative volume in the left side of the amygdala. Although increased connections does not definitively equate with statistically increased volume, it does raise the question of whether these are the same changes, measured differently, yielding in both cases, a more traditionally feminized, conflict-averse r-strategy which merely differs in degree.

Interestingly, homosexual females showed more widespread connections to the right amygdala, compared to heterosexual females. This would indicate a more masculinized brain structure (when viewed from a K-perspective). Given that the r-selected female is designed to fill the K-male's roles of provision and protection of offspring, and would need to exhibit a more masculinized, aggressive, and confrontational attitude, this is not surprising.

Again, the amygdala emerges as the seat of both the behaviors of r/K and the seat of ideology. We even find a structural alteration that is associated with homosexuality, and which is very similar to, if not the same as, that seen with both the liberal ideology and the r-strategy. We even see the reversal in sexual dimorphism and sex-specific behaviors that you see in r/K. We even see these traits emerging in our society, exactly as it trends leftward, all during an extended period of free resource availability courtesy of governmental deficit spending. Finally, yet again, the DRD4-7r allele appears, linking traits we already see linked in r/K, with ideological traits, and homosexuality.

158

Given the sum of the evidence, one cannot help but wonder if homosexuality is the result of a periodic overshoot of the r-selected mark in both men and women. As the society goes r, r-selected men become more effete, promiscuous,[246] and hedonistic[247] while r-selected women become more aggressive, masculine,[248] promiscuous, and competitive. Since r-strategists are better adapted under these conditions, r-females are programmed to seek more effeminate mates, as r-men seek more masculinzed mates. As they do, a simple mechanism, designed to shift behavior towards a more r-strategy, periodically over-expresses itself for reasons unknown, producing a complete reversal of mating behavior and sexual tastes. However, that small number of self-sterilizing overshoots fails to negate the reproductive advantage of the remainder of the more moderated r-specimens.

Here, we see yet another area of our society in which the traits and characteristics of the r/K dichotomy present themselves. With just a simple understanding of r/K, mystifying changes we see in our successful societies suddenly fall into context as distinct adaptations, with clear purposes and reproductive advantages.

Chapter Twenty Two

*The Games Ideologues Play*_____

In the book Games People Play,[249] Dr. Eric Berne postulated that many behavioral actions are merely pre-programmed responses to emotional stimuli, which humans developed during their childhoods. For example, if a child were to crave an emotionally distant mother's attention, he might one day, misbehave accidentally. His mother chastises him, he apologizes, and they then share a tender embrace, as all is forgiven. If this child craved that tender embrace, he might subconsciously feel rewarded following his misbehavior.

Later on, after numerous attempts to reacquire that embrace through more direct approaches failed, he might spontaneously act out, get chastised, apologize, and acquire his embrace yet again.

According to Dr. Berne, if this occurred often enough, the child would develop a subconscious urge to misbehave, which he would become accustomed to satiating, so as to acquire his mother's attentions. As an adult, his wife might one day find him making her angry for no apparent reason, and in the light of his adult environment, his motivations would seem illogical. However, by then he would have become conditioned, programmed with a desire to act out, even though his mother's hug no longer awaited him after his misbehavior. He called this behavior a game.

Dr. Berne observed numerous cases of different games, as he referred to them, and spent a career attempting to characterize the phenomenon. When I first read Dr. Berne' book in my teen years, I disregarded it as an unlikely hypothesis, at best limited to a select few instances within society.

Later in life, I came to know an individual whose entire life was spent satiating various urges that were obviously created in his childhood, and which had no relevance to the adult environment he traveled through. It was bizarre, and extreme enough that I began to see these games present in others around me, albeit to far lesser degrees and limited to much more specific areas of their lives. I suddenly realized that I was entirely wrong to dismiss Dr. Berne's work.

As time went on, I came to realize that many of us, to varying degrees, spend our adulthood perceiving life through a prism crafted in our childhood. Dr Berne's finely honed perception of psychological nuances had perceived something that my unrefined perceptual skills couldn't see, even when it was directly pointed out to me by an expert, in an entire book that he devoted to the subject.

According to the theory of this book, children develop an ideological predisposition early in their life, and one of the main components of this ideology is a perception of competition as either positive or negative in nature.

We have already cited research indicating that those with a liberal ideology exhibit a less capable and robust physical structure – The researchers indicated that may have produced a more conflict-averse psychology and liberal predisposition. Although more anecdotal, I have also heard it asserted several times, by different individuals, that many strongly ideological liberals in their social circles seem to be athletically challenged. If, as referenced earlier, liberals suffer from a dopamine receptor mutation, this might negatively affect dopamine signal transduction. Since proper dopamine signaling is important to smooth, well coordinated motor function, this could easily affect a liberal's physical coordination and proficiency at competitive athletic endeavors.

Derangements in dopamine function are well documented to affect locomotion, coordination and reaction times. Dopamine function is key to the etiology of the tremors of Parkinson's disease, and medications such as L-dopamine have long been known to have profound effects on muscular strength, reaction times, and physical coordination.

I point this out, as Dr. Berne's theory would indicate that physical incompetence at childhood play would profoundly affect an individual's perception of the competitive environment as an adult. If a child were to routinely find themselves humiliated in childhood play, whether it be roughhousing, pee-wee football, wrestling, or other competitive, physical, rule-governed play, the child might come to dread the conflict and challenge of the competitive environment. They might also be conditioned to envy those children who excelled in that world.

Conversely, were a child to step out into that arena, and routinely experience the ecstasy of a touchdown, or the thrill of a victory, they might find themselves conditioned to desire a rule-governed, conflict-laden environment of competition as an adult.

It is often said that play within the animal kingdom is a means by which the young develop physical abilities, in preparation for the rigors of a physical, competitive adulthood.

It is also possible however, that childhood play is a programmed behavior, designed to help the young test their competence in free competition in a safe, non-threatening environment, during the final period of heightened neurological plasticity they undergo in childhood.

If they prove competent relative to their peers, then they will grow up conditioned to enjoy free competition and they will follow the path of a K-selected competitor. If, however the outcomes they endure indicate that defeat will be likely in free, rule-governed competitions as adults, then these children will grow up designed to pursue a different strategy. They will be conditioned to avoid direct, head to head competition, break rules, violate loyalties, and do whatever is required to survive and reproduce, as quickly and as early as possible.

There is other evidence which would support such a premise. Dopamine, which we have shown is intimately involved in adherence to a political ideology, is best known as a neurotransmitter designed to provide a reward signal to the brain.[250] Thus, children who were successful in social activity and play would receive large pulses of it with each victory. In children who failed in such endeavors, they would only receive it rarely, when they violated the rules of the endeavors - or if overly envious, stifled the successes of those around them.

Activated repeatedly by competitive successes during a period of high developmental plasticity, a dopamine reward stimulus would have the effect of forming a highly malleable brain into a risk-taking, competitive, dopamine-driven machine.

Neuroscientists have linked dopamine activity to competitiveness and incentive salience (the want of a reward).[251, 252] Children who find they get a dopamine fix from setting out in competition and succeeding, will find the competitive environment more alluring due to its ability to satisfy their addiction. By contrast, those who found nothing but failure in competition as children will not be so rewarded, and thus they will be less inclined to tolerate the risk of the competitive environment.

As previously discussed, depression is associated with liberalism, is associated with low dopamine function, and is a cognitive state which could be conditioned during critical developmental periods. Depression is also associated with those who assume a lower social standing within a social hierarchy, such as the hierarchy that success in play establishes among children.

Additionally, liberals exhibit hypertrophy of the Anterior Cingulate Cortex, a brain structure highly associated with envy production in response to perceptions of others with superior levels of self relevant resources. Children forced to sit by and watch others effortlessly attain successes which they can only dream of, would tend to exercise those brain structures associated with envy. This envy could then offer the impetus to break rules, such as in competitions - a hallmark of the r-strategy, and a trait associated with liberals by researcher John Jost, as we will discuss shortly.

As discussed, the ACC is also activated widely during periods of psychic pain, especially the psychic pain of social exclusion, such as would be experienced by a child who failed repeatedly in free competition, and thus was excluded by peers. Combined with the ACC's role in envy, this does offer a compelling example of a mechanism by which early developmental experiences could adapt an individual's brain in ways which would predispose them to a particular political ideology later in life.

Imagine a child programmed by experience to view the world through a prism of envy, and prone to sympathize with the unsuccessful while not empathizing with the desires of the successful, who defeat them regularly. They would tend to mature into an adult with a more leftward leaning political inclination, unable to understand why anyone of modest means would lean conservative. Additionally, such a child, socially excluded by peers, would be conditioned to not perceive his peers as a part of his in-group, and thus would exhibit less loyalty to in-group as an adult.

In short, early developmental experiences which occur outside of the rearing environment, and which involve exposure to the competitive environment among peers, should be given ample consideration as a possible contributor to the adoption of our political ideologies.

Chapter Twenty Three

John Jost and the Personality Traits of Political Ideologues

John T. Jost of NYU has aggregated an extensive body of research on the personality traits of liberals and conservatives,[253] and here we will devote a chapter to some of his research, and how it relates to, and supports this theory.

Jost has found that research indicates conservatives tend to be less tolerant towards out-groups, more prone to seek stability, order, familiarity, conformity, and decisiveness. His work has also shown that conservatives are more prone to be motivated by fear-inducing and threatening stimuli, more prone to abide by rules, more loyal to their in-group, and less open to out-group interests.

These are all traits one would expect, were conservatives designed to engage in group competitions such as warfare for limited resources. Each trait would be adaptive in seeking the success of their group, while also engaging in individual, rule-governed competitions with in-group peers, designed to select for fitness and reward it with reproductive opportunities.

Stability, order, conformity and decisiveness are all traits which will produce a successful group. As we have shown, evidence indicates that fear motivates distrust, aggression, and conflict, while abiding by rules fosters more successful competitions among peers, and can motivate altruistic behaviors. Of course, increased loyalty to in-group, and less openness to out-group interests is what one would expect from a psychology designed to engage in group competitions with an eye to winning, and defeating their out-group.

Liberals tended to be less motivated by fearful or threatening stimuli, less prone to abide by rules, they exhibited more tolerance for ambiguity, and exhibited more tolerance towards out-group interests. They also sought conditions with less stability, less order, less familiar circumstances, less conformity, and they exhibited less loyalty toward their in-group. (Taken together, that is a description disturbingly similar to that of a psychopath, thrust into a group-competitive environment, something consistent with some research which has shown increased psychopathology[254] among those on the left.)

These are traits which would tend to produce an individual less prone to perceive and respond to competitive challenges such as threat, both individually, and at the group level.

Being less motivated by fearful or threatening stimuli (just as those with amygdala damage are unable to recognize threatening faces, and experience fear in response), they would be less prone to recognize and respond violently to threats, both individually, and at the group level. In seeking conditions with less stability, less order, and less familiar circumstances, liberals would be more tolerant of changes in governing circumstances, such as the sudden seizure of governing authority by a conquering force of outsiders.

By exhibiting more tolerance for out-group interests, and less loyalty to in-group, they would be more capable of breaking from the K-type rules and mores of warfare, such as loyalty to group, if it suited their interests. They would also be more likely to sympathize with the plight of an enemy who would produce a change in a country's leadership.

Given the lethality of engaging in warfare, feeling a freedom from rules within a society would be a potent Darwinian advantage during a time when all other citizens find themselves reflexively conforming to competitive behavioral patterns that lead them to risk death and Darwinian failure in battle. It would not be surprising to see such a strategy arise within a belligerent species, given the advantages it would offer to the individual capable of practicing it.

Combined, these traits could clearly facilitate a strategy of using betrayal in group competition, by creating a world view in which enemies are right, one's own people are wrong, and where blind loyalty is foolhardy and unintellectual. Indeed, the liberal's tendency to support out-group interests while feeling less loyalty to in-group can be seen as expressly designed to thwart the K-selected warrior's drive to pursue their group's competitive success by disregarding out-group interests, and showing blind loyalty to in-group.

It is also noteworthy that many of the personality traits noted by Jost would seem to be more related to issues of group competition than individual competition, indicating that perhaps group conflict has molded our political psyches even more than individual conflict.

This would not be surprising, given that under this theory, individual competition would be more rule-governed, limited in tenor, and not as prone to result in mass mortality. It would not be advantageous in a warring species to depopulate one's own tribe, through frequent lethal individual competitions. By contrast, the mortality of war would produce a far more lasting Darwinian impact on a species' nature.

It is also not surprising that our political inclinations, directed as they are to the structuring of our social order, would have been molded by group competitions, which were so dependent on the proper functioning of that social order.

That political ideology is related to fear and threat perception, is also consistent with research showing that amygdala stimulation is strongly associated with political ideology. It is also consistent with our assertion that this ideological divide is produced by the liberal's diminished amygdala function diminishing the liberal's ability to perceive threat, or drive the embrace of personal sacrifice that is needed to meet it.

Interestingly, it was noted by Jost that when fearful, mortal salience stimuli was presented to adults (stimuli designed to provoke fear of mortality, such as the attacks of September 11th), it had the ability to shift their ideological predisposition towards conservatism. This ideological shift did not just render them more conservative on the issue of threat presented to them. Rather, they espoused more conservative ideology on other issues unrelated to the threat presented.[255]

It should not escape notice that such stimuli would become increasingly prevalent as a population reached the carrying capacity of its environment, and conflicts began erupting over constantly limited resources. As the free and easy plenty of the r-selected environment shifted to the scarcity and conflict of a K-selected environment, it would make sense that the collective reproductive strategy of the populace would perceive this change and shift itself, so as to enhance competitiveness and belligerence, as well as their offspring's capability and survivability within such an environment.

167

No contrary stimuli were noted, which would precipitate a shift from conservatism towards liberalism. This raises the question of whether reception and acknowledgment of threat stimuli by individuals may yield increased amygdala functionality through stimulation-induced development of the structure. It also raises the question of whether such development will exhibit an increase in permanence that is not easily reversed.

This would be consistent with research into amygdala function. Once the amygdala is sensitized to a stimulus, deconditioning will not erase the sensitization pathway, but rather will only suppress it.[256] As a result, deconditioning of the amygdala to a stimulus will leave the sensitization pathway intact, allowing for fast and easy reactivation of the conditioned response. As a result, amygdala development and response is engendered with far more ease than atrophy. Jost may have been seeing this effect first hand - finding that developing the amygdala and inducing K-selected conservatism is far easier than atrophying the amygdala, and erasing the development.

Finally, on the subject of formulating personality tests based on this theory, one must understand that both the K-strategy and r-strategy are competitive, in the sense that they both seek to compete and win.

The difference is that the K-strategist seeks to win within their in-group, in rule-governed competitions that are designed to select for fitness. In seeking these individual, rule-governed competitions, the K-strategist is driven to accept defeat, if that is what the rules, (and the outcome of their own ability and effort) dictate.

In group competitions, the K-selected warrior is programmed to seek the success of their group over others, above all else. Thus, they will exhibit a blind adherence to traits such as loyalty, selflessness, respect for authority, and love of their group. They will always desire the success of their group at all costs, and the failure of their group's enemies, at all costs.

By contrast, the r-strategist is driven in individual competitions to succeed, regardless of rules, or any merit based determination of their own personal fitness. In group competition, this strategy is continued. The r-strategist's desire is to use the conflict for their own personal, individual advantage. (Though this drive is wholly subconscious – they likely think they are loyal, even as they castigate their own as wrong, their enemy as right, and view blind loyalty to their own as unintellectual foolishness).

As a result, the r-selected liberal will exhibit less loyalty to their in-group, more sympathy towards out-groups, and a general inability to perceive threat, or respond to it aggressively. None of these traits implies an absence of competitive drive. In fact it is the r-strategist's more aggressive competitive drive which will motivate him to turn his back on all of his species' historic K-type mores and values, as he desperately seeks his own personal success, at any cost, regardless of any "rules."

Thus both the r and K-type psychologies will prove competitive. The main differences in personality will be the K-strategist's desire to abide by rules that are designed to enhance the ability of their competition to select for fitness, and the K-strategist's tolerance for ability-based disparities in Darwinian outcomes, even when it results in personally disadvantageous outcomes.

These rules and the disparities that they produce may prove deleterious to the K-strategist's personal advantage, should they prove less fit than another K-strategist. However they will offer a distinct advantage to the K-trait, as they increase the evolutionary advancement of the K-selected cohort of humans as a whole. It is for this reason that the K-strategist was programmed by evolution to accept them.

This will produce the one delineation of tremendous importance between ideologues - the r-strategist's immense discomfort with Darwinian themes applied to social structures and human interactions. One example will be the more capable enjoying freely acquired rewards for their abilities and effort, while the less fit languish in poverty due to their competitive failure. By contrast, the K-strategist will exhibit far less discomfort with the concept of Darwinian themes playing themselves out within a culture.

Again, the K-type psychology is designed for a competitive K-type environment, where its purpose is to hone the biological vessels which carry the competitive trait. The r-strategist pursues their own individual advantage, and is designed for a non-competitive, r-selective environment, absent group competition.

Thus here, even in the study of the personality traits of political ideologues, we see further support for the theory that our political ideologies are simply intellectual manifestations of r and K-type reproductive strategies, further adapted by the environment of group competitive pressures.

Chapter Twenty Four

Historical Events and r/K Selection

Under the tenets of this theory, the political psychologies of populations should prove malleable beneath the force of environmental conditions, just as a population's reproductive strategy should prove malleable by the conditions that the environment presents to it.

Indeed, in examining history, we do see a tendency for the turmoil of chaos, laden with individual competition and scarcity of resources, to eventually give way to well structured societies, based on order and freedom.

As these governments form and then continuously provide for all, they allay the most aggressive forms of K-selective effects, in theory offering advantage to the r-type psychologies within them. As they do, we then see a tendency for such a government to gradually devolve into an ever more controlled and costly entity, until its size, scope, and cost are so great as to produce a collapse. At that point, the Darwinian environment of competitive chaos returns to cull the populace through K-selection, and the cycle will begin again. This slowly declining path of societal r-selection will also usually involve concomitant reductions in societal unity, loyalty to nation, morality, K-type parenting, personal shame and greatness. From oxytocin, to dopamine, to amygdala development - by now the physical mechanisms by which these changes arise, as well as the reasons they evolved, should be apparent to you.

Here, in the following three sections, we will just take a moment to examine how historical events can mold a population's psychology, and craft the nature of the history to come.

The Counterculture Movement of the 1960's

There is ample evidence of some means of transmissibility from parent to child, of political ideologies. Many studies show that a familial tendency towards a political ideology exists.[257, 258, 259] In a study on twins, it was shown that both direction of political leaning and strength of adherence to ideology would appear to have a genetic root.[260] Other studies indicate that a familial tendency towards a particular social attitude, and the strength of adherence to that attitude, are heritable.[261, 262, 263]

If there is a transmissible component of political psychologies, then historical events which favored the survival and/or reproduction of K-strategists or r-strategists could be expected to skew their relative proportions, just as populations can be either r or K-selected. This would then be expected to alter the general psychology of the affected generation, relative to its culture's baseline standards and mores. Under this theory, this effect would also alter the political ideologies of societies more generally.

This scenario would offer competitive advantage to groups (and the individuals within them), as it would allow a rapid psychological adaptation to changing historical and evolutionary circumstances. For example, the r-strategy (which in group interactions is similar to, if not identical to, the Stockholm Syndrome) would be beneficial under conditions of defeat in war. If all of a society's K-selected warriors were killed in the battle, it would be advantageous if that population's overall psychology adapted, changing from a more belligerent, competitive, K-psychology, to a less threatening, more pacifistic r-psychology, tolerant of being governed and controlled by hostile outsiders. In other words, were a population to lose a war, it would be in the interest of that group to immediately adopt a mentality and behavioral drive willing, or even desirous of ceding to the wishes of the conquering force.

Thus, under the tenets of this theory, should a selective pressure that culls r-strategists or K-strategists ever be applied to a population of humans, their political ideologies should change radically. Furthermore, given that we assert that group competitive processes have exerted an even stronger role over our ideological evolution than mere r/K stresses, any selective pressure which specifically removed K-selected warriors from a population should be expected to exert an even stronger force over the political ideology of a population than mere r or K-selecting environmental selection pressures.

Indeed, when America deployed as many K-selected warriors as possible during WWII, the sudden depletion of physically capable K-strategist males which ensued could be construed as similar to the conditions that would occur under the r-selection of a population, such as tremendously increased predation, or even defeat in war by foreign forces. Under the tenets of this work, this massive deployment of force would have had the effect of a clear r-selection pressure within the US population.

Those who stayed behind during the war contributed heavily to the gene pool of the generation born in the early to mid 1940's. These individuals produced a generation whose psychology was so inclined against the traditional American culture, that 20 years later, they were referred to as being the "counter-culture" revolution.[264]

The counter-culture revolution did exhibit many thematic influences similar to that which we maintain would accompany an r-selected psychology. They sought a competition-free, commune-like social structure.[265] They denigrated capitalism and economic ambition,[266] through embrace of anti-materialism.[267] They adopted a radical form of sexual promiscuity denigrating of monogamy, and demanding that women provide "free love," absent any careful fitness-based selection of potential mates.[268] Finally, in an extreme form of out-group tolerance, they allied with a foreign enemy (the NVA and Vietcong), and protested on this enemy's behalf at the very moment the United States was at war with this enemy.[269] There even existed an animus between physically aggressive males who embraced K-selecting Darwinian competitions, such as military members and police officers, and members of this "counter-culture" r-strategist generation.[270] Indeed, so great was this animus that these r-selected counterculture Hippies even spit on returning servicemen, and derided them as baby killers.[271]

There are some who have tried to assert that the Counterculture revolution was produced by the children of WWII vets. According to this assertion, it was some aberrant aspect of the returning vet's parenting

174

styles, perhaps produced by their traumatic exposure to war, which produced the modern Hippie. There are several aspects of this argument which conflict with a simple factual analysis of the era.

First, is the timing. The Hippie/Counterculture movement began in the early sixties, often being cited as a direct outgrowth of the Beat Generation of the late fifties. This Counterculture movement peaked around 1967, and by 1969 the Hippie movement was well in decline,[272] with the final "death knell for Hippies" being cited as the Hippie association with the Sharon Tate Murders in 1969.[273]

This Counterculture period begins just over 20 years after the beginning of American involvement in WWII. It ended just over twenty years following the peak yearly birth rate of the baby boom (births from 1946 to 1964),[274] in mid-1948.[275] This would indicate that as the individuals conceived at home during the US deployment reached around 20 years of age (20 years and nine months from conception), they created an r-selected social movement, which grew in strength with each subsequent year of r-selected births added. As the offspring of returning veterans became prominent 20 years after their births in 1968 and 1969, this r-selected movement saw its ascension end. At that point, the twenty-something social culture began a gradual return to more traditional K-selected mores and values, and the counterculture Hippie once again became aberrant in our species.

Second, one must confront the fact that the American period surrounding World War II had three distinct periods, consisting of a period of peace preceding the War (when K-selected psychologies would have reproduced at a normal rate), a period of War involvement (during which K-selected American warriors were removed from the breeding pool while r-type psychologies enjoyed enormous favor), and a period of peace following the war (when K-selected American warriors were allowed to reproduce again, and did so in large numbers).

Likewise, America showed three distinct periods of political and social behavior in its twenty-something youth during this period, consisting of a period of normative K-type conservative behavior during the fifties, a period of unusually r-type behavior during the early to mid sixties, and a following period consisting of a gradual return to more K-type behaviors which began in the late sixties. These three periods all occur a little over twenty years after their corresponding wartime periods, which consisted of a normative K-favoring reproductive environment, an r-favoring reproductive environment during the war, and a final return to a K-favoring environment. The individuals who comprised the social movements that motivated these changes were themselves, all around twenty years of age.

Of course all of that ignores the following simple logical argument. The War effort removed all males who showed even the slightest loyalty to their in-group. Those who refused to fight during WWII would have shown a highly diminished loyalty to in-group. Since lack of loyalty to in-group (and even desire for rebellion) is associated with a liberal political affiliation,[276] which has been shown to have a heritable component,[277, 278, 279, 280] it could be expected that a period of selective breeding favoring those who demonstrated diminished loyalty to in-group would have produced a generation which embodied this trait. Indeed, this is what we see here. Since lack of loyalty to in-group is associated with liberalism, one could expect this less in-group-loyal generation to show increased levels of liberalism, and likewise, we also see this. Since this text makes the case that liberalism is actually an intellectual manifestation of an r-selected reproductive strategy, this work would predict an increase in r-type behaviors. Here, we see an aggressive predisposition towards r-type behaviors such as promiscuity and disloyalty, and a greatly diminished respect for K-type behaviors such as competitiveness, monogamy, and loyalty in the Counterculture population.

Interestingly, since diminished loyalty to in-group is associated with liberalism, and the development of liberal ideology is associated with a long-form polymorphism in the Variable Number Tandem Repeat (VNTR) of the D4 dopamine receptor gene,[281] it could be expected that the Hippie would also exhibit similar long form VNTR polymorphisms in their DRD4 genes. This would lead to predictions of increased novelty seeking,[282, 283] promiscuity,[284] and drug abuse[285, 286] in the Hippie population. Of course, again, this prediction fits with observations.

As a result, given the perfect timing, the aspects of the selective pressures applied to the populace before, during, and after the war, as well as the behaviors and psychologies one finds in the populations before, during and after the counterculture revolution, it is extremely likely that the counterculture revolution arose as a direct result of an r-trait favoring, selective breeding of the populace during WWII.

As the surge of young K-selected descendents of the war veterans turned twenty in 1968 and 1969, they viewed the Hippie as an inferior specimen. Feeling something more within them, they broke free of the r-selected Counterculture of hedonism, disloyalty, and selfishness, and instead followed their own K-selected path. In doing so, they destroyed the Counterculture Hippie movement, and preserved American greatness, all without ever firing a shot.

This example does give excellent insight into how the r-strategist is designed to navigate group competitions. Jost[287] said that one delineation between political ideologies is loyalty vs. rebellion. In the counter-culture model of the r-strategy emerges a picture of a psychology prone to cultivate positive relations with an enemy force which sought to destroy their government, while being driven by subconscious, innate perceptions and urges that were designed to bring defeat to their own indigenous population. These urges are complemented by a desire to implement a strict anticompetitive economic and social structure on the populace, where even female mate choice was to be rendered uncompetitive. (In an r-selected movement, "the position of women is prone.") It is the position of this work that all of these urges are examples of how the r-strategist will seek to use rebellion and betrayal against their in-group, as one facet of a broader, r-selected, anticompetitive Darwinian strategy.

Here it helps to view liberalism in the context of the early evolutionary environment which produced it. In ancient times, wars were fought in close geographic proximity. To bring about defeat of one's society, while having acquired the favor of the conquering enemy, would have been a very effective Darwinian strategy for a less capable specimen, seeking to defeat the more capable indigenous K-strategists within their society. If the enemy chose to lay waste to one's society, they might spare such a cooperative r-strategist, while eliminating the r-strategist's Darwinian nemesis, the indigenous K-strategist. Were there an occupation, such an r-strategist could even have been promoted to a position of authority, overseeing some aspect of their occupier's new domain, and in the process gaining free access to copious resources, and numerous mating opportunities.

Here, using a force of foreign K-selected warriors as a proxy to subdue or eliminate local K-selected warriors would be an astonishingly brilliant Darwinian strategy. Like the r-selected transvestite cuttlefish, the r-type liberal Hippie could defeat their K-type warrior nemesis in war, without ever competing or risking Darwinian defeat themselves. All they had to do was sit back, and let the enemy do their work for them. In addition, an occupation would facilitate the imposition of an anticompetitive societal environment, where men were not free to compete with each other, lest they outshine their new occupiers. Nothing appeals to political leftists like government-mandated mediocrity.

In the Vietnam/counterculture example, had America been defeated and occupied by NVA/Vietcong forces (as would have occurred in our ancient evolutionary history), the counter-culture revolutionary would have been astonishingly well positioned to seize competitive advantage from their fellow indigenous K-strategists - a group for whom they exhibited open animus. While the few remaining K-strategists resigned themselves to the oppression of outsiders, the r-strategists would have thrived on the favor they curried with the new occupying force, while benefiting as well from the anticompetitive environment an occupation would have brought.

It is this clash of Darwinian strategies that Jost identified as a battle between "loyalty vs rebellion," and it is the purpose which the liberal's increased levels of openness towards out-group interests likely serves. Combine an urge towards rebellion with an openness to out-group interests, during time of war, and you have an r-selected psychology designed to use betrayal to gain advantage during group competition.

It is likely that no member of the counter-culture was conscious of how their innate perceptions and behavior would facilitate a seizure of competitive advantage in this fashion, however. Indeed, in the newly formed world of globalized warfare, where occupation was not so easy due to geographical constraints, this anticompetitive urge proved maladapted to that modern change in circumstances. However, such r-selected individuals in our distant evolutionary past, where wars were fought in close geographic proximity, certainly would have been well served to pursue such an anticompetitive Darwinian strategy during group competitions such as war.

Thus, we maintain that the counterculture was unconsciously driven by ancient r-selected anticompetitive behavioral drives which had evolved in a very different time. Such individuals were completely

178

unaware of the Darwinian strategy they were employing. Given the strongly r-selecting genetic effects of the draft in WWII, it is fascinating to see such a massive ground-swell movement of r-selected psychologies arise, and then disappear into the ether as the children of the K-type warriors of WWII began to enter the population in the 70's and 80's.

The theory contained within this text is the only theory extant which would explain why a movement, so opposed to traditional American culture that it would be termed "counter-culture," would suddenly erupt within our nation, dominate the political debate within its generation for a short period, and then disappear, just as the children of WWII veterans came to dominate the young-adult scene.

The competitive nature of the competition between r and K, which is inherent to the group-competitive aspect of this theory, would predict all aspects of the counter-culture's political and social platforms. This theory predicts their sympathy with the causes of out-groups during group conflict, their favoritism for less competition-driven economic models, and their adoption of a mating strategy entailing sexual promiscuity and monogamy aversion. It predicts their hostility to the military and police, as well as their rejection of social rules designed to produce societal cohesion.

This is also the only theory extant which explains how each anticompetitive aspect of their behavior would have conferred survival advantage on them under similar conditions, in our evolutionary past. This theory shows where similar psychologies can be found in other species, demonstrates how these psychologies pursue similar behavioral strategies, and highlights that they would be produced under similar environmental conditions. This theory also explains the ephemeral nature of the counter-culture movement, and why it disappeared, never to be seen in such strength again.

No other theory to date can explain just why young men of subsequent generations did not continue to hop on the train of free and easy sex, drugs, anti-Americanism, pretty colors, and no responsibilities - thereby keeping the movement, and all of its hedonistic pleasures alive and well for decades to come.

One interesting aspect of this example is the fiercely strong expression of the r-selected liberal psychology that was exhibited in the counterculture. This ideological shift is only highlighted by the relatively conservative nature expressed just one generation prior. Although the period of the fifties was highly prosperous, and would have afforded an environment that provided numerous environmental cues indicating free resource availability was forthcoming, such cues have not seemed to produce such radical shifts in ideological predisposition elsewhere, by themselves. Such a strong expression of the r-strategy here may speak to the effects of genetic selection being extraordinarily potent on the expression of a political/reproductive strategy by a population.

Finally, peer pressure influences likely played a considerable role in the evolution of the counter-culture movement. This will make it difficult to analyze each case of ideological divergence at the individual level. However, it is still notable that enough of a shift in the overall psychology of a generation occurred to produce this dramatic, yet temporary, shift in culture and political ideology. That this temporary shift in psychology so closely aligned with such a momentous occurrence as the temporary deployment of American military might during WWII, and that it proved reversible with the return of our military members at the end of the war, lends further support to this thesis of political ideology as Darwinian strategy.

The Renaissance

The Renaissance is attributed by some to an outbreak of disease caused by the gram negative bacillus Yersinia pestis, which produced the pandemic commonly referred to as the Black Death, or Black Plague.[288]

This pandemic ravaged European populations, killing 30 to 60 percent of the population, with estimates of the mortality in certain regions rising as high as 80%.[289]

Those who describe an interrelationship between the plague and the Renaissance claim that the ever present mortality made people think about death.[290] This focus on mortality then altered the psychology of the afflicted population, especially in Florence, and this new psychology then spread, and led to the increased artistic and intellectual expression which characterized the Renaissance period, between 1400 and 1700 AD.

This theory is consistent with John Jost's finding that focusing on mortally salient stimuli will produce a shift towards a more conservative ideology, focused on success and pro-social traits designed to unite groups in pursuit of goals.

This theory ignores any selective effect by the pathogen, however. When the Black Plague arrived, food prices had already grown to all time highs, due to both scarcity and increased demand for food. This had begun during the years 1315 to 1322, when there was a great famine, which reduced the population by as much as 10%.[291] Clearly, at the beginning of the pandemic, conditions of K-selection had already begun. Given this work, one would have already begun to predict an imminent rise in intellect, ability, group-functionality, and overall fitness in the population.

The conditions of famine were as would be expected in an r-selected population which had multiplied sans selective effect for some time prior, due in part to the Medieval Warm Period lading to bountiful crops. As the Medieval Warm Period came to a close, this produced a population which suddenly found an temporarily increased population, at or exceeding the carrying capacity of its environment. Adding to this difficulty would be an enlarged r-selected contingent of the population produced by the bountiful harvest of years past. If today's experiences are any guide, they would likely fail to contribute sufficiently to production, would continue to multiply at a high rate, and yet would simultaneously exhibit a sense of entitlement to their society's produced resources.

Due to this food shortage, many of the lower castes exhibited impaired immune function, and this elevated the mortality within their cohort when confronted with Y. pestis exposure. Those of lesser means would likely have lived in more dense populations, and in closer proximity to rodents, and this would also have facilitated infection more easily, through the plague's primary vector, the flea.

Others, more affluent and more productive, would have been well nourished. They would have been of sufficient means to limit interactions with rodents, and even other humans during an outbreak. They would have had a better chance of either never being exposed to the infection, or of fighting it off if infected. Those who would have been most malnourished would have been the uncompetitive, less capable, unproductive, more prolific, r-selected contingent of the populace.

Although some hard-core ideological liberal leaders in America today are affluent, their political support (and their effect on the society and culture) arises from a much more substantial, lower income population which congregates in cities, where rodent populations thrive and people are concentrated in high densities. It is safe to assume that the same would have been true of the r-selected individuals during the Black Death.[292]

If this is accepted, then the period preceding the Renaissance would have seen a massive culling of those who lacked resources, due to their failure to produce products or services of sufficient value to others.

If one were to seek out this subset of our populace today, one would find a group of individuals who do not produce value or earn sufficient quantities to survive on their own, sans federal assistance. These individuals will also tend to demand welfare from the state in disproportionate numbers, be over-represented in crime statistics, live in dense concentrations to limit costs of living, mate as frequently as possible, and generally exhibit an r-selected, leftist-supportive psychology politically.

Such individuals will favor enlargement of the state, increases in resource redistribution from rich to poor, and elimination of any discrimination by individuals between good/bad, right/wrong, liked/unliked, or moral/immoral (all according to our species' K-selected standards).

Additionally, the majority of these unproductive r-selected individuals will likely exhibit limited facility in science, mathematics, philosophy, and other intellectual endeavors, such as flourished within the Renaissance. Clearly, removal of these less productive traits from a population would skew its nature more towards that of the Renaissance man. Additionally, as this r-selected cohort shrank in size, one could expect the social structures of the time to punish success less, and reward industriousness more. This motivational force would only enhance the productivity and greatness of the resultant society.

It is for these reasons that this text will assert that the selective mortality inflicted on the human populace by Yersinia pestis would have preferentially culled the unproductive, unmotivated, uncompetitive individuals within the human populace, thereby leaving behind a more K-selected population overall. The K-selected individual is the individual most prone to strive for a standard of accomplishment that is superior to that of their peers and most prone to compete with peers for resources. They are, therefore, most prone to produce products and services of substantial advancement and merit, as a means of economically competing with fellow K-selected individuals.

The K-selected individual is also the individual most likely to self assort with other high-producing K-selected individuals, so as to form a group with superior functional abilities, and superior accomplishment. They are also most prone to abide by rules, and therefore produce functional societies, designed to incubate industriousness and greatness through its reward.

As a result, the K-selected human will also be more prone to adopt pro-social thought processes and behaviors such as adherence to morals and honor in interpersonal interactions, acceptance of outcomes in free competition, and a generalized willingness to behave in an altruistic fashion, on behalf of peers, so as to promote societal cohesion among their group. Additionally, enhanced amygdala function allows the K-type individual to discern more effectively, which, combined with K-type tendencies to aggressively discern between "good" and "bad," would likely have had a sizable effect on the quality of everything, from moral virtue, to the artwork of the time. Looking at the period, this is exactly what you see, from an embrace of capitalism,[293] to societal accomplishments which leave people in awe, even today.

Indeed, were such a strong K-selection pressure applied to America today, it could be expected to radically alter our culture, and society, as it virtually eliminated the envious and self-destructive tendencies of liberalism from our culture. Our culture would immediately show increased competitiveness and ability, and this effect would only magnify as our citizens began to compete amongst one another, motivated by the increased rewards for success that such a society would favor. As time went on, our rate of evolutionary advancement would skyrocket as well due to competitive selection effects, combined with an increased competitive drive to out-produce, and defeat rival cultures and nations.

It is likely that after such an event, America would see its art revert from crucifixes soaked in urine and crude finger paintings splattered with elephant feces, to works more akin to Davinci's, Michaelangelo's, or Rembrandt's. Per-capita production would likely increase due to competitive motivation, while economic success would grow due to increased free-market competitiveness.

Individual freedom would increase as well, since there would be fewer r-selected liberals, who uniformly tend to favor government intervention in the lives of private citizens. And finally, American greatness would also emerge on the international stage, as the K-selected populace adopted a more competitive, in-group focused foreign policy, less desirous of appeasing outsiders and enemies.

This highlights one of the main differences between ideologies. One ideology is designed to provide a temporary hedonistic period absent any displeasure, before creating much worse conditions of chaos and collapse. The other will produce a less hedonistic environment, but will forestall the destruction and horror that is inherent to the chaos and collapse promulgated by the former.

184

The Roman Example

Many have examined the fall of the Roman Empire, with the hope that in divining the cause of the fall, valuable lessons could be learned which would preserve great civilizations in the future. Such examinations have identified various symptoms of the fall, from "barbarism and religion" triggering a decline in civic virtue,[294] to a declining military character within the populace combined with increasing reliance on foreign barbarians for protection,[295] to unsound economic policies,[296] to increasing government complexity, cost, and taxation.[297] The decline in the quality of the Roman citizenry has proven so perplexing that it has even been postulated that lead poisoning from the preparation of foodstuffs in lead containers might explain what had gradually produced a populace which was so much duller, less motivated, and less capable of preserving their empire's majesty, than the standard of citizen which had come before and created it.[298]

Viewed in the context of this theory, one should note that it would not be unusual for a populace producing copious resources (or seizing copious resources and slave labor), to see all selections for fitness within their society eliminated – a situation akin to what would be called an r-selection pressure in nature. We have national debt today, providing this environmental condition, and we see these effects in our population. The Romans had something similar in their seizure of foreign booty and slave labor. The only real difference is, they didn't promise to repay the resources they acquired from other nations.

The effect of these free resources would be slight, in the beginning, as the K-selected populace would not want to provide undue resources to those who did not produce themselves. Nevertheless, the effect would be to protect those who did not produce from the rigors of Darwin.

These r-selected individuals however, once provisioned even just to subsistence levels, would begin to rapidly reproduce. As history has shown, rarely will the resources provided to such a group diminish as the population of r-selected resource-consumers grows.

Adding to this effect would be the aggressive deployment of Rome's K-selected warriors to man garrisons, secure borders, conquer enemies, and secure further resources to support the increasingly unproductive, r-selected Empire. As the K-selected individuals removed themselves from the competition for mates to go forth and protect the Empire, the r-selected individuals would gain even further advantage.

Once having gained a reproductive foothold, these unproductive r-selected individuals, being of the r-strategy, would reproduce quite quickly, out-reproducing the K-selected contingent of resource-producers. As the r-selected contingent grew in proportion, it would shift the psychology of the populace, gradually reducing military virtue, decreasing the ability to judge threats, welcoming outsiders to hold positions of authority within government, and increasing the size, scope, and control of government in an effort to eliminate all competition.

Taxes on the productive and the wealthy would increase to strip them of any advantage, while welfare would become ever more generous. Price controls would be enacted to allow the unproductive equal access to resources. As this failed to stall the inevitable onset of K-selection, the r-type leadership would inevitably call for more resources seized from abroad to sustain the free resource availability required for r-selection.

As this r-selected civilization attempted to increase its elimination of all competition, it would further enhance the reproductive advantage of the r-selected cohort within the population, and this would further increase the shift in the populace's psychology towards a more r-selected, anticompetitive bent.

Of course, in nature resources cannot remain limitless forever. Sooner or later, either each individual begins to pull their own weight, or nature restores the balance herself, through far less benevolent means.

In this light, all of the symptoms of the Roman collapse could be seen as an unavoidable byproduct of civilization, the success it produces, and the natural human tendency to try and eliminate the unpleasantness of selection effects that inevitably favor a competitive, driven, and productive, group-oriented specimen.

No population anywhere in nature will survive absent some selective effect upon its genome. Given the higher proportion of detrimental mutations prone to arise, compared to beneficial mutations, it is simply scientifically impossible for any genome to not devolve, once natural selective effects are removed.

The slide towards r will be exacerbated by the innately higher rate of r-selected reproduction over K-selected reproduction. Further feeding the fires of destruction will be the feed forward effect such a psychology's rise has on the further elimination of selective effects within a society. As the society goes ever more r, this is detected by ancient mechanisms in the population, and it results in the production of even more r-offspring. Any successful civilization will inevitably produce a gradually more r-selected, anticompetitive society, until such time as a collapse intervenes, and resets the competitive order.

Unfortunately, the purpose of the r-selected psychology is not to create a perfect utopia of pacifism and plenty which lasts in perpetuity. The purpose of the r-selected psychology is to increase a population's size to the point that the population will meet the carrying capacity of its environment and begin to be culled by the effects of competition for what will always, inevitably, prove to be limited resources.

In nature, where the carrying capacity of an environment exists as a static plateau, this will eventually produce a highly K-selected population, and a gradual stabilization of population numbers at the carrying capacity of the environment. In humans, however, this may work a little differently.

Chapter Twenty Five

The Misery Index vs The Conservative Policy Mood Visualizing the r/K Shifts in Societal Ideology ___

Thus far, this analysis would indicate that liberalism and conservatism are suites of instinctual inclinations, designed to foster survival and reproduction under conditions of resource excess, and resource scarcity. Each has been engineered into humans in such a way as to spontaneously emerge in our populations in response to environmental signals indicating that their respective conditions of resource availability have begun to emerge. In other words, as resources grow scarce, a population will spontaneously shift towards a conservative worldview, and as resources become freely available, the ideological balance will shift towards liberalism.

It will happen at a variety of levels, and on a variety of time scales, all of which will vary among individuals. Amygdala adaptation to the environment, and immediate learning will produce fast, but limited changes. Epigenetic adaptation will slowly change how the DNA code is stored, and how accessible the important and unimportant parts are, from generation to generation. Genetic selection will take even longer still, but will presumably have its effects as well.

It will not happen evenly in everyone, of course. There will be those stalwart souls whose grasp on reality cannot be shaken free by even the most copious resource availability, and those who will not be able to think rationally, even when their lives literally depend upon it. Intellects will further complicate matters, as some smart individuals see reality despite changes to their nature which could cloud their vision, and vice versa. But some correlation should still be visible, at the population level, between resource availability, and political inclination.

This will be, to most people the most inarguable evidence presented in this work. On the next page are two graphs, laid over each other. Beneath, is a bar graph of the Economic Misery Index, year to year. On the right is its scale. Combining the measures of Inflation with Unemployment, it is a rough economic measure of resource scarcity, and

189

resource excess. As a result, it can also be seen as a rough measure of dopamine activity in the population. When it is low, resources are flowing freely, as is dopamine in the brains of the citizenry. When it rises, resources will be getting short, as will dopamine activity.

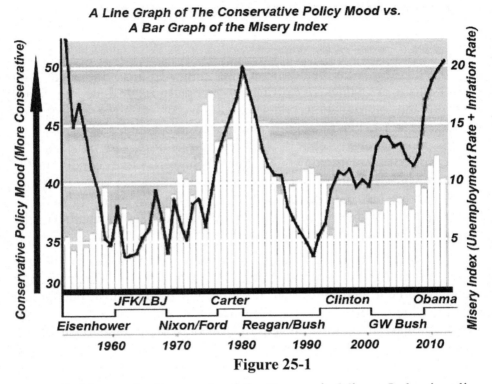

Figure 25-1

Laid over the bar graph of the Economic Misery Index is a line graph of the Conservative Policy Mood, as described in this article.[299] It is a complex measure, not of political affiliation, but of the expression, by the individuals in the population, of specific policy inclinations identified as fundamental underpinnings of the Conservative political ideology. When it is high, the population will grow increasingly open to conservatism, and when it is low, liberalism will be enjoying favor.

Obviously, there is much of interest in figure 25-1, as can be seen explained in figure 25-2, on the next page. First, periodic bursts of Misery (resource restriction) will often precipitate a K-shift in the population. Following WWII, the Conservative Policy mood was sky high, as one would expect – conflict is an environmental signal of K-selection, and should precipitate a commensurate K-shift in the populace. As the CPM was elevated, misery was reduced markedly, due to production by a populace which produced as if its life depended on it, literally. This massive production and prosperity (ie free resource availability) precipitated a commensurate decline in the CPM. Clearly, resource availability roughly correlates with overall adoption of political inclinations as defined by the r/K model.

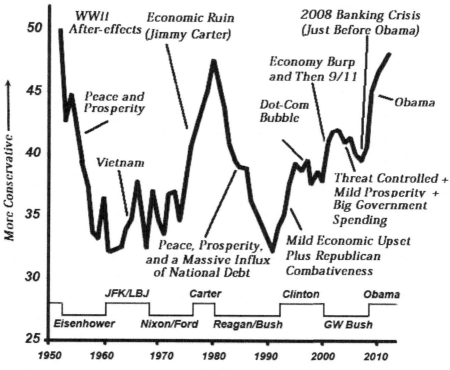

Conservative Policy Mood, 1952-2012, with annotations.
For the full story, see the Washington Post article linked above.

Figure 25-2

War, and violent stimuli, from Vietnam to 9/11 can apparently precipitate a "K-shift" in the population, regardless of underlying economic indicators. When strongly precipitated, such as during WWII, this K-shift alters the psychology of the population in such a way as to produce unusually low misery, and unusually high Conservatism. Since crime has been shown to parallel the Misery Index,[300] it is not clear if the violent stimuli present in a crime-filled environment mediates the change, or if merely forcing a sinecure life on a population alone can activate amygdalae, and have this effect. As one would expect, Jimmy Carter, almost solely through economic mismanagement, created a jump in Conservatism which nearly rivaled that produced by a World War, and Conservatism jumped after the 2008 banking crisis.

There is one strange aspect to the graph. Beginning in 1994, the misery index seems to be less related to the Conservative Policy Index than in years prior – a trend which grows. Indeed, although the Conservative Policy Index continues to rise and fall with Misery, it seems to rise more aggressively, as if Misery is now under calculated.

Indeed, although we are told that today's economy is well into recovery, the CPM has risen again to nearly WWII-era heights. In 1994 the Unemployment calculation method was changed, (and as a result the way the Misery Index was calculated was changed). That year, the change radically diminished the Unemployment calculation, although the underlying reality had not changed at all. As subsequent years passed, it again became a measure of relative misery in comparison to the previous year, but some have argued that its effectiveness was degraded, and it was only accounting for a fraction of the real unemployment. This recalculation may be, in part, what is behind the divergence of the two graphs, beginning in 1994. It is also possible, in these strange times, that other calculations, such as the government proffered measure of inflation, are today, less reliable measures of the unpleasantness of economic misery than they have been in the past. That would contribute to the effect as well.

Of greatest irony in this figure is that although his own governing policies were quite effective, Ronald Reagan may have fostered our current national decline, as he both defeated the Soviet Empire, and began to open the spigot on a flood of free resources, courtesy of our national debt. In creating massive quantities of success, peace, and comfort, he created an environment which facilitated liberal ascendancy. It is likely, that as the economic disaster which will eventually flow from that gradually unfolds in the future, we will see a reversal of that process, and conservatism will rise again.

Even as we suffer economically, our nation and our world will grow stronger, more moral, more demanding of freedom and decency, and less tolerant of any form of stupidity applied to our social, political, or familial structures. Given how the world's national economies are interwoven, this Conservative revival will probably spread across the entire world. Competitiveness/aggression/protectiveness, monogamy, family values, and loyalty to in-group will all begin a resurgence, as will respect for traditional gender roles, demand for fairness in earned rewards, and functional social structures. Disregard for out-group interests will also likely make a resurgence, as will, more ominously, hostility to out-group interests.

One really need not see graphs of these metrics however, to see this mechanism. Should resources snap back, people will grow more miserable. It is only commonsense that under those conditions, individuals will see their amygdalae become twitchy, leading to increased aggression and competitiveness. As the world becomes harsher, people will begin to desire, and seek out, loyal familial bonds for stability. Little things they ignore now will become more bothersome, such as people who shouldn't be raising children, selfishly forcing children to endure substandard rearing experiences. As crime increases with resource scarcity, so will danger and threat. When people begin to realize that their lives are on the line, they will demand that law enforcement be selected for IQ, aggressiveness, and physical ability alone.

Sadly, Liberal foolishness of the last few decades, mixed with its consequent future resource limitation will probably not allow for a smooth, peaceful return of the success and happiness of the 1950's that we all so desperately desire to see again. That world will come, but it will not come cheaply, given the debt that we have taken on. As the unpleasantness unfolds, it might be of utility to make sure that liberals are made aware that people realize that the unpleasantness is ultimately brought about by their loony, resource-intoxicated worldview Ultimately it is the embrace of the r-strategy, which undoes all the success that the K-strategy creates. What Conservatives will want to do, at the neurological level, is burn an amygdala pathway in the brain of humans linking Liberal policy measures with the suffering they produce, so in the future, contemplation of liberalism and liberals will initiate an immediate burst of aversive stimulus within the population. Perhaps, if that point can be driven home sufficiently, any subsequent K-shifts will arrive more gently, and prove to be less unpleasant than the next one likely will be.

Chapter Twenty Six

What is K?

There is a deeper, philosophical aspect to this work which arises, if one tries to examine exactly what the K-strategy is. Is it an ability, or desire to engage in violence? Is it technological sophistication? Is it IQ and intelligence? Conservatives will all know, on a very deep, primal level that K is good, and r is measurably bad – even evil. We look at r, and feel little but overwhelming contempt, hatred, and disgust. But why? Is K something more than a mere suite of traits? Is it imbued with some overriding purpose? Is it measurably good, in any tangible way?

A study of this will gradually reveal a more fundamental truth about the universe, and its Creator. In the end, K is something programmed into the computer code of the universe – a fundamental force integral to the world, and designed to arise spontaneously, due to the designed nature of it. Once arisen, it guides the evolution of every self-sufficient organism's form and function. K may even be the fundamental force really driving the universe's organization, if not the underlying purpose of the entire Creation. In its most basic form, K is about the fostering of a specific quality within the Universe's organization. The quality can loosely be described as "greatness," - encompassing such variables as complexity, ability, resiliency, sophistication, creativity, adaptability, etc.

If one examines the world around them, they will quickly come to the realization that, over the long haul, it favors K innately, and that this is likely an engineered design. God does not want to crack the hood on His Creation, only to look out upon a Universe of worlds that all look like the world in the movie Idiocracy, filled with imbeciles denigrating the lone eloquent smart person. Indeed, were the universe designed to favor r, evolution would never have even made it that far. All God would see in a perpetually r-universe would be ever more rapidly expanding blobs of goo, each unit of goo competing fiercely with the others, to see which can expend less energy on greatness and complexity, to focus on reproducing more of an ever less-evolved goo.

Where K inevitably emerges, it not only produces greatness – it produces a deep, abiding love and respect for it in the very products of its creation. This innate drive, fundamental to our being, favoring greatness, leads us to seek to nurture, protect, and defend it where necessary. Like it or not, the imbeciles of Idiocracy do not produce, protect, or favor greatness. Their's is a nihilistic world absent any purpose or accomplishment.

The true r-strategy however, goes further than merely lacking the greatness-producing or protecting traits of K. Wherever r takes hold, greatness actually becomes the enemy. Greatness becomes an epithet, to be reviled, and castigated as inconsiderate and evil. Create a successful business, and your creation will be reviled as "big business," and portrayed as inveterate evil. Create a great nation, head and shoulders above all others, and it will be castigated as a selfish, evil, greedy, oppressive empire. The mere word patriotism, due to the desire to foster and celebrate greatness among one's own, will become an epithet. Create greatness in your culture, and the r-strategists will seek to infect it with degeneracy. They insist that immigrants be drawn from the least great individuals in the least great corners of the world. Should you object you will be castigated as intolerant and mean.

From the school tests which measure and foster the pursuit of greatness in our young, to the economic benefits which accrue from exhibiting it in adulthood – The r-strategist believes that it must all be torn down with the express goal of making greatness disadvantageous, while conferring benefit on those who either fail or refuse to exhibit it. And should you strive and succeed yourself, you too will be castigated - unless you apportion sufficient quantities of your own success to the express goal of destroying greatness yourself. The destruction of greatness is the only spiritual cause, of any real meaning, to the r-strategists. A commitment to that cause is even how they recognize each other.

Again, as with the temporal elements of political ideologies, this creates a situation where the two ideologies, in their purest forms, are in a very real sense wholly incompatible, and unable to share the same terrain. It could be argued that all calls for tolerance and compromise are really calls to cede to the r-strategist's goal of destroying the greatness of one's own people, and reducing one's own nation to ashes.

The only benefit is that God designed this world to favor K, so even as the governing structures of one's nation are reduced to ashes, all this really does is trip a switch in the universe, which spontaneously forces the return of K, and the forceful eradication of the r-strategy, so that greatness can once again emerge. Apparently, God does not wish to look upon a universe of featureless goo.

Chapter Twenty Seven

The Cycle of Life, and Governmental Death

In nature, the carrying capacity of an environment is determined by the resources available to the population. In ecosystems, it is common for such environments to exist in a mostly stabilized state. Such an environment produces a balanced ecosystem, where carrying capacities and environmental stresses for the various species are relatively predictable and stable. This results in species adopting relatively stable reproductive strategies, and consequently exhibiting fairly stable psychological natures. As a general rule, rabbits do not exhibit violently truculent and competitive natures, nor are many lions noted for their overly pacifistic and docile nature.

In humans however, the carrying capacity of our environment is determined by our population's productivity, which can prove variable, with the nature of a society, and its stage of development. Ironically, a population's r/K status is profoundly involved in its productivity, which in turn, determines its r/K status.

In a K-selected population, where all individuals are competing with each other and where those who do not produce endure privation, per capita productivity will be high, and the carrying capacity of this productive output will be well in excess of the population's numbers. As evolution works its magic, production will only increase, as long as conditions of K-selection persist, and success is rewarded, while failure is punished.

Of course as history shows, these circumstances cannot last. We are a species which cannot deny its decent nature. We are driven by our group psychology to protect those within our in-group. If we begin producing an excess of resources, we will offer some of that excess to those disadvantaged individuals within our society who would otherwise be culled by their inability to produce sufficiently to sustain themselves. It is through these means that the inevitable result of K-selection pressures will be to routinely produce an onset of conditions of r-selection within human populations.

The r-selected individual originally evolved to exist within an environment where resources were readily available, due to lower population densities leaving their population well below the carrying capacity of their environment. When their intellectual thought process meets this primitive urge to consume freely available resources, it produces a governing philosophy designed to provide everyone with more than ample resources, to continue a meteoric explosion of the population's numbers. But this is only adaptive as long as resources can continue to be freely available.

As r-selected individuals begin to increase in relative numbers, they will gradually diminish the productivity of the population. First, they will promote the proliferation of less productive, less capable, less competitively-vetted specimens. Second, they will diminish the competitive drive motivating the remaining K-type population through the use of government to interfere in free interactions between men. By effectively punishing success and rewarding failure, they will further diminish their society's production beyond what would have occurred due to the relative increase of r-type psychologies.

As this progresses, productivity carries less and less competitive reward, and per-capita productivity will decline. Individuals, whose amygdalae previously motivated them to produce due to the threat of privation, will suddenly find themselves in an environment where the lack of productivity produces no punishment, and their amygdalae will take note.

Eventually a time will come where the carrying capacity of the population's productivity and the population are equal to each other, and the curves will cross. From that point forward, the unproductive r-type individuals will out-reproduce the productive K-type individuals, and consumption will begin to exceed production. As these two curves diverge, the society's declining productivity will no longer be sufficient to support the expanding population of r-type consumers. This point may be able to be forestalled through debt, printing, and policy, but all of those are only temporary cosmetic fixes to a deep, structural imbalance in the financial ecosystem. Sooner or later, the r-selected party will end.

At that point, competition will again enter the arena, and there will be a return of K-selection, by force of reality. The K-selected contingent will find itself forced to choose.[301]

200

They may abide by an r-type government's directives, and continue to support all of the r-selected individuals while enduring mortality themselves due to insufficient resources. Or they may abandon the strictures of the r-government, and choose to support their own offspring with their own earned resources. At some point, their choice will be inevitable, since the nature of such a government heads in only one direction; increasingly illogical, increasingly oppressive, and increasingly detached from reality. Their eventual choice will signal a tipping point in the stability of the government.

It is at this point that the government will collapse, as those who produce will refuse to continue to support those who do not. In the collapse, K-selected conditions of free competition will again return, and this will both cull the population, and trigger ideological/strategy conversions in those who are capable. Once again, the K-selected psychology will emerge as the predominant psychology of the population.

Of course, then the cycle will repeat, as K-type productivity returns, and K-type individuals again provide excess resources to those who cannot produce. The r-type psychologies will begin multiplying again.

This cycle would follow logically from the scientific evidence presented within this work thus far. If K-selection of a population produces a K-type psychology within a populace (and it clearly does), and the K-type psychology generated by group competition produces cooperativeness, altruism, and pro-sociality, as well as enhanced innate ability and incentive salience (due to competitive selection effects), then we see this rather shocking model of societal growth and collapse emerge logically and spontaneously.

In nature, absent the human effect, this would likely eventually reach a point of homeostasis. There would be a point of mild K-selection which would cull the r-types just enough to maintain productivity at a level which could sustain the remaining population. In humans however, r-selected individuals have the ability to extend their period of parasitism of the K-selected members through governmental interference. This will cause us to repeatedly overshoot the homeostatic mark, as the r-strategists use government to prolong the r-selection unnaturally, producing an overly-selective period of K-selection. This overly extreme

K-selection will then, again, produce resources in such excess as to overly fuel the subsequent r-selection.

Similarly, the compassionate urges of the K-type population, produced by their pro-sociality, will also tend to unnaturally prolong the persistence of the r-type individuals as the collapse approaches. This too, will exacerbate the magnitude of the collapse when it finally comes. Psychological effects will also play a role, as the r-type individual's reward of failure, and punishment of success, will depress each K-type individual's productivity below what they are capable of when motivated by free competition, and the rewards of success.

The degree to which the cycle occurs will vary, depending on circumstances. If there are frequent periods of limited resources forcing a periodic limited competitive culling of the population, the disruptions they cause will likely be minimal. But if the population goes for a long period, absent any selective effect, the consequences of this on the population may prove to be quite severe.

In the Roman example, the raiding of neighboring lands and the seizure of their resources by force allowed the population to forestall the onset of K-selective pressures for much longer than would otherwise have been possible. As production became insufficient to support the increasingly r-selective social structure, r-selection was prolonged with foreign resources, labor, and productivity. As a result, the Roman government continued to grow, as did their population's contingent of less productive and less competitively competent, r-type individuals.

When the seized resources finally ran out, the population's productivity was so low that the Empire could not possibly continue as it was, and Rome underwent a full scale governmental collapse from which it could not recover. Productivity had simply collapsed well below the levels required to support the population. competitive hoarding effects after such a collapse likely further exacerbated the subsequent shortage, enhancing the degree of K-selection.

Many have noted that no nation can survive forever. No matter the greatness which has imbued any nation, the civilization of a people will generally, inevitably, decline towards collapse before beginning over again, and again striving for greatness.

It is the position of this work that when viewed from the biological perspective of r/K theory, the origins of this phenomenon are patently obvious.

This effect is best exemplified within the movie Idiocracy. There, r-strategist idiots out-reproduced the intelligent by such a margin that eventually, the IQ of the entire world was reduced to a comedic level. Absent any selective effect, such devolution is a natural consequence of a species encountering unlimited resources, while experiencing no selective effect. Indeed, a case can be made that we are seeing it today.[302, 303, 304]

In reality, the Idiocracy effect will only last until the population reaches the carrying capacity of its productivity. Once the population reaches that point, competition will reenter the arena by force, and the genome of the species will resume its ascent towards evolutionary advancement.

The end result of this is that governments will follow an endless cycle of production and consumption, productivity and scarcity, growth and collapse, and order and chaos.

There are two methods by which the cycle could theoretically be stalled. If non-selective, state-sponsored charity was eliminated, most charity would come from the K-selected, productive contingent of the populace. If these K-selected competitors carefully disbursed their charity in a selective manner, only to K-selected psychologies which favored a K-type social structure and reproduced accordingly, then they might diminish the competitive advantage of r-type psychologies through resource limitation. Under such circumstances, a society would likely continue for an extended period in a K-type cycle of productivity and advancement. (It is likely no coincidence that K-type conservatives favor private charity over freely available government handouts.)

Unfortunately, this would also require leaving the children of r-strategists to potentially suffer the consequences of their parent's irresponsibility, consequences which they would not have brought on themselves. Reeking of eugenics, such a strategy will never take hold among K-type psychologies due to an evolved in-group loyalty. This is despite the distasteful nature of the alternative, which involves inevitable anarchy, governmental collapse, and wholesale societal failure.

The second means by which the cycle of government might be stalled can only provide a temporary effect, judging by history. If the r-selected individuals gain enough power to implement a government in which the K-selected individuals cannot withdraw productive effort for fear of death, then the r-selected individuals can continue to parasitize the productivity of the K-selected individuals, as long as the government can maintain sufficient control, and as long as the relative proportions of r and K-type psychologies can be maintained.

This circumstance can only exist as some form of violent governmental oppression and control, and it will have to be accompanied by some form of controlled r-selection pressure, in the form of massive, unselective mortality. This mortality would need to include many unproductive r-type individuals, though not so many as to lend political advantage to K-selected psychologies. Rather, such mortality should seek to limit the explosive growth of r-type psychologies, so as to prevent the r-type population from growing to the point that the productive cannot support them. Again, although it might work, this is a morally reprehensible option.

As one can see from the many examples of Communist and Socialist governments past, the r-type psychology is not so hesitant in going for the jugular when in pursuit of a more r-selective environment. In history however, even this strategy has proven an unsustainable form of government, fortunately.

There is a third means by which to prolong r-selection effects which merits mention, though as with other methods, its effects will prove temporary. If a nation can acquire excess resources beyond its productivity, a period of r-selection can be extended, much as the Romans extended their period of r-selection through foreign conquest. This can arise through a variety of means, ranging from acquiring foreign aid to exploiting a natural resource. The easiest to produce predictably however, would be the use of foreign debt.

Unfortunately, the use of debt to prolong r-selection can probably be expected to produce a more thorough collapse when conditions of competition finally return. Upon collapse of the governing structure which attempts this, not only will the r-type population have expanded to even greater numbers than their productivity can support, but the currency used to exchange value will likely also collapse with the government. Between the increased r-type population seeking access to limited resources, and the difficulties in exchanging value absent any currency, competition will be fierce.

That also ignores the prospect of having to pay off the debt incurred in the process. What limited individual productivity was available may be even further reduced by the outflow of debt payments, exacerbating the K-selection pressures even more. Even the Romans weren't saddled with the need to pay back the resources they had plundered.

Undoubtedly, a transition to K-selection following a period of debt-prolonged r-selection will prove an unusually selective period indeed.

Chapter Twenty Eight

Where Evolution Meets
r/K Selection

There are technological and philosophical developments in our species which have altered how these base psychological urges operate, and the effects they have on our evolutionary development. Here we will examine what this theory may tell us about how some of these newer developments will affect the evolution of our species' nature and our inherent ideology.

Birth Control

The most obvious development is the sudden emergence of effective birth control. The r-selected strategy is a selfish-individualist psychological strategy. In nature, its practical focus is on maximizing mating opportunities, and minimizing rearing investments. Today, bearing children involves financial cost and legal responsibility for both parents, as well as nine months of extraordinary physical stress for mothers during gestation. Additionally, low parental investment drives will mean that r-type psychologies will be less desirous of engaging in parenting, often due to negative views of children and child rearing. For these reasons, the advent of birth control has altered how the r-selected behavioral drives will function within our species.

Today, individuals who wish to be free of responsibilities for offspring can follow a simple, painless regimen to prevent conception, and forestall even the hint of risk for any responsibility for a child. Combined with the ultimate form of low-investment parenting, abortion, this will diminish the reproductive rate of the r-selected individuals within our society, even as liberals will advance an ever more promiscuous society. (Interestingly, this diminished desire to rear children would also predict declining birthrates in economically successful societies, where birth control is easily available.)

This reduced reproduction among r-strategists will likely produce a longer period during which resources will prove plentiful, and the associated adverse effects resulting from r-type proliferation will prove less potent.

This will however, gradually select for any r-selected variants that still proliferate, despite the option of easily avoiding it. This means that variants of the r-type psychology, such as the component of the r-selected population which is too irresponsible to make use of such a simple regimen as modern birth control, will continue to proliferate at a faster rate than their K-selected, and even r-selected, birth-control-using peers.

This may mean that the responsible, intellectual liberal, who uses birth control, can perceive cause and effect, and produces resources while acquiring wealth, is a dying breed. As long as resource availability is sufficient to support unlimited population growth, this will result in an ever increasing ideological divide within our populace. The K-selected individuals will remain relatively similar, though more advanced. However it is likely that the r-selected contingent of the populace will gradually become less industrious, less intelligent, less capable of controlling behavior to alter life outcomes, more envious, more prolific, and more entitled. Given how this is trending, the liberal of today may one day appear to be a trustworthy, responsible, and reasonable intellectual when compared to this future model.

Peaceful Competition

Another change today which our ancestors did not adapt to is the relatively peaceful nature of our societal competitions. For eons, competitions were violent affairs. This produced an exceedingly fast rate of evolution, but it also adapted us to violent, physical competitions, and left us less adapted to the more peaceful, intellectual competitions we engage in today. This profoundly affected how we subconsciously determined our potential competitiveness as children, and the mechanisms underlying the molding of our psychology during early development.

As a result, a child who excels in physical activities may come to relish the competitive environment, while a child who is physically incompetent may find competitions with peers humiliating. According to this theory, this will affect their later political psychology, especially regarding freedom and the necessary scope of governmental authority.

However, in today's world, where violence is relatively absent from our peaceful economic competitions, one need not be gifted in the physical activities of childhood play in order to prove economically competitive as an adult. Evolution however, made physical activities the foundation of childhood play, and a strong determinant in one's comfort with the competitive environment as an adult.

This may produce unusual chimeras. One is an individual who is very capable of economic competition as an adult, due to a facility in intellectual endeavors, but who loathes the competitive environment due to their adverse childhood play conditioning. The other may be a less economically successful individual who supports freedom and limited government due to their dominance on the athletic field as a child, even though their own personal situation today would benefit more from supporting r-selected liberalism.

I would suspect, were we a less violent, less warlike species, children would eventually evolve to be more prone to seek out intellectual competitions, instead of physical competitions. Due to the nature of the world however, violence will always be a selective pressure, leaving our species to ultimately adapt into more intellectually capable, physical specimens and more physically capable, intellectual specimens. It should be expected that as time passes, our children's competitive drives will mirror this.

Cities

As Maynard Smith first pointed out, and subsequent research has shown, groups of altruists, each of whom places the well being of the group before themselves, will inevitably be infected by selfish individuals, who will proliferate faster than the altruist. This can only be forestalled if the group practices, the three R's, reputation, reciprocity, and retribution, as a means to curtail the advantages of selfishness.

Policing of the group by the group is the only way to use Darwinian selection to favor those members committed to the group's success. If selfishness is punished in Darwinian style, through expulsion from the group or death, then groups will maintain their societal cohesion and unity of purpose, and Darwin will continue to smile down on altruism.

Research indicates that this policing is best accomplished in small groups, where everyone knows one another. As the sizes of groups increases, policing becomes more difficult. As reputations become less important to interpersonal interactions due to the anonymity of the masses, retribution becomes ever easier to avoid, and consequently, reciprocity becomes less of an individual benefit, and more of a detriment. This effect is only enhanced if the group one inhabits is composed of numerous different sub-groups, making discrimination of in-group and out-group difficult.

It is a well accepted fact that liberalism flourishes in large cities, much more so than it does in small towns. If liberals were programmed by evolution as migrators, designed to seek out freely available resources and lives of ease, their migration to cities is likely due to the image cities exhibit of copious services, and freely available resources.

Cities are often hubs of commerce, with higher median incomes than rural areas. Also, few city dwellers need worry about proficiency in many tasks outside a small area of specialization. (Some research indicates that r-strategists may have a type of technical, "specialist intelligence" designed to excel at specialization as a means of competition avoidance.)

Indeed, in cities, matters as simple as the disposal of garbage, which would be handled so easily by those in rural areas, have the potential to destroy the very fabric of civilization within a modern city, were authorities to suddenly cease providing such a service. As a result, cities offer a life that is freer from responsibilities, where self-sufficiency is unnecessary due to copious services provided by authority.

Additionally, cities often will offer the image of an anticompetitive paradise, where weapons are outlawed, competitiveness is viewed as antisocial and primitive, and herds of peaceful city dwellers are free to peacefully graze on some portion of the city's freely available resources.

Of course, once having migrated to the increased resource and service availability of a city, the large populations of cities likely make it easier to avoid the three R's, and pursue individual advantage at the expense of the group with greater ease. Such large groups would inevitably allow for the persistence of psychological strategies which would not prove as advantageous in smaller, more closely knit communities.

Thus the advent of large cities has allowed the r-strategist a competitive advantage they would not have enjoyed, had Homo sapiens been maintained in small groups of individuals in frequent, direct competition with each other. It is also possible that liberals have evolved a comfort in such a highly populous, densely packed, diverse environment because it protects them.

This advantage is not enough to overcome any future diminution in resources and resultant contraction in environmental carrying capacity (indeed, a sudden Roman style collapse will hit cities especially hard). However it does, at present, allow an environment particularly hospitable to the r-selected psychology. Those who favor the K-type psychology should be unusually grateful to the founders, and their desire to give less populous areas the ability to exert high levels of influence on national policy.

Government Welfare

Clearly, any scheme which allows free reproduction, as well as sufficient provisioning to survive comfortably, absent any evidence of productivity, is going to favor the r-type psychology. When one is actually paid by the government to simply produce children while not contributing to society, this will do far more than merely upset a balance.

K-strategists are left torn between conflicting urges here, as the K-selected high-investing parental drive will seek to see all children given maximal opportunity to compete. However, r-type parents, copiously producing government subsidized offspring, absent any productivity or effort on behalf of society, are guaranteed to produce an r-type entitlement class which will eventually, inevitably, prove unsupportable.

Today, there are people who cannot support themselves, who have children as a means of acquiring revenue in the form of government support. To reward such unproductive reproduction, will only exacerbate an already financially unsupportable situation, and hasten an unusually unpleasant period of history.

In nature, this problem is self limiting, however, we have not yet been exposed to this stress long enough to have adapted a means by which to control it within our civilizations. Combined with the selective effects of birth control, mentioned above, this will eventually create a rather deep ideological divide within our nation.

There may be no solution to these issues, and this may be why nations inevitably collapse, stagnate, and then are reborn, as freer, more productive incarnations of their previous selves.

Laws

The advent of voluntary adherence to the will of a populace, through legal strictures, creates a unique situation. As r-selected individuals gain ground in a population, they gain control over others through numerical superiority in elections.

This control, however, is not effective in overriding an individual's drive to survive. For this reason, this control is only effective as long as it does not impact K-type survivability.

It is a fundamental conclusion of this text that the r-selected, liberal human is maladapted to a world of limited resources. For this reason, liberal policy is designed to pursue a mirage, in which resources are forever unlimited, mortality is easily eradicated by fiat, and competition between individuals is forever banished to the past.

Invariably, the pursuit of this mirage will lead to policy implementations designed to forestall the onset of resource limitations, and the K-selected, competitive environment which would inevitably follow. In forestalling the onset of the K-selected environment, liberal policy temporarily fuels the increase in the r-type populace. This will only amplify the magnitude of the K-selection event which will inevitably take place at some point.

As this selective period arrives, K-selected humans are faced with a choice. Adhere to liberal dictates mandating the elimination of competitiveness, and endure a negative effect on personal survivability, or reject the will of the (by now) highly r-selected electorate, and seize the resources necessary to survive, in competitive struggle. Since this all heads in one direction, it is inevitable that at some point the need to survive will force a return to K-selection.

It is not clear if individuals, voluntarily abiding by laws (the moral nature of which will vary, depending on whether the majority tends r or K) may produce some psychological adaptation, designed to blunt the highs and lows of the governmental cycle, or eliminate the periods of stagnation in accomplishments that are induced by collapse.

Perhaps all individuals, r and K, will become less compassionate and more averse to supporting the unproductive subset of the r-psychology. Perhaps K-strategists will evolve a tighter loyalty to each other, and diminished respect for the law. Perhaps, if the productive r-types evolve an animus towards the unproductive r-types, they will seek to limit the supply of governmental resources to them. Or perhaps periods of high productivity, followed by growth and collapse will prove a stable and predictable aspect of our nature and our governance. Only time will tell.

Chapter Twenty Nine

Implications for Warfare

The r-selected psychologies usually arise due to a population experiencing an external mortality which substantially reduces their population's numbers. In nature, this is most often seen in the form of an r-selected species experiencing predation via another species.

Although this is the evolutionary root of modern liberalism, it is likely that within humans, depopulation by neighboring tribes during warfare produced a similar environmental effect, and both perpetuated the r-selected psychology within our species, and further adapted it. The r-strategy specifically adapted several social aspects to its nature, allowing the r-selected human to function, and even thrive, under the circumstances presented within the mortality that occurs with a society's defeat.

As we have discussed previously, were a population to see all of its warriors die, and then be occupied by a force akin to the NVA and Vietcong, the anticompetitive Hippie strain of human would quickly become the predominant presentation of human within such a population. Although generally less motivated, less combat capable and less intellectually capable, they would still enjoy substantial advantage within the population, under the protection of their occupying patrons.

Given this, it is likely that the Hippie psychology may be of immense value to the study of political ideology. Just as the warrior culture within the most aggressive combat units of the Armed Forces will most perfectly embody the conservative psychology, it is the Hippie culture which may most effectively embody the most ardent manifestation of r-type political leftism.

The similarities between the r and K-selected psychologies and the liberal and conservative psychologies extend well into the martial realm, because it is likely that this realm is where this psychological divergence within our species was finalized in its current form.

The behavioral effects of political psychologies may also extend into the realm of tactics and strategies. It is possible that enemies which embody an anticompetitive psychology may be more prone to adopt "rule breaking" strategies and tactics, designed to seize advantage absent any merit based assessment of fitness.

From suicide bombers, to attacks on unarmed civilians, it is likely that an r-selected, anticompetitive enemy will seek to wage war by avoiding any merit based assessment of fitness. In so doing, they will embrace exactly the type of mass, random, unselective depopulation of their enemy which is embodied in r-selection. To the r-type enemy, such random mortality, unrelated to competition or fitness is normal, and tolerable.

Conversely, K-selected civilizations may instinctively tend to adopt strategies designed to meet their enemy, and kill them directly, in a manner designed to demonstrate a clear superiority in fitness. K-selected individuals will also seek to face specifically those few highly fit individuals who pose the greatest competitive threat, while avoiding violent contact with those individuals who pose no competitive threat. Indeed, most conservatives will likely find the indiscriminate killing of non-combatants, such as one sees in terrorist attacks, to be particularly vexing. To a K-type psychology, their own fittest going into battle and dying valiantly is inherently more tolerable than a large group of innocent women and children in a market being butchered by a cowardly terrorist.

This difference in perceptual frameworks and innate behaviors will manifest elsewhere as well. The dichotomy between r and K-strategies is often referred to in biology as a dichotomy between producing quantity over quality vs producing quality over quantity. This refers to child production, obviously. However it may also manifest in societal features such as the nature of manufacturing. There, r-type nations emphasize a mass produced product of inferior quality, vs a K-selected nation's strategy of producing a smaller number of a vastly superior, and vastly more effective, product.

This effect is probably best understood through imagining the amygdala atrophy which is really behind it. If your amygdala doesn't produce sufficient quantities of aversive stimulus due to atrophy, then when things break, prove substandard, and fail, you will not be motivated sufficiently to rectify that in the future. When you seek replacements, you will not seek out quality, nor will you seek expressly to avoid the failure you just experienced. Additionally, if free resource availability is in force, that will further enhance the effect. Did your freezer break? Get another. It isn't a problem, since resources are everywhere, and it might even be good because the new ones are so shiny. If you have no amygdala, you have no ability to feel aversion, and if resources are free, you will not be conditioned by the environment to gain that ability.

In contrast, in a society with limited resources, more developed amygdalae, and a more K-psychology, failure will lead the amygdala to produce a more motivating aversive stimulus. Did your freezer break? Well, you will never buy that brand again. Added to the mix will be how resource limitation will force you to make sure the next freezer doesn't break, since you can't go on buying freezers forever. As you experience consequences more, your amygdala will develop more, and you will operate with a careful desire to see what you invest in succeed.

One can easily visualize this effect in America by picturing the rise of cheap imported Chinese goods which occurred as the United States began to flood its economy with the free resources produced by deficit spending during the eighties and nineties. As the nation's amygdala atrophied, so did its demand for quality in the products that it consumed. The result was a society which emphasized quantity over quality, and which saw the rise of cheap Chinese goods as an opportunity for everyone to acquire some form of goods. These r/K strategies are deeply imbued, and will affect every aspect of a culture and society.

It can also manifest in military strategy, where r-selected societies will emphasize their numerical advantage and place less emphasis on the quality of each individual soldier. r-type forces will also place less value on each soldier, viewing them as disposable, just as offspring are disposable to an r-type organism. By contrast, a K-selected society will produce a smaller number of very highly trained troops, view each of its warriors as invaluable, and will risk everything to bring every one of them back safely.

If K-selected civilizations are to intellectually plot a means by which to promote the advantage held by their K-selected trait within the species, it may pay to adapt to this dichotomy, by simply seeking the eradication of the r-selected enemy, regardless of any instinctual K-type

217

assessment of a method's propriety or decency. In other words, when confronting a rule breaker, it may pay, for the good of our species and our trait, to abandon the rules, and simply eradicate them on their own terms.

Counter-intuitively, this strategy might actually diminish overall mortality within a conflict between an r-type movement, and a K-type movement. r-type psychologies instinctually seek to ally with violent out-groups, while showing diminished loyalty to in-group, as part of their evolutionary strategy – a psychological drive very similar, if not exactly the same, to that underlying the Stockholm Syndrome. Given that the r-type psychology has evolved to avoid violent conflicts and competitions at any cost, this Stockholm-Syndrome-like behavior will probably manifest most strongly as a drive to grovel and serve before strength, but only when combined with a threat of violence and conflict.

In the bank robbery in Stockholm, where this phenomenon was first observed, the decent police officers (who carefully tried to protect and rescue the victims who were taken hostage), were castigated by the hostages as dangerous and stupid. Meanwhile the robbers, (who actually strangled a hostage for effect on a phone call) were hailed by the hostages as kind and decent, if innocently misguided. In that case, it was the most brutal violent individual with whom the r-type appeaser bystanders allied, and supported, as the theory in this book would predict. (It is likely that those prone to Stockholm Syndrome will exhibit reduced amygdala volume, as do leftists. It is the same phenomenon, merely differing in degree and deniability.)

This Stockholm type effect can also be seen today among r-type psychologies. Often, the most r-type leftists will routinely take the side of terrorists, criminals and other violent threats, while castigating military servicemen and law enforcement for the most minor of transgressions. This is done despite the fact (or as this theory asserts, because of the fact) that the Military personnel and Law Enforcement Officers pose no violent threat to the r-type individuals, beyond simple competitive superiority.

It is possible, that in attempting to deal with such an r-type enemy on the battlefield peacefully and decently, or in being magnanimous when waging war, that one will only increase the animus they feel towards you and your side. Rather, if one deals with an r-type

218

enemy as violently and cruelly as possible at the onset of hostilities, one could trigger a Stockholm-like effect within the r-type psychologies in theater, leading them to become more open to their out-group's (your) interests and desires, and less willing to fight.

This effect may work on both, the active participants, and the non-combatants, if both are sufficiently r-selected in their natures, and you present a suitable facade - sufficiently brutal and lacking in remorse.

The Middle East is filled with nations which were ruled by a cruel dictator. The dictator however, easily maintained control and order through brutality (ie applying an r-type, appeaser-favoring selection pressure). Often such leaders could not only walk their own streets, they would even see grovelling displays of affection from their citizens while walking the streets.

Once such a leader begins to treat the populace with decency and justice or shows weakness (ofttimes due to international effort), the citizenry will quickly rise up against him, kill him, and then promptly reinstall a brutal dictatorial regime, which all citizens will then publicly support.

This effect can also be seen in liberals, who have no qualms with castigating the civil K-type citizens within their own country, but who will bend over backwards to not offend a violent enemy or radical ideology. Often they will not even acknowledge any negative observation about such an enemy, despite that enemy opposing everything the r-type liberal stands for.

Thus it should be considered that in quashing r-type enemies abroad, or waging war in an r-type society, violence and ruthless brutality might serve as effective means by which to exploit evolutionary psychology to avoid and curtail conflict, and gain the indigenous' populace's favor.

Again, the urges which motivate these behaviors are not conscious, but they are not accidental either. The r-selected individual is programmed to be extremely uncomfortable within a competitive environment, where resources are disproportionately awarded, based on merit or fitness. The K-type individual however, will look on such an environment and only see freedom and opportunity.

Criminals, Terrorists, and Other Predators

One aspect of the ideological divide sure to fascinate is the liberal's comfort with predators, both two legged and four legged, despite the liberal's apparently non-violent, and less martially-competent nature. Given that the r-psychology has evolved to avoid violent conflicts and competitions at any cost, this Stockholm-Syndrome-like behavior will probably manifest most strongly as a drive to grovel and serve before strength, but only when combined with a credible threat of violence and conflict.

This Stockholm-type effect can be seen today among r-selected liberals when examining a wide variety of issues. There are numerous cases of hard-core liberal ideologues supporting the release of captured terrorists into the world (such as the Uighurs of Guantanamo recently, some of whom were almost released into communities near Washington, DC). There are other cases where liberals have opposed their ruthless eradication, despite the dangerous natures of such terrorists, and the random mortality they would inflict on our population. Several US soldiers are incarcerated right now, for attempting to aggressively eradicate enemies of America, while serving in uniform.

Likewise, liberals will also often exhibit sympathy towards criminals, despite overwhelming evidence of their guilt and a likelihood that they will randomly prey upon citizens within our populace (The infamous case of Jack Abbot comes to mind, as does Mumia Abu Jamal). This extends into liberal support for lax sentencing, support for measures limiting Law Enforcement's ability to effectively combat crime, and even a generalized animus towards Law Enforcement within predominately liberal cities. Liberals even oppose law-abiding citizens carrying firearms to defend themselves and their families from such criminals.

Stranger still, when confronted with a situation where conflict exists between a natural predator, such as a shark species, cougar population, or wolf pack, and a human population, the liberal will unhesitatingly take the side of the predator, and seek to protect it. In California, where mountain lions have even taken to eating the odd jogger here and there, liberals vociferously oppose any attempt to cull back the cougar population. Likewise, liberals oppose hunting bears in New England, and wolves in the Midwest.

This is in clear contrast to the behavior of more competitively selected, K-type populations, especially such as our own nation's early frontier inhabitants. There, the most minor threat was quickly driven extinct through the use of bounties and firearms. That was viewed by the K-type individuals of that era as being wholly logical, just as the r-type psychologies of this era will view an occasionally eaten jogger as logically unimportant compared to the death of a cougar.

This drive to support predators, two legged, four legged, and even finned, would seem to run contrary to liberal desires for a pacifistic world, where all violence is eliminated. For some reason, to the liberal, violence visited upon a human population is acceptable, so long as it does not focus itself solely on liberals, or the less fit and able. This behavior is even less capable of being understood from a Darwinian perspective of individual competition, given such liberals are risking their own safety and survival, by allowing such predation of their populations.

As we have maintained, within our species is a battle, between the r and K-selected traits. In this battle, each trait would appear to be seeking to engender environmental circumstances which would aid its strategy to succeed within the population, from a Darwinian standpoint.

It is very interesting that one of the best means by which to further the advance of an r-selected trait within a population is to expose the population to some form of relatively unselective external mortality, such as aggressive predation.

Given that liberals, in all of the above cases would seem to be pursuing actions which would increase just that sort of predation of their own population, it does beg the question - does the hard-core liberal ideologue philosophically support predators of their own population due to some primitive, subconscious drive to engender a steady depredation of their populace? Are they seeking a means of bringing about conditions of r-selection within their populations?

Is their contrasting visceral disdain for any form of competitive selection, even when merely consisting of individuals keeping resources they earned, a similarly imbued urge to avoid conditions which might

221

foster advance of the K-trait within their populations? If you look closely at the most extreme leftist, how can they oppose capitalism, and yet support female joggers being killed and eaten by 180 pound felines? How can they support death panels and health rationing, and yet oppose a free market in healthcare? From any other perspective, it would make no sense.

On occasions when the r-selected movement has acquired power, it has tried to hold on to it by perpetuating conditions similar to the unselective mortality of r-selection. The r-selected ideologies, from Communism to Socialism, have a long history of self-imposing an aggressive mortality on their populace, with some estimates holding that up to 262 million people have been executed by r-strategist regimes. That this mortality would have included many of the more competitive, K-selected, freedom-seeking members of the population would have only enhanced the selective effects of the mortality. Even in modern times, the r-selected psychology has favored such random, population limiting methods as the aggressive promotion of birth control, eugenics, health rationing, and abortion.

This history of embracing either random mortality, or mortality targeted at those who seek freedom, is not seen among the more K-selected individuals. To them, competitive selections should be allowed to have their effects, as the populace navigates the path towards its evolved destiny freely. To them, freedom is sacred.

Those of a more K-psychology, who seek to further freedom, must recognize three things about the r-strategist. First the r-strategist thinks and acts in a completely different fashion, groveling before strength and oppression, and contemptuously lashing out at decency and reason. There is a lesson in that, if one seeks the adoption of the K-virtues by the population.

Two, the r-strategy is a slippery slope, leading to evil. r-strategists never acquire an r-enough society to satiate their desires. As soon as they gain one measure of control, and oppressively quash one amygdala stimulant, they immediately set about looking for another. As they eradicate amygdala-stimulant after amygdala-stimulant, their amygdala atrophies ever more, and becomes unable to handle even the slightest of stimulants, or perceive the greatest of dangers.

Eventually, a simple tweet becomes so overwhelmingly amygdala panicking, that it is reason to expel a college student. Suddenly a hunting T-shirt is reason to suspend a high-school student, and a gun shaped pop-tart enough to expel an elementary student. The path of r-selection is a path of ever increasing neuroses and panic attacks over trifles, because an atrophied amygdala finds itself unable to cope with the simple stresses which government is eradicating for the liberal. As this occurs, liberals demand that government and institutions with authority exhibit the same neurosis so as to protect them. From there, oppression will not be far behind. The horrors of the past lay buried in the human mind, waiting to spring forth again. This time, they will be no different from the past, because they will come from the same source.

Finally, the K-strategist must realize that he is designed to interact with fellow K-strategists, just as the r-strategist is designed to exploit this group K-psychology. If K-strategists are to win, they must recognize that the r is different, and treat him accordingly.

Applying K-behavioral urges to the r-strategist, such as treating him with decency, not aggravating his neuroses, or ceding to his demands for polity and comity, is to cede victory to him without ever raising a hand. One must treat the r as one would never treat a fellow K-strategist - rudely, with disdain, contempt, and ridicule. Only there, lies the path of amygdala stimulation, amygdala development, and ultimate victory. One must continually stimulate the undeveloped r-amygdala to develop it, mature it, and condition it to accept and tolerate the unpleasantries of reality. Only then can the r come to embrace the K-strategy.

In stimulating the r-strategist's amygdala through this path, one can train their amygdala to actually cease being r. When they demand politeness, apply rudeness. When they demand you cede ground, take even more, and ridicule them in the process. Every time they try to oppress socially, stimulate their amygdala, and teach their brain to pursue another path. Understand that when they are at their most agitated and agonized, their amygdala is developing. Understand, what you are doing to them is good for them.

Eventually, a time will come when you will not even need to argue, as their brain will have developed to better cope with the stresses

223

of life and reality. Cede ground to them, however, and you only feed their amygdala atrophy, and further the nation's descent into r.

Chapter Thirty

*The Nature of Oppression*_____

The nature of the world dictates that resources are not unlimited, and what little can be acquired will not be acquired without commensurate effort. Given these facts, competition is an immutable law of nature among all higher organisms. Due to this, it is unavoidable that in any population some individuals will acquire the resources necessary to survive and thrive, and others will not. This will create winners and losers.

As we have written, due to the divergent nature of r/K psychologies, humans exhibit two philosophies of social organization, and this will produce two different definitions of the word oppression.

To a K-selected, conservative competitor psychology, life is meant to be lived free from any external control, in free competition with peers. This freedom will allow individuals to craft their own futures by their own hands, to the best of their own personal abilities. The merit-based, disproportionate resource allocation that this will produce is viewed as a just state of affairs.

This generates a perception among conservatives that oppression is any form of interference with this lifestyle of free, unfettered competition between individuals, or the merit based apportionment of resources it entails. It is for this reason that conservatives will view any liberal governmental action as oppressive.

By contrast, the r-selected, anticompetitive liberal psychology is designed to live in a world of diminished populations, where copious resources are freely available, and no one competes with anyone else, because competition is unnecessary. To this psychology, everyone's life should be spent in equal pacifistic ease to everyone else, peacefully gathering freely available resources, mating copiously, and avoiding all confrontations and competitions with peers.

To this psychology, the K-selected competitor is oppressive, since the competitor enters the arena, and begins freely consuming the limited resources that are available. By denying resources to the r-strategist through competitive consumption, the K-strategist disrupts the r-strategist's ability to live the free, hedonistic life of ease that their psychology was designed to live. Thus, to the r-selected, liberal, the K-strategist is oppressive. Obviously, this is more the fault of an environment where resources are inherently limited, than the K-strategist's fault, but regardless, the r-type individual want's free resources, and in a K-type environment they will blame their inability to acquire them on the consuming K-strategist.

Since humans are, overall, a K-selected species, our species' definition of oppression trends towards that of the K-selected competitor. Indeed, where r-strategists take control of government, and attempt to eradicate their definition of oppression, we can find instances of some of the worst oppression in history. Here we will briefly discuss several r-selected movements in history, and examine how their r-selected, pacifistic, anticompetitive, benevolent intentions came to produce less than benevolent results, when viewed from the perspective of our K-selected, competitive species. It is interesting to note how our almost universal agreement regarding their oppressiveness arises out of our species' highly K-type morals and values, themselves derived from our species' long and storied history of K-selection.

Communism, Socialism and Anticompetitiveness

Karl Marx was obsessed with Darwin's study of natural selection.[305] The description of an environment where the strong succeeded by out-competing the weak clearly struck a nerve. Immediately Marx saw Darwin's account of K-selection within the natural world as analogous to the unfair and unnecessary struggle for survival within a human society, where individuals interacted freely and resources accrued to them unequally, based on ability, effort, and determination. As a result, when Marx (already a respected intellect within the leftist movement) encountered Darwin's work, it fascinated him.

Being of an r-selected psychology, Marx operated from an assumption that all would feel as he did, and seek to produce a government which would outlaw this struggle. To Marx it was simple - eliminate any chance of failure in competition with peers by using force of government to end the competition. Take all the resources by force, and provide them freely to all.

Digested by similar r-selected psychologies, the work of Marx (and his fellow r-strategist co-author Friedrich Engels) struck nerves in r-strategists the world over, in part due to a subconscious commonality between all of their psychologies. Today, wherever one finds a despot quashing freedom and competition among citizens, that despot will usually cling to power by using some variant of these clearly elucidated r-ideological concepts.

What is of most interest with Marx is how a clear elucidation of the r-strategy by an r-strategist can attract other r-strategists to their work, and lead them to continue to champion it over a century later. Marx's psychology was not new or unique. However his ability to create within fellow r-strategists an emotional response to the K-strategy, and rally them around the r-strategy's themes made his work unique and timeless.

Likewise, it is highly likely this work's elucidation of the underlying evolutionary forces and themes motivating the emergence of liberalism and conservatism will have a similarly strong, if polar opposite effect. In likening political ideologies to the evolutionary environment which produced them, this will create the purest of emotional metaphors, and thereby maximize the emotional reactions of the readers. Once so emotionally invested, it would be surprising to see any rational discussion of the veracity of the basic ideas presented herein arise. Rather, this work will produce reflexive emotional battles, and personal attacks.

These psychologies are remarkably standardized throughout time, and over the generations.

Nazism

Anton Drexler co-founded the Deutsche Arbeiterpartei (The German Worker's Party), which would later be renamed the National

Socialist Party, or Nazi Party. The purpose of this party was to unite German "workers" against wealthy interests within Germany, which were portrayed as being associated with out-groups opposed to German success. The study of this movement is important because it was motivated by a unique amalgam of both r and K-selected psychologies, and this proved unusually dangerous. This is also a strategy liberals seem prone to employ today, absent conscious awareness. So the study of it is important to understanding an instinctual leftist strategy.

On the one side of this Nazi ideology were the "workers," who sought to rise up against the successful within their society, using force of government as a proxy to fight their battles for them. On the other side were nationalists, who felt that the successful had betrayed their nation to outsiders. This unique chimeric ideology, appealing to elements of both r and K, arose due to unique circumstances in Germany at the time, as well as clever political maneuvering by the early Nazi leaders.

In post-WWI Germany, there was a perception that Germany was being betrayed and oppressed by their leadership, due to various rumors regarding the War's end, and the signing of the Treaty of Versailles. This led many to perceive that their nation's leaders were treasonously allying with outsiders for personal gain (ie., r-strategists). Often these leaders were established leftists, which created an even stronger foundation of animosity with K-strategists within the nation, and likely lent credence in their minds to the allegations.

These circumstances allowed other indigenous r-strategists within various socialist workers' movements to couch their movement against the successful in terms of a K-selected movement operating against r-strategists who had betrayed the in-group. It was this circumstance which led K-selected nationalists to become allied with the left leaning, r-selected leaders of the National Socialists.

One of the fundamental problems that r-selected movements have is that they are composed of individuals who are instinctually competition and conflict-averse. Thus, they can only oppress a populace so much through laws, before the populace's K-strategists rise up, and compete openly with them. At that time the nation will quickly revert to a K-type governing structure. As a result, the r-type movement can only hold power, and actively oppress if they can find a way to lead enough K-type warriors of their nation to enforce their oppression for them.

Again, no anti-gun, liberal bunnymen will ever have the courage to come to your house, and demand that you surrender your firearms to them, no matter how anti-gun they may be. However they will try to manipulate affairs so that a SWAT team will come in their stead. This is the same phenomenon.

Normally, the psychological divergence between ideologies is enough to keep them separated and in opposition to each other. However, occasionally, elements of the K-strategy can find themselves taking orders from r-strategists. Historically, when r-type humans have the strength of K-type warriors at their disposal, to enforce their ruthless selfishness and oppression of free competition, the results can be quite horrible.

Had Germany been wholly autonomous, or had the successful been seen as staunch supporters of the state/group in a competition with the outside world, they would have been perceived as successful K-strategists within the in-group of the nation. Under those circumstances, Socialists and Workers Parties motivating indigenous K-selected animosity against them would have been much more difficult.

The German Worker's Party quickly became influenced by a man named Rudolf von Sebattendorf. He sought to use the party to support an aggressive nationalism (Völkisch) designed to unite both the r-strategist "workers" and the more mainstream K-strategist nationalists against "outsiders" who were oppressing Germany.

His real targets however, were the German leaders who were running the country in collusion with the outsiders. The end result was to unite those who had r-selected Communist or Socialist sympathies with those who had the more K-type nationalistic inclinations to purge outsiders and traitors from their nation.[306]

This strategy united these two Darwinian psychologies, due to the perception that outsiders (and their allies within the German in-group) occupied positions of power over the people. This produced a movement with a broader base of support than would otherwise have been possible, should one have simply espoused strict K-selected or r-selected emotional themes. It combined K-selected nationalism and competitive desires to attack outsiders, with the prospect of using r-selected policy initiatives to strip these powerful traitors of their resources and punish their success.

Unfortunately, when these two ideologies combine, it is the r-selected individuals who desire the power to tell others what to do, so it is these individuals who seek to lead the movement. K-strategists tend to be inherently respectful of other's freedoms and rights (an outgrowth of their desire for a free environment for all), and thus they tend to shy away from positions of power, and jobs which involve controlling their fellow citizens. When both ideologies collide, it is usually the r-type human who ends up in the leadership position. (Even today in America, the leadership of the Republican Party is considerably more liberal and r-selected in their psychology than the grassroots of the conservative movement.)

This movement to combine ideologies in Germany was not a strategy which was directly employed from the start, however. Initially, the Nazi's attempted to gain political power by waging class warfare, while attacking big business, the bourgeois, and capitalism. This was met with limited success, due to the small pool of dedicated r-selected ideologues. So the founders then adapted to the political terrain, emphasizing a strategy of aggressive nationalism and anti-Semitism, while toning down the attacks on business and industry, in an effort to expand their political support.[307]

This unusual amalgamation of ideologies is described by Hitler in Mein Kampf, where he wrote disparagingly of both the left and right, saying that the left abandoned Germany to foreign interests, while the right's embrace of the populace's freedom to choose its government allowed the nation the freedom to support the left.

Obviously if Nazism were the opposite of the failures Hitler derided, it would consist of a K-selected opposition to out-groups, combined with an r-selected unwillingness to let men chart their own courses freely.

Nazism increasingly became predicated on the premise that regardless of any competitive outcomes, the Aryan was a superior form of human, and that other inferior forms of humans needed to be either exterminated or segregated by government. Chief among these inferior races in the opinion of the Nazis, were the Jews, who were relentlessly portrayed as an out-group, to facilitate K-type hostility against them. Indeed, as the Nazis went on to kill 6 million Jews in the Holocaust, they were sent to their deaths with nationalistic fervor, due to their status as different from "real" Germans.

This is an excellent case study in the Group r-strategist's subversive strategy for competing against more fit individuals. K-selected group competitors seek honest, open group competitions. They seek these competitions so that they may test their group's fitness and ability against the fitness and ability of other groups.

As we have stated, the r-strategist seeks to exploit group conflict for personal advantage. If a war erupts, they will seek to use their enemies' forces as a proxy force to combat their own population's successful competitors. Within populations they will stoke divisions, foment animosities, and then attempt to ride to power themselves, on the battles of the K-selected subgroups within their populations.

Here, we see this strategy perfectly executed. A movement of r-strategists begins by seeking to strip freedom from fellow men and motivate others to attack the successful. Once it became obvious a wider swath of Germans could be compelled to join them by limiting attacks to those they could portray as an out-group (such as Jews and German leaders), they quickly adapted their strategy. However the leaders of this new movement were still the r-selected Socialist and Communists, and their motives were the same. Use force of government to seize power and resources, limit free competitions among men, and control everyone.

This diminished the success of others, while advancing their relative position, all absent any direct competition by the r-strategists themselves. No Nazi needed to open a shop next to a Jew, and offer a better product at a lower price. All he needed to do was convince a soldier that the Jew was an enemy of the state, and the soldier would kill the Jew for him, and redistribute the Jew's earned wealth to others.

There are two main lessons to be found in the rise of Nazism. First, r-selected movements will attempt to unite themselves with K-strategists, for the purpose of using the K-strategist to eliminate a competitive threat. To avoid this, K-strategists must firmly and clearly define their in-groups, define the rules of the competitions of their society, and assiduously avoid letting their movement be led by r-strategists. Even if an r-selected movement offers the ability to eradicate treasonous r-selected liberals who are betraying your nation, K-

231

strategists need to understand where joining forces with r-strategists will lead.

Wealthy Jews stood little chance once the r-strategists succeeded in portraying them as a cheating out-group, and turned the K-strategists upon them - especially since Hitler had already taken measures to fully disarm his future victims. The success Jews often enjoy within a society, combined with their minority status, may make them a common target at the beginning of r-strategist surges, when the political terrain is being surveyed, and enemies of the in-group are being sought by the r-strategists.

The second lesson is that K-selected movements tend to be poorly led. K-selected humans respect freedom, and exhibit little drive to control others subversively, as this drive would clash with their drive towards unrestricted free competition. As a result, those who seek to lead such K-movements (and who are programmed to desire such control over others), will tend to be r-type psychologies, feigning K-type status to acquire power.

To prevent their movement from being led astray, grassroots K-selected psychologies must force themselves to seek control of their movements, and vigorously demand that their leaders adhere to their ideology. Alternately, they must refuse to take part in movements whose leaders are not purely of their psychology. The risks are simply too great.

If K-selected humans fail to do this, r-selected psychologies may gain control of their movement. If history is any guide, such a circumstance will presage a particularly bloody and terrifying period.

Oppressive Divisions Today

One of the more confusing aspects of the K-strategy and the r-strategy in group competitions is that both are competitive strategies. K-selected group competitors seek group conflicts with outsiders, which they want to wage themselves. Confusingly r-strategists will also foment group conflicts, although the group competitions they seek to foment are between different groups of K-strategists, and their goal is to not fight these battles themselves. Rather, the r-strategist's strategy is to foment a

232

group conflict, and then manipulate others of K-type psychologies into fighting these battles for them.

In Nazism, the National Socialists began by attacking the bourgeois, and big business (read the successful K-strategists). When this strategy failed, they isolated an ethnic group which was competitively successful, and then attempted to use nationalistic themes to incite one group of their nation's K-strategists into a battle against this other group. In dragging the Jews down, the r-strategists raised their relative economic and social status, and even managed to secure leadership positions within the Nazi party and the government.

As we have discussed, there is evidence that much of modern liberalism is driven by feelings of envy mediated by the ACC, and aversions to free competition that are rooted in the amygdala. Given that the r-strategy is a competitive strategy, yet it seeks to avoid direct competition, it is only natural that such an envious, yet competition-averse strategy would seek to pit the competitors they are envious of against other competitors they are envious of, in such a way as to benefit themselves.

Within domestic politics, this will most often manifest in the r-strategist fomenting dissension within their populace, and then using that dissension to their advantage, without directly partaking of competitive risk themselves.

Thus, Communists will seek to stir dissension against the rich, and then use a group of less rich individuals to defeat the rich, and thereby acquire power for the Communist. Nazi's and their National Socialist Party will attempt to do the same, and when it fails due to nationalistic unity, they will seek to find a sub-group of rich which they can portray as an out-group, and thereby provoke the K-type nationalists into attacking.

As an example, within America, liberals are envious of "Big Business." A K-strategist would open their own business, and seek to outcompete the existing business. The liberal, however, will attempt to demonize "Big Business" as morally evil, and unite the less successful against them, so as to destroy the business using the proxy of government to tax it or regulate it into submission. Likewise, "Big" oil will be demonized, as will "Big" banking, as will "Big" pharma, as will any successful entity that enjoys enough success to be labeled "Big," and therefore is deserving of envy.

Even gun owners in America see this strategy employed against them. No liberal would have the courage to go to a gun owner's house, demand their guns, and take them by force, in face to face competition. Rather, the liberal seeks to turn the K-strategists of Law Enforcement on the gun owner through politically manipulative games. There is little doubt, were such a strategy to erupt into open hostilities between the conservative gun owner, and the Law Enforcement apparatus, the liberal would view that as a positive development. Of course, as these events transpired, the liberal would hide, and avoid the conflict themselves. Whether cop or conservative gun owner were killed, the liberal r-strategist would have won.

This is all done with the hopes that K-strategists will depopulate each other's groups. In so doing, they will carry the r-selected liberal to relative success over the previously successful K-competitors, without the liberal having to actually fight for it themselves in fitness-based, competitive battle.

In truth, this is fundamentally the cuttlefish mating battle, where the K's fight, while the r's exploit. It is merely played out in a more complex competitive environment, with more complex rules of society and politics to abide by.

This strategy can emerge in a variety of ways. From supporting national enemies in war, to fomenting divisions between racial sub-groups, to exploiting religious or regional differences in identity, in every case, the liberal r-strategist is playing a game of, "Let's have you and him fight." In every case, the liberal is fomenting competition between different groups of K-strategists, in the hopes of stealing competitive success, without actually competing.

If that strategy fails to garner the r-selected liberal political power, liberals will even attempt to import foreigners of a competitive/aggressive mindset, and then foment dissension between the foreign competitors, and American citizens, in the subconscious hope that the foreign competitors will subdue the successful Americans, on the liberal's behalf.

When this psychology gains a sufficient footing, these divisive strategies will be applied to every aspect of the governance of the society. This will gradually create a nation, which instead of unifying under the banner of freedom and opportunity will splinter into many battling factions. Due to the free-for-all atmosphere, each faction will feel justified in taking freedom, opportunity, or earned property from the other, and this will be encouraged by r-selected liberals at every turn. Suddenly girls think others should pay for their birth control, the poor are entitled to free cellphones with text messaging courtesy of the taxpayer, healthcare that is paid for by others is a right, and everyone remaining begins looking for a slice of the government pie, paid for by someone else, of course.

It is very ironic that only by pulling the free resource availability, can the citizenry be reunited into groups who are loyal to each other.

The Superiority of Oppressors

Human societies do have several common psychological drives which will tend to motivate their populace against this r-selected strategy of divide and conquer. Most of these drives are derived from our species' K-selected evolutionary history. These will include drives to see merit recognized with reward, to see fairness in competition, and to see an honestly won competitive outcome honored.

Due to their K-selected evolutionary history, humans will also have a very strong desire to be allowed to lead their life freely, crafting their own destiny by their own hand, as well as an innate respect for the freedom of others. These K-type desires will produce within the K-selected individual, a desire for personal freedom as well as a desire to retain any earned rewards for their decisions and actions. This will also create drives to recognize the earned success of others and recognize the freedoms of others. Combined with the inherent tendency to respect fellow K-strategists, and seek to form in-groups with them, these traits will all tend to unify a population.

Even though the r-selected liberal will have very different psychological themes guiding their behavior, they still must couch all appeals to the populace in terms of K-selected psychological drives, if

235

they are to sway the K-selected populace into following an r-selected governing strategy of oppression, control, and uniform mediocrity for all. As we just discussed, due to an innate cowardice/docility, the r-strategy is nothing, without at least the tacit support of some K-strategists.

For this reason, the most common tool one finds r-psychologies exploiting is deception. Whether it is a transvestite cuttlefish pretending to be a female, or a liberal supporting a foreign enemy while maintaining that his dissent is patriotic (and he is a loyal American) - deception is the most fundamental tool of the r-psychology, because it is needed to fool K-strategists into fighting the r-strategist's battles for them.

Probably the most interesting deceptive adaptation which the r-psychology has had to evolve, in order to operate within this K-selected psychological milieu is the r-type concept of innate "superiority."

Humans are hardwired by their K-selected psychology to adhere to concepts of fairness in free competition. Our K-type psychologies dictate that those who are superior are going to be entitled to the spoils of victories earned in honest competition with peers.

The r-strategist however, agitates against this system. Their basic desire is that rewards earned in free competition need to be redistributed, to varying degrees, among less competitively capable segments of the populace. This runs contrary to our species' innate programming to see honestly won competitive outcomes honored.

Even in the r-strategist, who is driven to subvert all competitions, there is a recognition that this urge to alter competitive outcomes is fundamentally unfair, according to our evolutionary programming. As a result, the r-strategist will experience a cognitive dissonance, as their urge to alter competitive outcomes and their urge to allow defeat to stand, clash within their mind. Furthermore, the K-type psychology held by the majority of our species is programmed to innately rebel at the thought of weak, lazy, and cowardly imbeciles attacking the productive unfairly, and seizing their hard-earned resources by force of government.

Thus the r-strategist needs to present their demands to violate our behavioral programming in a manner which will not conflict with these urges. In doing this, they can both, better sway the populace, and assuage their own conscience over their clearly "unfair" (by our K-selected standards) actions.

Due to these forces, every r-selected movement will be based on an aggressive assertion of the r-strategist's superiority. So long as the r-strategist tells themselves that they are superior, they can also tell themselves that they are not actually altering a fairly won competitive outcome to reward the loser. Rather, they will tell themselves that as a superior individual, they are sparing the inferior individuals, whom they oppress, from an inevitable defeat at the hands of innately superior r-strategists. They can even tell themselves that it is magnanimous of them to give so much of these resources to the proletariat, rather than keeping all of it for themselves.

It is likely that this psychological construct allows the liberal to avoid overstimulating an amygdala which is ill prepared to be flooded with negative stimuli. Negative stimuli would abound, were a liberal to honestly examine themselves, or their actions. Their entire ideology consists of stealing earned income from others who toiled for it, all under a cowardly cover of government authority - and simply out of envy.

From the concept that stealing another's earned resources is wrong, to the concept that the liberal might be inferior to a K-competitor (who would bravely choose to win the resources fairly in free competition), to the aversive stimuli produced by rule violations such as theft (itself a tacit admission of competitive inferiority), or the cowardice of hiding behind government agents when stealing, a liberal position invites a whole host of amygdala-stimulating perceptions if not viewed through a self-deceiving prism. Liberals do not believe that their theft is altruistic (despite their own lack of altruistic charity), or that their hiding behind government is intellectual (instead of cowardly) because they want to. They believe it because they have to.

A blind assertion of personal superiority can short-circuit all of these concerns, quieting the agony of an amygdala overwhelmed. Suddenly, the liberal is not a cowardly loser, cheating to steal success while oppressing free men unfairly. In preventing any free competition, the "superior" liberal is really an innately blinding success. They are compassionately sparing those who would inevitably lose, from the humiliation and defeat that would result were they pitted against the superior r-type liberal.

As a result of this psychological defense mechanism, this theme of unverified superiority will consistently reappear wherever an r-selected movement seeks to upset any K-selected, competitive social structure.

First, the r-strategist will maintain that they are superior. Almost always, there will be no verifiable proof of this assertion, in the form of any free competitive outcome. This is because, if the r-strategist could win in free competition with peers, and prove their superiority within the competitive arena, they would not seek to subvert the competition through political means, but would rather, seek to continue it. They would not hide behind the government, or the population. Rather, they would seek to minimize these competition stifling forces, so they might engage their opponent directly, and win.

It is for this reason that White Supremacists will aggressively maintain that whites are superior to non-whites, whose potential success they wish to forestall through government-sanctioned discrimination. Among the r-type community organizers, the poor are portrayed as morally superior to the evil and greedy rich, thus justifying their government mediated theft from others. To a Marxist, the workers are superior to their company's owners, who are undeserving of their status and wealth, no matter what risks they took, or abilities they demonstrated in the course of their ascension. Of course, Aryan Nazis maintained that Aryans were simply superior to the Jews, even though the Jews were more successful in the business environment of free economic competition.

Indeed, in examining the psychology behind the Nazi movement, M. W. Fodor wrote in 1936, "*No race has suffered so much from an inferiority complex as has the German. National Socialism was a kind of Coué method of converting the inferiority complex, at least temporarily, into a feeling of superiority.*"[308]

Using a Coué method of repeating that one is great, in the hopes that your belief of it will make it true, is not generally the psychology one finds within the K-selected individual. K-selected individuals jump into the arena and compete, even when the odds do not favor them. When having failed, a K-selected psychology will accept their defeat, only to throw themselves back into the competition, with zeal. Their definition of superiority is reality based, and is proven through the hard metric of personal accomplishment relative to their peers. Only the r-selected individual will seek to deny everyone else the ability to compete, under the auspices of the r-type's own innate "superiority," absent any free competitive evidence.

The constant verbal repetition of one's own superiority, as one seeks to deny any free competitive opportunities to others, is a common theme among the r-type movements for this reason. From a cognitive neuroscience perspective, this mantra is a practical method by which to quiet a weakened amygdala that is overwhelmed by the realization of one's own inferiority, and terrified of the concept of a freely competitive environment around them which might yield hard proof of this.

Of course, we see this today in our political battles as well. Political liberals maintain that they exhibit an intellectual and moral superiority to conservatives, and this superiority justifies the liberal's demand to determine all free competitive outcomes, control all free competitions, and reapportion any winnings which may have already been awarded. Indeed, the evidence of the liberal's superiority is their adherence to the superior ideology of liberalism. Of course, the evidence of liberalism's superiority is the superior liberal's adherence to it. There can be no arguing with that kind of logic. If you do argue, and do so effectively (such as by pointing out the liberal can't be superior if they exhibit utter terror at the thought of free, Darwinian competition with conservatives), you will stimulate the liberal's less capable amygdala. The stress and anxiety which will be exhibited in their agitated emotional response will serve as strong evidence in favor of this work.

Even among conservatives, the more liberal moderates deride the true conservatives as less intellectual and less understanding, thereby implying their own superiority.

Therefore, whenever one heads towards the left of the political spectrum, one will find assertions of superiority, absent any competitive test. As one heads towards the more K-type psychologies, one will find individuals content to merely let the results of competition determine the hierarchy of superiority, even if such a hierarchy is not personally advantageous.

Simple human morality (evolved from the K-selected, psychology) demands rewards be apportioned according to ability, determination, and effort. In order to override this basic human behavioral drive, some psychological construct must be created which will justify violating this innate perception. The false superiority of the r-selected movement is this psychological construct.

Now if this assertion of superiority is being made to assuage an uncomfortable psychological process, it is possible that a strong refutation of that superiority, done in such a way as to eliminate its palliative powers, might create a condition within the r-strategist's brain which would cause them to be either less motivated to pursue r-selected strategies, or unable to pursue them, due to cognitive discomfort. It is quite surprising to me that no one to date has examined how to manipulate these political psychologies, or what purposes some of the stranger assertions by ideologues may serve to modify brain function within their own minds.

In summary, r-selected movements seek to sustain their divisive, anticompetitive campaigns for power on the premise that the r-strategist is innately superior, and deserving of victory. The repetition of this premise may serve the purpose of altering the r-strategist's brain function to assuage the cognitive discomfort associated with violating K-type behavioral standards. It is possible that aggressive refutation of this premise may result in a reversal of this process, and produce extreme psychological discomfort within the liberal, and that this should be considered as part of a broader ranging political strategy.

Chapter Thirty One

Conclusions

Given the available evidence, it is hard to argue against the idea that political ideologies are merely evolved psychologies. Clearly they both exhibit a full suite of r/K traits. These traits will imbue those who hold them with behavioral programs that are optimized to the two main evolutionary environments that can confront us. That each strategy seems to emerge during its respective environment would only further support this idea. If this is accepted, what does it tell us about the way forward?

There is one ideology which is practically implementable, which is designed for a world in which resources are limited in quantity, and which will advance our species evolutionarily. Conversely, there is one strategy which is impractical, which is designed for an environment where every individual is provisioned by nature with limitless resources forever, and which, even if it could be implemented indefinitely, would devolve and destroy our species' very genome. It would endlessly produce quantity over quality, forever diluting intellect, morals, and drive. It would leave us a mere shadow of the evolutionary greatness we exhibit today.

The differences of course, go on. One ideology is designed to effectively regulate reproduction in a world where resources are limited, thereby preventing catastrophic collapses of our societies. The other is designed to facilitate reproduction of the least capable in ever-increasing quantities. Designed for a world we will never see, where resources are available freely in limitless quantities forever, it will inevitably produce a collapse of civilization.

One ideology will comport, both morally and spiritually with the morals of the majority of our K-selected species. The other will require the majority of our species to be oppressed and controlled - controlled, lest they follow their natural desire for freedom, and attempt to craft their own future by their own hand.

One ideology will lead us to a nation which flawlessly works together, in harmonious unity, and embodies the best of noble virtues, from loyalty to love. The other would fill every man's heart with little more than selfishness and envy, producing an endless supply of petty grievances and divisions between comrades, all designed to apportion misery in equal measure to everyone.

One has inspired an immortal awe, with the greatness of the civilizations which have followed its ascendancy. The other has filled mass graves the world over with innocent victims, as it destroyed once great societies in collapses that are legendary.

Up until now, it has been assumed that most humans are exactly the same. As a result, the political argument was based on logic and reason. Conservatives believed all men wished to be free to plot their own destiny, while liberals believed that all men wished to be protected from the dangers of other free men. One believed everyone wanted to be protected from government, the other that all people sought to be protected by government.

If this theory is correct however (and it almost certainly is, given the scale of the evidence), then some element of our society is always going to be unhappy with how their government is structured. Bipartisanship is a myth.

Thus the primary determinant of how our government should be structured is what the purpose of our government should be. This begins with the question of individual freedom. Is there anyone who, given a choice between freedom or subjugation, would choose subjugation? Given our status as K-selected, overall, the answer will be obvious. Freedom is an almost universally respected virtue, and protecting it would seem a reasonable purpose for our government to serve. It would seem the fairest of compromises and in debate, the best of beginnings.

If we desire a government designed to allow humans to live their lives in freedom, then government's job will be to safeguard each individual's ability to craft their own future by their own hand. In following this path, we will find ourselves protecting the noble virtues that the vast majority of our K-selected species has evolved to hold dear, from respect for freedom, to morality, to loyalty, to honor. The protection will require nothing more than living a life free from the constraints of government.

To my eye, this theory also highlights that liberalism is largely incompatible with the K-selected nature of our species. Liberalism cannot honor freedom for all individuals, because by its very nature liberalism must use governmental force to constantly subvert an innately competitive human nature.

From our desire for and love of freedom, to our drive to succeed in group competition, to the immense worth we all ascribe to life – an r-type human will tell you that these are all urges which must be eradicated and suppressed, by force of government. Those who are stupid enough to believe them will watch as their societies collapse, their leadership is taken over by ruthless despots, and freedom becomes little more than a fantasy, spoken of in hushed tones.

This raises one of the most interesting aspects of this work. Liberalism, as an ideology, sustains itself on the premise of its own superiority. The superiority of liberalism is in fact, the primary reason we are told we must subjugate ourselves to the whim of the liberal.

Liberalism is superior in many ways, we are told. It is intellectual, and relentlessly logical. It is hyper-moral, and hyper-compassionate. Those who espouse it are to be respected, if for no other reason than the fact that they are wise enough to espouse it. It is the path forward, the future incarnation of mankind's evolution. Someday, we are told, everyone will be liberal, so we should want to show our advanced nature as well today by espousing it ourselves.

By contrast, conservatism is a crude, prehistoric, caveman-ideology. It is borne of un-evolved urges to pursue primitive behaviors, which people should be ashamed of. It is a mark of an inferior individual with an undeveloped mind, who marks themselves as undesirable by their very adherence to the ideology.

Yet, if this theory is accepted, liberalism is not any of the things it asserts. It is not intellectual, any more than conservatism. The psychological drives motivating both arise from the same biologically imbued well of r/K instincts.

Even among Reproductive Strategies, liberalism is not superior. In fact, among species, it is the K-selected organisms which exhibit the superior levels of evolutionary advancement, produced by their history of competitive selection. Their relentless drive to compete is what motivates further evolutionary advancement. Few will argue that an r-selected bunny rabbit is "superior" to a K-selected wolf, if any will even accept such a gradation in perfectly adapted organisms.

Humans notice these things on a very primal level. Deride a liberal, to their face, as a "Bunnyman." Present to them an image of the collapse of the governing structures they hide behind. Ask how they will compete with the conservative wolves, once government ceases its oppressive protection. Then watch as the fireworks begin. Those are amygdala stimulants in action, and they have their effect because on a deep level, humans recognize these metaphors. It is as if our DNA were a magnetic tape, these images imprinted on it during our evolution.

Nor is liberalism a future incarnation of mankind. Liberalism will continue to grow, until it collapses our society, at which point conservatism will return, with a vengeance. Liberalism is merely one phase in the life cycle of our species, and it is a devolving phase, at that.

If liberalism is not hyper-intellectual, hyper-logical, or the future incarnation of mankind, then what is it? The answer is simple. Just like conservatism, it is a pre-programmed way of thinking. It is a natural psychological predisposition, consisting of a cowardly urge, an irresponsible urge, a selfish urge, and a horny urge - all imbued by genes and environment, yet claimed by those who hold it to be intellectual and superior.

One cannot blame liberalism for marketing itself in such a way, however. If the majority of a population exhibits a tendency to prefer loyalty to in-group, or freedom from oppression, and you want them to willingly cede an oppressive authority over themselves to you, you have little choice. You must make a case that you are superior in some fashion, and that their urges are inferior. Otherwise, everyone will ignore your plaintive wails, and instead, just go with their instincts, pursuing a life of honor, courage, moral decency, and loyalty.

Unfortunately, we will not be rid of liberalism so easily. Mankind's greatest failing (and greatest attribute) is the uncontrollable, all or nothing drive towards total moral perfection, regardless of logic, reason, or likelihood of success. Viewed coldly, absent such a moral and decent drive, this work would indicate that suffering will always exist, but that its total quantity could be limited through the acceptance of a small amount of K-selective cruelty permanently laid upon the lowest among us. This cruelty would effectively keep the proliferation of the less-productive r-type individuals in check, through competitive denial of resources.

However, man's innate sense of compassion will always reject this option. Instead, man will choose to willingly endure waves of abundance and freedom, as well as the horrible periods of scarcity, collapse, and mass suffering that nature will forever throw at our species. If the choice is to compassionately protect the individuals who will collapse the very society which protects them, or callously leave them to the wolves so as to prevent mass misery later, we simply cannot help ourselves. To accept some misery is to admit defeat in our quest for a morally perfect world.

Of course, the r-type trait can never truly succeed. Should the r-type individuals ever gain full control over the populace, their mechanisms of control require a constant supply of the fuel of resources, produced by the very populace they oppress.

In removing the reward for effort and ability, such an r-type government will inevitably diminish its people's productive output and thereby starve itself of the very currency it requires to operate, and oppress. At that very moment, proliferative r-parasites will be multiplying without bound, attempting to consume ever greater amounts of resources that are no longer being produced. As the power to control recedes, the populace will increasingly abide by its competitive nature.

As we have seen, such a mechanism will not tend towards a steady homeostasis, where r and K type natures exist in a perpetually harmonious balance, but rather will careen wildly between periods of oppressed shortages, and freedom-fueled abundance. When the highs come, they will be wonderful, but within each will lay the r-selected seed of overly abundant resources. Just as surely as day follows night, that seed will inexorably grow, alongside the r-type subset of the population, until stability has given way to governmental collapse, and abundance and plenty becomes shortage, inefficiency, and desperation.

The least immoral path is to honor each man's freedom, limit governmental intervention, and let each man bear the burden of responsibility for himself and his future. Combined with personal charity, awarded by the productive to those who they feel are worthy, such a scheme would produce a society where everyone was committed to the success of our nation, and sloth was unrewarded, beyond a bare subsistence level of support to those who are worthy in some regard.

Not only does such a path comport with the majority psychology of our K-selected species, but it will also aid our descendents to one day, millennia hence, enjoy the immense evolutionary advantage of the K-selected genetic greatness that it will produce.

Of course, it is up to the reader to make up their own mind on these issues. Whether they will support selfless loyalty to in-group or individual selfishness and betrayal in group competition, whether they will embrace freedom for all or choose oppression for most, whether they seek to see our species be embodied by the unmotivated Hippie, or the fiercely focused and accomplished warrior, these are decisions for each individual to make.

It is my greatest hope, however, that this book will aid in perceiving the issues and motives involved in this decision, and perhaps, increase our people's respect for, and love of, individual freedom, personal responsibility, moral decency, loyalty, and the accomplishment and greatness this produces when it merges with our governing structures.

Please help spread r/K Selection Theory, to friends, loved ones, coworkers, and acquaintances. The mainstream media will never talk about it, the establishment conservatives will never promote it, and academia will not teach it until they are forced to by its ubiquity in the political dialog.

This concept can change the face of politics, alter people's very perceptions of themselves, and forever shift our civilization's paths toward freedom and greatness, but not without the help of all those who have seen it. Take any opportunity to join the battle and spread r/K Theory where you can, because the freedom you save will be your own.

For further information, visit the blog at:
http://www.anonymousconservative.com/blog

Like us on Facebook:
http://www.facebook.com/AnonymousConservative

Follow us on Twitter:
@anonymousconservativ

Follow us on Gab.ai
@AnonymousConservative

You can leave a review on Amazon.com or share this link with friends:
http://amzn.to/2e0JYpH

Lots of other Conservative thinkers are doing interesting things online:

If you enjoy this work, you will love Bill Whittle. A veteran of National Review who submits regular commentary to NRATV, Bill's videos are so insightful and entertaining that they are happily funded by members:
http://www.BillWhittle.com

Stefan Molyneux's Free Domain Radio is incredibly addictive. With millions of fans who subscribe to his channel, Stefan is the king of Political Analysis, News, Interviews, and Current Events. His YouTube Channel is at:
https://www.youtube.com/user/stefbot

Or visit Stefan's website at:
https://freedomainradio.com/

For more on news about the growth of K in Europe, see Red Ice Radio:
https://redice.tv/

Author Matt Forney's great viewer funded, in-person political reporting:
http://www.mattforney.com

Visit the Facebook r/K Theory and Politics discussion page:
https://www.facebook.com/groups/187782054968995/

Heartiste is a staple of the new, reality-based right. Brilliant, off-color, insightful, and right, he explores the way women think when times are r:
https://heartiste.wordpress.com/

Castalia House Publishing produces quality conservative books:
http://www.CastaliaHouse.com

Author/blogger/podcaster Davis Aurini covers news and culture:
http://www.staresattheworld.com/

Bernard Chapin Covers Male Rights Activism at:
http://www.maledefender.com/

Day by Day political cartoons:
http://www.daybydaycartoon.com/

Xenosystems takes a systematic approach:
www.xenosystems.net

The Burning Platform:
https://www.theburningplatform.com/

Ex-Army covers the decline from a Libertarian Nationalist perspective:
http://ex-army.blogspot.com/

Ramblings on explosives, guns, politics, and sex by a redneck farm boy
http://blog.joehuffman.org/

Krauser on "game," which K's need to find and keep a wife in r-times:
https://krauserpua.com/

For a wild rollicking ride on the conspiracies behind society's decline:
http://vault-co.blogspot.com/

Human Biodiversity, Consanguinity and its effect on society:
http://hbdchick.wordpress.com/

The graphical designers at Better Book Covers produced our cover art:
BetterBookCovers@gmail.com

Notes

Chapter One

[1] Jeanna Bryner. "Conservative or Liberal? Workspace Reveals All" 25 September, 2008. <http://www.livescience.com/2894-conservative-liberal-workspace-reveals.html> (15 January, 2013)

Chapter Two

[2] Altmeyer focuses more on the in-grouping, ethnocentric urges of conservatism (such as the drive to see all abide by the group authority), but also touches on other social issues, couching them as demands by conservatives that the public cede to the (traditional K-selected) authority's views of how the world should be. What he does not discuss is why the authority would concern itself with mating strategies or the need for supposedly deleterious group competitions with others. These works we cite here are useful, but they must be viewed as characterizations of the wolf's world, viewed from the perspective of the bunny. Only in that context to they foster a true understanding.
Altemeyer, B. (1981). Right-Wing Authoritarianism. Manitoba: University of Manitoba Press.

[3] For another good general review of the literature on ideology and issue associations see:
Jost, J. T., Glaser, J., Kruglanski, A. W., and Sulloway, F. J. (2003). Political conservatism as motivated social cognition. Psychological Bulletin, 129 (3), 339–375.

[4] Here, Jost makes the case that ideological affiliation is real, partisanship is not disappearing, and it is highly predictive of voting behavior.
Jost, J. T. (2006). The end of the end of ideology. American Psychologist, 61 (7), 651–670.

[5] This paper offers an interesting statistical analysis of many issues and their association with ideologues.
Treier, S., Hillygus, S. (2005). The structure and meaning of political ideology (Working Paper). <http://satreier.myweb.uga.edu/mpsa05TreierHillygus.pdf> (12 May 2013)

Chapter Three

[6] MacArthur, R., Wilson, E. (1967). The Theory of Island Biogeography. Princeton, NJ: Princeton University Press.

[7] Pianka, E. R. (1970). On r- and K-selection. American Naturalist, 104, 592–596.

[8] Reznick, D., Bryant, J., Bashey, F. (2002). r- and K-selection revisited: the role of population regulation in life history evolution. Ecology, 83(6), 1509–1520.

[9] Kelly, K. (1987). Females, Males and Sexuality. New York: SUNY Press. p64

Chapter Four

[10] Ricklefs, R. E., Miller, G. L. (1999) Ecology. New York: W.H. Freeman. 658-676.

[11] Molet M., Van Baalen M., Peeters C. (2008). Shift in colonial reproductive strategy associated with a tropical-temperate gradient in Rhytidoponera ants. The American Naturalist, 172 (1), 75-87.

[12] This offers just one example of how r and K are used today as a shorthand to describe the difference between the need to focus effort on producing a small number of quality offspring, or the ability to spread efforts more broadly on producing raw quantities of offspring. *"In r-selected environments..., (where the ability to mate more and produce more offspring is favored), 7R+ genotypes would be expected to rise in frequency."* From : Garcia, J. R., MacKillop, J., Aller, E. L., Merriwether, A. M., Wilson, D. S., Lum, J. K., (2010). Associations between dopamine D4 receptor gene variation with both infidelity and sexual promiscuity. Plos One, 5 (11), e14162.

Chapter Five

[13] If, as we assert, liberalism is an adaptation to free resource availability, and conservatism is an adaptation to resource scarcity, this paper has a very interesting premise. Notice, r-strategists evolve to exploit the good environmental conditions, while K-strategists evolve to confront bad environmental conditions. See : Dodd, M.D., Balzer, A., Jacobs, C., Gruszczynski, M., Smith, K. B., Hibbing, J. R. (2012). The political left rolls with the good, the political right confronts the bad. Physiology and Cognition in Politics, Philosophical Transactions of the Royal Society, Biological Sciences, 367 (1589), 640-649.

Chapter Seven

[14] For a detailed review of Cuttlefish mating habits see Hall, K.C. & Hanlon, R.T. (2002). Principal features of the mating system of a large spawning aggregation of the Giant Australian Cuttlefish Sepia apama (Mollusca: Cephalopoda). Marine Biology, 140 (3), 533-545.

[15] Tomkins, S. S. (1963). Left and right: A basic dimension of ideology and personality. In R. W. White (Ed.), The study of lives (pp. 388–

411).Chicago: Atherton.

[16] Greater survival rates for K-competitors are inferred from the fact that over the preceding eons, neither the r-anticompetitor, nor the K-competitor has come to fully dominate the population. This despite studies showing that the female of the species, though she acquires sperm from many males, has been shown by genetic testing to produce more anticompetitor offspring than competitor offspring. This would fit with the model of anticompetitors as r-strategists, designed to eschew competitions which enhance survival of offspring through ability and fitness. As a result, they must possess increased reproductive rates compared to competitors, to account for increased mortality rates in the wild. For details of Sepia apama fertilization, see: Hanlon, R.T., Naud M.J., Shaw, P.W., Havenhand, J.N. (2005) Behavioural ecology: Transient sexual mimicry leads to fertilization. Nature, 430, 212.

[17] Cardwell, J. R., Liley, N. R. (1991). Hormonal control of sex and color change in the stoplight parrotfish, Sparisoma viride. General and Comparitive Endocrinology, 81 (1), 7-20.

[18] Gibson, K. N. (2010). Male mating tactics in spider monkeys: sneaking to compete. American Journal of Primatology, 72 (9), 794-804.

[19] Huffard, C. L., Caldwell, R. L., and Boneka, F. (2008). Mating behavior of Abdopus aculeatus (d'Orbigny 1834) (Cephalopoda: Octopodidae) in the wild. Marine Biology, 154 (2), 353-362.

[20] Knapp, R., Neff, B. D. (2007). Steroid hormones in bluegill, a species with male alternative reproductive tactics including female mimicry. Biology Letters, 3 (6), 628-631.

[21] Kurdziel, J. P., Knowles, L. L. (2002). The mechanisms of morph determination in the amphipod Jassa: implications for the evolution of alternative male phenotypes. Proceedings of the Royal Society, Biological Sciences, 269 (1502), 1749-1754.

[22] Plaistow, S. J., Tsubaki, Y. (2000). A selective trade-off for territoriality and non-territoriality in the polymorphic damselfly Mnais costalis. Proceedings of the Royal Society, Biological Sciences, 267 (1447), 969-975.

[23] Rios-Cardenas, O., Webster, M. S. (2008). A molecular genetic examination of the mating system of pumpkinseed sunfish reveals high pay-offs for specialized sneakers. Molecular Ecology, 17 (9), 2310-2320.

[24] Simmons, L. W., Emlen, D. J., Tomkins, J. L. (2007). Sperm competition games between sneaks and guards: a comparative analysis using dimorphic male beetles. Evolution, 61 (11), 2684-2692.

[25] Wada, T., Takegaki, T., Mori, T., Natsukari, Y. (2005). Alternative male mating behaviors dependent on relative body size in captive oval squid Sepioteuthis lessoniana (Cephalopoda, Loliginidae). Zoological Science, 22 (6), 645-651.

[26] Whiting, M. J., Webb, J. K., Keogh, J. S. (2009). Flat lizard female mimics use sexual deception in visual but not chemical signals. Proceedings of the Royal Society, Biological Sciences, 276 (1662), 1585-1591.

[27] Jones, A. G., Walker, D., Kvarnemo, C., Lindström, K., Avise, J. C. (2001). How cuckoldry can decrease the opportunity for sexual selection: data and

theory from a genetic parentage analysis of the sand goby, Pomatoschistus minutus. Proceedings of the National Academy of Sciences of the United States of America, 98 (16), 9151-9156.

28   Fischer R.A. (1930). The genetical theory of natural selection. Oxford: Clarendon Press. p. 131-132.

Chapter Eight

29   Researcher William Eckhardt spent a lot of time trying to show that militarism was associated with nationalism and conservatism, and all were a part of a psychopathology in need of a treatment. Again, just because a bunny rabbit has said somewhere that the wolf's loyalty to his pack is aberrant and stupid doesn't mean the wolf isn't loyal, or that the study showing such is wrong. See:
Eckhardt, W., & Alcock, N. Z. (1970). Ideology and personality in war/peace attitudes. Journal of Social Psychology, 81, 105–116.
All of our political debate is just the bunnies vs. the wolves.

Chapter Nine

30   Shavit, A. (2004). Shifting values partly explain the debate over group selection. Studies in history and philosophy of biological and biomedical sciences, 35 (4), 697-720.

31   There has been speculation by historians that many researchers in this field viewed the altruistic group competitor as a group conformist, and that they viewed conformity as a tool of totalitarianism. In viewing non-conformists as a vital check on totalitarianism, it became important to these researchers to de-emphasize the importance of conformity to the pursuit of group success, and the altruism it entailed.
In denying the possibility of group conflict playing a role in producing the altruistic goodness of man as well as civilization, this de-emphasized the noble aspects of group competition itself.
See:
Keller, E. F., (1988). Demarcating public from private values in evolutionary discourse. Journal of the History of Biology, 21, 195–211.
And:
Mitman, G., (1992), The State of Nature. Chicago: University of Chicago Press.

32   *"When two tribes of primeval man, living in the same country, came into competition, if (other things being equal) the one tribe included a great number of courageous, sympathetic and faithful members, who were always ready to warn each other of danger, to aid and defend each other, this tribe would succeed better and conquer the other."*
And

"It must not be forgotten that although a high standard of morality gives but a slight or no advantage to each individual man and his children over the other men of the same tribe, yet that an advancement in the standard of morality and in increase in the number of well-endowed men will certainly give an immense advantage to one tribe over another. There can be no doubt that a tribe including many members who, from possessing in a high degree the spirit of patriotism, fidelity, obedience, courage, and sympathy, were always ready to give aid to each other and to sacrifice themselves for the common good, would be victorious over other tribes; and this would be natural selection."

From Darwin, C. (1871). The Descent of Man. The Heritage Press, New York, 1972.

[33] Maynard Smith, J. (1976). Group selection. Quarterly Review of Biology, 51 (2), 277-283.

[34] Maynard Smith, J. (1964). Group Selection and kin selection. Nature, 201, 1145-1147.

[35] Wilson, D. S. (1975), A general theory of group selection. Proceedings of the National Academy of Sciences, 72, 143–146.

[36] Boyd, R., Richerson, P. J. (1992). Punishment allows the evolution of cooperation (or anything else) in sizable groups. Ethology and Sociobiology, 13, 171–195

[37] Boyd, R., Richerson, P. J. (2009). Culture and the evolution of human cooperation. Philosophical Transactions of the Royal Society: Biological Sciences, 364, 3281-3288.

[38] Lewis, G. J., Bates, T. C. (2010). A common heritable factor influences prosocial obligations across multiple domains. Biology Letters. 7 (4), 567-570.

[39] Lewis, G. J., Bates, T. C. (2010). Genetic evidence for multiple biological mechanisms underlying in-group favoritism. Psychological Science, 21 (11), 1623-1628.

[40] Jackson, J. W, (1993). Realistic group conflict theory: A review and evaluation of the theoretical and empirical literature. The Psychological Record, 43 (3), 395-413.

[41] Egas M., Kats R., van der Sar X., Reuben E., Sabelis M. W. (2013). Human cooperation by lethal group competition. Scientific Reports, 3, 1373.

[42] Koenig L. B., McGue M., Krueger R. F., Bouchard T. J. (2007). Religiousness, antisocial behavior, and altruism: genetic and environmental mediation. Journal of Personality 75 (2), 265-90.

[43] Cornwallis, C. K., West, S. A., Davis, K. E., Griffin, A. S. (2010) Promiscuity and the evolutionary transition to complex societies. Nature 466, 969–972.

[44] Stanish, C., Levine, A. (2011) War and early state formation in the northern Titicaca Basin, Peru. Proceedings of the National Academy of Sciences of the USA, 108 (34), 13901-13906.

[45] Bowles, S. (2006). Group competition, reproductive leveling, and the evolution of human altruism. Science, 314 (5805), 1569-1572.

46 Bowles, S. (2009). Did warfare among ancestral hunter-gatherers affect the evolution of human social behaviors? Science, 324 (5932), 1293-1298.

47 Gneezy A. and Fessler, D. T. (2011). Conflict, sticks and carrots: war increases prosocial punishments and rewards, Proceedings of the Royal Society: Biological Sciences, 279 (1727), 219-223.

48 The Greenbeard effect occurs when an altruistic organism evolves a perceptible trait (such as the tendency to express the behavior of altruism or loyalty), the ability to perceive the trait in others (such as the human ability to share the information which comprises a reputation), and a drive to provide preferential treatment (such as an expression of altruism or loyalty) to those who have the trait. By this means, those who have a trait will help to perpetuate the trait in all who carry it through assisting other carriers, and providing them advantage.

It is commonly seen within human warrior groups, where a reputation for loyalty to the group is a prerequisite for both membership and altruistic reciprocity. Within that milieu, reputation plays a vital role in acquiring the favor of fellow altruists, as it is how altruists spot each other.

What is generally not discussed in the Greenbeard effect is punishment, which is probably something mankind is highly programmed to engage in. Of course, active punishment of non-Greenbeards should have as much, if not more effect, than providing advantage to fellow Greenbeards.

For more on Greenbeard traits, see:

Hamilton WD (July 1964). The genetical evolution of social behaviour I. Journal of Theoretical Biology 7 (1), 1–16.

Hamilton WD (July 1964). The genetical evolution of social behaviour II. Journal of Theoretical Biology, 7 (1), 17–52.

Dawkins, Richard. (1976). The Selfish Gene. Oxford University Press, Oxford.

Grafen, Alan (6 August 1998). Green beard as death warrant. Nature, 394 (6693), 521–522.

49 *"...cooperators have a recognizable phenotypic tag that allows them to adopt the conditional strategy of cooperating with fellow tag-mates while defecting against others, a mechanism known as the 'green-beard effect'. The resulting intra-tag cooperator strategy is particularly effective in structured populations where local clumps of cooperative tag-mates can find refuge. While intra-tag cooperation is robust against unconditional defectors in the spatial Prisoner's dilemma (at least when the cost of cooperation is low), the role of extra-tag cooperators - individuals who cooperate only with those bearing a different tag - has received little attention, despite the fact that these traitors form mixed-tag aggregations whose heterogeneous makeup potentially allows the exploitation of multiple other strategies. Using a spatial model of the two-tag Prisoner's dilemma, I show that extra-tag cooperation readily evolves under low to intermediate cost-benefit ratios of mutual cooperation (r)."*

From: Laird R. A. (2011). Green-beard effect predicts the evolution of traitorousness in the two-tag Prisoner's dilemma. Journal of Theoretical Biology, 288, 84-91.

In other words, if a group of individuals sharing a cooperative trait form an in-group and cooperate with each other, it is inevitable that others will evolve to penetrate their groups, and work together to exploit a strategy of betrayal for personal advantage.

[50] Carney, D. R., Jost, J. T., Gosling, S. D., Potter, J. (2008). The secret lives of liberals and conservatives: Personality profiles, interaction styles, and the things they leave behind. Political Psychology, 29, (6), 807-840.

[51] *"There is now the possibility of explaining ideological differences between right and left in terms of underlying psychological needs for stability versus change, order versus complexity, familiarity versus novelty, conformity versus creativity, and loyalty versus rebellion."* From: Jost, (2006). Notice, as war with an out-group approaches, the creative-thinking, novelty-seeking, change-desiring individual, who is programmed to embrace rebellion against their own social order, is perfectly designed to exploit selfish betrayal for personal advantage in group competition. The stability-desiring, order embracing, familiarity-loving conformist, who is programmed for loyalty to his own, is the warrior who rejects betrayal.

Chapter Ten

[52] Henrich, J., Boyd, R., Richerson, P. J. (2012). The puzzle of monogamous marriage. Philosophical Transactions of the Royal Society Biology, 367 (1589), 657-659.

Chapter Eleven

[53] Laird (2011).

[54] Liberals are less likely to own or display national flags. See: Carney, et al. (2008).

[55] Fourth of July parades energize conservatives and suppress liberalism, perhaps through shame. See:
Madestam, A., Yanagizawa-Drott, D. (2011). Shaping the nation: the effect of fourth of July on political preferences and behavior in the United States (Working Paper IGIER WP 399). Retrieved from Harvard University website: http://www.hks.harvard.edu/fs/dyanagi/Research/FourthOfJuly.pdf

[56] Seeing Flags promotes conservatism, suppresses liberalism. See:
Carter, T. J., Ferguson, M. J., Hassin, R. R. (2011). A single exposure to the American flag shifts support toward republicanism up to 8 months later. Psychological Science, 22 (8), 1011-1018.

[57] Kelly, K. (1987). Females, Males and Sexuality. New York: SUNY Press. p64

Chapter Twelve

⁵⁸ K-strategists have a pretty stable moral compass, which will always view all offspring as sacred. When you let the r-strategist's mind wander, what emerges is their lack of any real moral foundation beyond every bunny's right to happiness at any cost to anyone else. You will get some pontifications so opposed to the K-strategist's instincts, that they are nearly unbelievable. Among them is this idea of the ethicality of aborting babies, for some time after birth, even without parental consent. Notice, under conditions of limited resources, where the wheat is cleanly separated from the chaff, these psychologies would quickly be culled by Darwin. See:

Tooley, M. (1972). Abortion and infanticide. Philosophy and Public Affairs, 1, 37–65.

Singer, P. (1993). Practical Ethics (2nd ed). Cambridge: Cambridge University Press. pp 169-174.

Appel J. M. (May 2009). Neonatal euthanasia: Why require parental consent? Journal of Bioethical Inquiry, 6 (4), 477–482.

Giubilini, A., Minerva, F. (2012). After-birth abortion: why should the baby live? Journal of Medical Ethics, 39 (5), 261-263.

⁵⁹ Jost, (2006).

Chapter Fourteen

⁶⁰ Kanai, R., Feilden, T., Firth, C., Rees, G. (2011). Political orientations are correlated with brain structure in young adults. Current Biology, 21 (8), 677-680.

⁶¹ Amodio, D. M., Jost, J. T., Master, S. L., Yee, C. M. (2007) Neurocognitive correlates of liberalism and conservatism. Nature Neuroscience, 10 (10), 1246-1247.

⁶² Rule, N. O., Freeman, J. B., Moran, J. M., Gabrieli, J. D. E., Adams, R. B., Ambady, N. (2010). Voting behavior is reflected in amygdala response across cultures. Social Cognitive and Affective Neuroscience, 5, 349–355.

⁶³ Öhman, A. (2009) Human fear conditioning and the amygdala. In Whalen, P. J., Phelps, E. A. (Eds.), The Human Amygdala, (pp. 118-154). New York : Guilford.

⁶⁴ Adolphs, R., Tranel, D., Damasio, A. R. (1998). The human amygdala in social judgment. Nature, 393, 470–474.

⁶⁵ Adolphs, R., Baron-Cohen, S., Tranel, D. (2002). Impaired recognition of social emotions following amygdala damage. Journal of Cognitive Neuroscience, 14, 1264–1274.

⁶⁶ Broks, P., Young, A. W., Maratos, E. J., Coffey, P. J., Calder, A. J., Isaac, C., Mayes, A. R., Hodges, J. R., Montaldi, D., Cezayirli, E., Roberts, N., Hadley, D. (1998). Face processing impairments after encephalitis: Amygdala damage and recognition of fear. Neuropsychologia, 36, 59–70.

67   Winston, J. S., Strange, B. A., O'Doherty, J., Dolan, R. J. (2002). Automatic and intentional brain responses during evaluation of trustworthiness of faces. Nature Neuroscience, 5 (3), 277–283.

68   Yang, Y., Raine, A., Narr, K. L., Colletti, P., Toga, A. (2009). Localization of deformations within the amygdala in individuals with psychopathy. Archives of General Psychiatry, 66(9), 986-994.

69   David, A. S., Brierley, B., Shaw, P. (2002). The human amygdala: a systematic review and meta-analysis of volumetric magnetic resonance imaging. Brain Research - Brain Research Reviews, 39(1), 84-105.

70   Dicks, D., Meyers, R. E., Kling, A. (1968). Uncus and amygdala lesions: Effects on social behavior in the free ranging rhesus monkey. Science, 165, 69-71.

71   Buchanan, T. W., Tranel, D. & Adolphs, R. (2009). The human amygdala in social function. In Whalen, P. J., Phelps, E. A. (Eds.), The human amygdala, (pp. 308-309). New York : Guilford.

72   Kohn, R. H. (1994). Out of control: the crisis in civil-military relations. The National Interest, 35, 3–17.

73   Trowbridge, G. (2004). Poll: Today's military: right, republican and principled. Army Times, 05 January 2004, 15.

74   Brown, S., Shäfer, E. A. (1888). An investigation into the functions of the occipital and temporal lobes of the monkey's brain. Philosophical Transactions of the Royal Society of London: Biological Sciences 179, 303–327.

75   Settle, J.E., Dawes, C. T., Christakis, A., Fowler, J.H. (2010). Friendships moderate an association between a dopamine gene variant and political ideology. The Journal of Politics, 72, 1189-1198.

76   Benjamin, J., Li, L., Patterson, C., Greenberg, B. D., Murphy, D. L., Hamer, D. H. (1996). Population and familial association between the D4 dopamine receptor gene and measures of novelty seeking. Nature Genetics, 12 (1), 81–84.

77   Benjamin, J., Osher, Y., Kotler, M., Gritsenko, I., Nemanov, L., Belmaker, R. H., Ebstein, R. P. (2000). Association between tridimensional personality questionnaire traits and three functional polymorphisms: DrD4, 5-HTTLPR, and COMT. Molecular Psychiatry, 5 (1), 96–100.

78   Ebstein, R. P., Novick, O., Umansky, R., Pirelli, B., Osher, Y., Blaine, D., Bennett, E. R., Nemanov, L., Katz, M., Belmaker, R. H. (1996). Dopamine D4 receptor exon III polymorphism associated with the human personality trait of novelty seeking. Nature Genetics, 12, 78–80.

79   Noble, E. P., Ozkaragoz, T. Z., Ritchie, T. L., Zhang, X., Belin, T. R., Sparkes. R. S., 1998. D2 and D4 dopamine receptor polymorphisms and personality. American Journal of Medical Genetics, 81 (3), 257–267.

80   Chen, C., Burton, M., Greenberger, E., and Dmitrieva, J. (1999). Population migration and the variation of dopamine receptor (DRD4) allele frequencies around the globe. Evolution and Human Behavior, 20 (5) , 309-324.

81   Trimble, M. R., Mendez, M. F., Cummings, J. L. (1997). Neuropsychiatric symptoms from the Temporolimbic Lobes. In Salloway, S., Malloy, P.,

Cummings, J. L. (Eds.), The Neuropsychiatry of Limbic and Subcortical Disorders, (pp. 123-132). Washington, DC: American Psychiatric Press.

82 Bucher, K., Myersn, R., Southwick, C. (1970). Anterior temporal cortex and maternal behavior in monkey. Neurology, 20 (4), 415.

83 Blair, R.J., Jones, L., Smith, M. (1997). The psychopathic individual, a lack of responsiveness to distress cues. Psychophisiology, 34 (2), 192-198.

84 Tiihonen, J., Hodgins, S., Vaurio, O., Laakso, M., Repo, E., Soininen, H., Aronen, H. J., Nieminen, P., Savolainen, L. (2000) Amygdaloid volume loss in psychopathy. Society for Neuroscience Abstracts, 2017.

85 Blair, R. J. R. (2007). The amygdala and ventromedial prefrontal cortex in morality and psychopathy. Trends in Cognitive Neurosciences, 11 (9), 387-392.

86 Greene, J. D., Nystrom, L. E., Engell, A. D., Darley, J. M., Cohen, J. D. (2004). The neural bases of cognitive conflict and control in moral judgement. Neuron, 44, 389-400.

87 Moll, J., Oliviera-Souza, R., Eslinger, P. J., Bramati, I. E., Mourão-Miranda, J., Andreiuolo, P. A., Pessoa, L. (2002). The neural correlates of moral sensitivity; a functional magnetic resonance imaging investigation of basic and moral emotions. The Journal of Neuroscience, 22, 2730-2736.

88 Michl, P., Meindl, T., Meister, F., Born, C., Engel, R. R., Reiser, M., Hennig-Fast, K. (2012). Neurobiological underpinnings of shame and guilt: a pilot fMRI study. Social Cognitive and Affective Neuroscience, Online Publication, Nss114.

89 Shirtcliff, E. A., Vitacco, M. J., Gostisha, A. J., Merz, J. L., Zahn-Waxler, C. (2009). Neurobiology of empathy and callousness: implications for the development of antisocial behavior. Behavioral Sciences and the Law, 27, 137-171.

90 Yang, Y., Raine, A., Narr, K., Lencz, T., Toga, A. (2006) Amygdala Volume Reductions In Psychopaths. The Twentieth Annual Meeting of the Society for Research in Psychopathology, San Diego, CA.

91 Yang et al., (2009).

92 Enebrink, P., Andershed, H., Langstrom, N. (2005). Callous–unemotional traits are associated with clinical severity in referred boys with conduct problems. Nordic Journal of Psychiatry, 59 (6), 431–440.

93 Frick, P. J., Bodin, S. D., & Barry, C. T. (2000). Psychopathic traits and conduct problems in community and clinic-referred samples of children: Further development of the psychopathy screening device. Psychological Assessment, 12(4), 382–393.

94 Marsh, A. A., Finger, E. C., Mitchell, D. G., Reid, M. E., Sims, C., Kosson, D. S., Towbin, K. E., Leibenluft, E., Pine, D. S., Blair, R. J. (2008). Reduced amygdala response to fearful expressions in children and adolescents with callous–unemotional traits and disruptive behavior disorders. American Journal of Psychiatry, 165 (6), 712–720.

95 Blair, R. J. (2007). The amygdala and ventromedial prefrontal cortex in morality and psychopathy. Trends in Cognitive Science, 11 (9), 387–392.

96 Blair, R. J. R. (2006) The emergence of psychopathy: implications for the neuropsychological approach to developmental disorders. Cognition 101,

414–442.

[97] Sterzer, P., Stadler, C., Krebs, A., Kleinschmidt, A., Poustka, F. (2005). Abnormal neural responses to emotional visual stimuli in adolescents with conduct disorder. Biological Psychiatry, 57 (1), 7–15.

[98] Reduced amygdala function related to cooperation : Rilling, J. K., Glenn, A. L., Jairam, M. R., Pagnoni, G., Goldsmith, D. R., Elfenbein, H. A., Lilienfeld, S. O. (2007). Neural correlates of social cooperation and non-cooperation as a function of psychopathy. Biological Psychiatry, 61 (11), 1260–1271.

[99] Marsh A. A., Kozak, M. N., Ambady, N. (2007). Accurate identification of fear facial expressions predicts prosocial behavior. Emotion, 7 (2), 239-251.

[100] Rummel, R. J. (1994). Death By Government. New Brunswick, NJ: Transaction Publishers.

[101] Sylvers, P. D., Brennan, P. A., Lilienfeld, S. O. (2011). Psychopathic traits and preattentive threat processing in children: a novel test of the fearfulness hypothesis. Psychological Science. 22 (10), 1280-1287.

[102] Blair, R. J. (2004). The roles of the orbital frontal cortex in the modulation of antisocial behavior. Brain and Cognition, 55 (1), 198-208.

[103] Jonason, P. K., Kavanagh, P. (2010). The dark side of love: love styles and the Dark Triad. Personality and Individual Differences, 49, 606–610.

[104] Jonason, P., Li, N., Webster, G., Schmitt, D. (2009). The dark triad: facilitating a short-term mating strategy in men. European Journal of Personality, 23 (1), 5-18.

[105] Ghods-Sharifi S., St Onge J. R., Floresco S. B. (2009). Fundamental contribution by the basolateral amygdala to different forms of decision making. The Journal of Neuroscience, 29 (16), 5251-5259.

[106] Craig, A. D. (2002). How do you feel? Interoception: The sense of the physiological condition of the body. Nature Reviews Neuroscience, 3 (8), 655–666.

[107] Eisenberger, N. I., Lieberman, M. D. (2004). Why rejection hurts: A common neural alarm system for physical and social pain. Trends in Cognitive Science, 8 (7), 294–300.

[108] Eisenberger, N. I., Lieberman,M. D., Williams, K. D. (2003). Does rejection hurt? An fMRI study of social exclusion. Science, 302 (5643), 290–292.

[109] Singer, T., Seymour, B., O'Doherty, J., Kaube, H., Dolan, R. J., & Frith, C. D. (2004). Empathy for pain involves the affective but not sensory components of pain. Science, 303 (5661), 1157–1162.

[110] Sanfey, A. G., Rilling, J. K., Aronson, J. A., Nystrom, L. E., & Cohen, J. D. (2003). The neural basis of economic decision-making in the Ultimatum Game. Science, 300 (5626), 1755–1758.

[111] Takahashi, H., Kato, M., Matsuura, M., Mobbs, D., Suhara, T., Okubo, Y. (2009). When your gain is my pain and your pain is my gain: neural correlates of envy and schadenfreude. Science, 323 (5916), 937-939.

[112] Decety, J., & Lamm, C. (2006). Human empathy through the lens of social neuroscience. Scientific World Journal, 6, 1146–1163.

[113] Brooks, A. (2007). Who really cares. New York: Basic Books

114 Glenn, A.L. & Raine, A. (2011). Antisocial personality disorders. In J. Decety & J. Cacioppo (Eds.) The Oxford Handbook of Social Neuroscience (pp. 885-894). New York: Oxford University Press.

115 Pujol, J., Lopez, A., Deus, J., Cardoner, N., Vallejo, J., Capdevila, A., Paus, T., (2002). Anatomical variability of the anterior cingulate gyrus and basic dimensions of human personality. Neuroimage, 154, 847–855.

Chapter Sixteen

116 Settle, J.E., Dawes, C. T., Christakis, A., Fowler, J.H. (2010). Friendships moderate an association between a dopamine gene variant and political ideology. The Journal of Politics, 72, 1189-1198.

117 Cloninger, C. R., Svrakic, D. M., and Przybeck, T. R. (1993). A psychobiological model of temperament and character. Archives of General Psychiatry, 50 (12), 975–990.

118 Wiesbeck, G.A., Mauerer, C., Thome, J., Jacob, F., Boening, J. (1995). Neuroendocrine support for a relationship between "'novelty seeking'' and dopaminergic function in alcohol-dependent men. Psychoneuroendocrinology, 20, 755–761.

119 Miller E. K., Freedman D. J., Wallis J. D. (2002). The prefrontal cortex: categories, concepts and cognition. Philosophical Transactions of the Royal Society London B, Biological Sciences, 357 (1424), 1123–1136.

120 Cacioppo, J.T. (2009). Handbook of neuroscience for the behavioral sciences, Vol 2. New York: Wiley Books. p. 873.

121 Tochigia, M., Hibinoa, H., Otowaa, T., Katoa, C., Maruia, T., Ohtania, T., Umekagea, T., Katoa, N., Sasakia, T. (2006). Association between dopamine D4 receptor (DRD4) exon III polymorphism and neuroticism in the Japanese population. Neuroscience Letters, 398 (3), 333-336.

122 Berridge, K. C. (2007). The debate over dopamine's role in reward: the case for incentive salience. Psychopharmacology, 191, 391-431.

123 Berridge, K. C., Robinson, T. E. (1998). What is the role of dopamine in reward: hedonic impact, reward learning, or incentive salience? Brain Research Reviews, 28 (3), 309-369.

124 Ben Zion, I., Tessler, R., Cohen, L., Lerer, R., Raz, Y. (2006). Polymorphisms in the dopamine D4 receptor gene (DRD4) contribute to individual differences in human sexual behavior: desire, arousal and sexual function. Molecular Psychiatry, 11 (8), 782–786.

125 Guo, G., Tong, y. (2006). Age at first sexual intercourse, genes, and social context: evidence from twins and the dopamine D4 receptor gene. Demography, 43 (4), 747-769.

126 Garcia, J. R., MacKillop, J., Aller, E. L., Merriwether, A. M., Wilson, D. S., Lum, J. K., (2010). Associations between dopamine D4 receptor gene variation with both infidelity and sexual promiscuity. Plos One, 5 (11), e14162.

127 Brooks, A. (2008). Gross National Happiness. New York: Basic Books. p. 32.

128   Napier, J. L., Jost, J. T. (2008). Why are conservatives happier than liberals? Psychological Science, 19, 565-572.

129   Pew Research Center. (2006). Poll : are we happy yet? Available online at <http://pewresearch.org/pubs/301/are-we-happy-yet> (Retrieved December 10, 2011)

130   Verhulst, B., Hatemi, P. K., Martin, N. G. (2010). The nature of the relationship between personality traits and political attitudes. Personality and Individual Differences, 49, 306–316.

131   In many studies, the term "authoritarian personality" is used as a proxy for politically conservative. Peterson B. E., Zurbriggen E. L. (2010). Gender, sexuality, and the authoritarian personality. Journal of Personality, 78 (6), 1801-1826.

132   Jost, J. T., Napier, J. L., Thorisdottir, H., Gosling, S. D., Palfai, T. P., Ostafin, B. (2007). Are needs to manage uncertainty and threat associated with political conservatism or ideological extremity? Personality and Social Psychology Bulletin, 33, 989-1007.

133   Pianka (1970).

134   Mackay, T. (2001). The genetic architecture of quantitative traits. Annual Review of Genetics, 35, 303–339.

135   Plomin, R., DeFries, J. C., McClearn, G. E., McGuffin, P. (2008). Behavioral Genetics. 5th ed. New York: Worth Publishers. p. 39.

136   Trumble1, B. C., Cummings, D., von Rueden, C., O'Connor, K. A., Smith, E. A., Gurven, M., Kaplan, H. (2012). Physical competition increases testosterone among Amazonian forager-horticulturalists: A test of the 'Challenge Hypothesis'. Proceedings of the Rotyal Society, Biological Sciences, 279 (1739), 2907-2912.

137   Travison, T. G., Araujo, A. B., O'Donnell, A. B., Kupelian, V. and McKinlay, J. B. (2007). A Population-Level Decline in Serum Testosterone Levels in American Men. The Journal of Clinical Endocrinology & Metabolism, 92 (1), 196-202.

138   Bhasin, S. (2007). Secular Decline in Male Reproductive Function: Is Manliness Threatened? The Journal of Clinical Endocrinology & Metabolism, 92 (1), 44-45.

Chapter Seventeen

139   Dennis Mangan, "Food and Porn as Supernormal Stimuli." 26 June, 2012. <http://mangans.blogspot.com/2012/06/food-and-porn-as-supernormal-stimuli.html> (21 April 2013)

140   Treadway M.T., Buckholtz J. W., Cowan R. L., Woodward N. D., Li R., Ansari M. S., Baldwin R. M., Schwartzman A. N., Kessler R. M., Zald D. H. (2012). Dopaminergic mechanisms of individual differences in human effort-based decision-making. Journal of Neuroscience, 32 (18), 6170-6176.

141   Kosfeld, M. Heinrichs, M., Zak, P. J., Fischbacher, U., Fehr, E. (2005). Oxytocin increases trust in humans. Nature, 435, 673-676.

[142] Zak, P. J., Stanton, A. A., Ahmadi, S. (2007). Oxytocin increases generosity in humans. PLoS ONE, 2 (11), e1128.

[143] Lee, H. J., Macbeth, A. H., Pagani, J. Young, W. S. (2009). Oxytocin: the great facilitator of life. Progress in Neurobiology 88 (2), 127–151.

[144] Feldman, R., Weller, A., Zagoory-Sharon, O., Levine, A. (2007). Evidence for a neuroendocrinological foundation of human affiliation: plasma Oxytocin levels across pregnancy and the postpartum period predict mother-infant bonding. Psychological Science, 18 (11), 965-970.

[145] Gubernick D.J., Winslow J.T., Jensen P., Jeanotte L., Bowen J. (). Oxytocin changes in males over the reproductive cycle in the monogamous, biparental California mouse, Peromyscus californicus. Hormones and Behavior, 29 (1), 59-73.

[146] Insel T. R., Hulihan T. J., (1995). A Gender-Specific Mechanism for pair bonding: Oxytocin and partner preference formation in monogamous voles. Behavioral Neuroscience. 109, 782–789.

[147] Bales K. L., Carter C. S. (2003). Developmental exposure to Oxytocin facilitates partner preferences in male prairie voles (Microtus ochrogaster). Behavioral Neuroscience, 117, 854–859.

[148] Scheele D., Striepens N., Güntürkün O., Deutschländer S., Maier W., Kendrick K. M., Hurlemann R. (2012). Oxytocin Modulates Social Distance Between Males and Females. The Journal of Neuroscience, 32 (46), 16074-16079.

[149] DeAngelis, T. (2008). The two faces of Oxytocin. American Psychological Association: Monitor on Psychology, 39 (2), 30.

[150] DeAngelis, T. (2008). Can Oxytocin Promote Trust and Generosity? American Psychological Association: Monitor on Psychology, 39 (2), 32.

[151] De Dreu, C. K. W., Greer, L. L., Van Kleef, G. A., Shalvi, S., Handgraaf, M. J. J. (2011). Oxytocin Promotes Human Ethnocentrism. Proceedings of the National Acadamy of Sciences of the USA, 108 (4), 1262–1266.

[152] Baskerville T. A., Douglas A. J. (2010). Dopamine and Oxytocin Interactions Underlying Behaviors: Potential Contributions to Behavioral Disorders. CNS Neuroscience & Theraputics, 16 (3), 92-123.

[153] Succu S., Sanna F., Melis T., Boi A., Argiolas A., Melis M. R. (2007). Stimulation of dopamine receptors in the Paraventricular nucleus of the hypothalamus of male rats induces penile erection and increases extra-cellular dopamine in the Nucleus Accumbens: Involvement of central Oxytocin. Neuropharmacology, 52 (3), 1034-1043.

Chapter Eighteen

[154] Meaney, M. J. (2001). Maternal care, gene expression, and the transmission of individual differences in stress reactivity across generations. Annual Review of Neuroscience, 24, 1161–1192.

[155] Meaney, M. J., Szyf, M. (2005). Maternal care as a model for experience-dependent chromatin plasticity? Trends in Neurosciences, 28, 456–463.

[156] Weaver, I. C., Cervoni, N., Champagne, F. A., D'Alessio, A. C., Sharma, S., Seckl, J. R., Dymov, S., Szyf, M., Meaney, M. J. (2004). Epigenetic programming by maternal behavior. Nature Neuroscience, 7, 847–854.

[157] Ellis, B. J., Jackson, J. J., Boyce, W. T. (2006). The stress response systems: universality and adaptive individual differences. Developmental Review 26, 175-212.

[158] Bogaert A. F. (2008) Menarche and father absence in a national probability sample. Journal of Biosocial Science, 40 (4), 623-636.

[159] Bogaert A. F. (2005) Age at puberty and father absence in a national probability sample. Journal of Adolescence 28(4), 541-546.

[160] Deardorff, J., Ekwaru, J. P., Kushi, L. H., Ellis, B. J., Greenspan, L. C., Mirabedi, A., Landaverde, E. G., Hiatt, R. A., (2011). Father absence, body mass index, and pubertal timing in girls: differential effects by family income and ethnicity. Journal of Adolescent Health, 48 (5), 441-447.

[161] Ellis, B. J. (2004). Timing of pubertal maturation in girls: an integrated life history approach. Psychological Bulletin, 130 (6), 920-958.

[162] Ellis, B. J., Shirtcliff, E. A., Boyce, T., Deardorff, J., Essex, M. J. (2011). Quality of early family relationships and the timing and tempo of puberty: Effects depend on biological sensitivity to context. Development and Psychopathology, 23, 85-99.

[163] Graber J. A., Brooks-Gunn J., Warren M. P. (1995). The antecedents of menarcheal age: heredity, family environment, and stressful life events. Child Development, 66 (2), 346-359.

[164] Jorm A. F., Christensen H., Rodgers B., Jacomb P. A., Easteal S. (2004). Association of adverse childhood experiences, age of menarche, and adult reproductive behavior: does the androgen receptor gene play a role? American Journal of Medical Genetics, Part B, Neuropsychiatric Genetics, 125B (1), 105-111.

[165] Romans S. E., Martin J. M., Gendall K., Herbison G. P. (2003) Age of menarche: the role of some psychosocial factors. Psychological Medicine, 33 (5), 933-939.

[166] Belsky, J., Steinberg, L., Draper, P. (1991). Childhood experience, interpersonal development, and reproductive strategy: an evolutionary theory of socialization. Child Development, 62 (4), 647-670.

[167] Draper, P., Harpending, H. (1982). Father absence and reproductive strategy: and evolutionary perspective. Journal of Anthropological Research, 38 (3), 255-273.

[168] Chisholm, J. H. (1999). Death, Hope, and Sex: Steps to an Evolutionary Ecology of Mind and Morality. Cambridge: Cambridge University Press. pp. 161-167.

[169] Belsky, J. (2007). Childhood experiences and reproductive strategies. In Dunbar, R., Barret, L. (Eds) Oxford Handbook of Evolutionary Psychology. New York: Oxford University Press. pp. 242-243.

[170] Hetherington, E. M., (1972). Effects of father absence on personality development in adolescent daughters. Developmental Psychology, 7, 313-326.

171   Hepworth, J., Ryder, R. G., Dreyer, A. S. (1984). The effects of parental loss on the formation of intimate relationships. Journal of Marital and Family Therapy, 10 (1), 73-82.

172   Belsky, J. (1997). Variation in susceptibility to rearing influences: an evolutionary argument. Psychological Inquiry, 8, 182-186.

173   Belsky, J. (1997). Theory testing, effect-size evaluation, and differential suscepability to rearing influence: the case of mothering and attachment. Child Development, 68 (4), 598-600.

174   Belsky, J. (2005). Differential susceptibility to rearing influences: an evolutionary hypothesis and some evidence. In Ellis, B. and Bjorklund, D. Eds, Origins of the Social Mind: Evolutionary Psychology and Childhood Development. (139-163) New York: Guilford

175   Belsky, J., Pleuss, M. (2009). Beyond diathesis-stress: differential susceptibility to environmental influences. Psychological Bulletin, 135 (6), 885-908.

176   Bakermans-Kranenburg, M. J., Van Ijzendoorn, M. H. (2006). Gene-environment interaction of the dopamine D4 receptor (DRD4) and observed maternal insensitivity predicting externalizing behavior in preschoolers. Developmental Psychobiology, 48 (5), 406-409.

177   Van Ijzendoorn, M. H., Bakermans-Kranenburg, M. J. (2006) DRD4 7-repeat polymorphism moderates the association between maternal unresolved loss or trauma and infant disorganization. Attachment and Human Development, 8 (4), 291-307.

178   Settle et al. (2010).

179   Dweck, C. (1999). Self-Theories: Their Role in Motivation, Personality, and Development. Philadelphia: The Psychology Press.
Dweck, C. (2006). Mindset: The New Psychology of Success. New York: Random House.

180   Beck, A. T. (1999). Cognitive aspects of personality disorders and their relation to syndromal disorders: a psychoevolutionary approach. In Cloninger, C. R. (Ed.), Personality and Psychopathology, (pp.411-430). Washington, DC: American Psychiatric Press. p. 187.

181   Clark, D. A., Beck, A. T., and Alford, B. A. (1999). Scientific Foundations of Cognitive Theory and Therapy of Depression. New York, NY: John Wiley & Sons. p. 49.

Chapter Nineteen

182   Brooks (2008). p. 32.

183   Napier & Jost (2008).

184   Pew Research Center. (2006). Poll : are we happy yet? <http://pewresearch.org/pubs/301/are-we-happy-yet>. (25 January, 2011)

185   Nesse, R. M. (2000). Is depression an adaptation? Archives of General Psychiatry, 57 (1), 14-20.

186   Henriques, G. (2000). Depression: disease or behavioral shutdown mechanism? Journal of Science and Health Policy, 1, 152–165.

[187] Beck (1999).

[188] Leahy, R. L. (1997). An investment model of depressive resistance. Journal of Cognitive Psychotherapy, 11, 3-19.

[189] Gilbert, P. (1992). Depression: The Evolution of Powerlessness. East Sussex: Lawrence Erlbaum Associates. p. 244.

[190] Price J. S. (1967). The dominance hierarchy and the evolution of mental illness. Lancet, 2, 243-246.

[191] Price, J., Sloman, L., Gardner, R., Gilbert, P., Rohde, P. (1994). The social competition hypothesis of depression. The British Journal of Psychiatry, 164, 309-315.

[192] Sloman, L., Price, J., Gilbert, P., Gardner, R. (1994). Adaptive function of depression: psychotherapeutic implications. American Journal of Psychotherapy, 48, 401-416.

[193] Maes M., Kubera M., Obuchowiczwa E., Goehler L., Brzeszcz J. (2011). Depression's multiple comorbidities explained by (neuro)inflammatory and oxidative & nitrosative stress pathways. Neuroendocrinology Letters, 32 (1), 7-24.

[194] Reinherz, H. Z., Giaconia, R. M., Hauf, A. M., Wasserman, M. S., and Silverman, A. B. (1999). Major depression in the transition to adulthood: risks and impairments. Journal of Abnormal Psychology, 108, 500-510.

[195] Yu, Y., and Williams, D. R. (2006). Socioeconomic status and mental health. In Aneshensel, C. S., Phelan, J. C. (Eds.), Handbook of the Sociology of Mental Health. New York: Plenum Publishers. p. 154.

[196] Drevets, W. C. (1998). Functional neuroimaging studies of depression: the anatomy of melancholia. Annual Review of Medicine, 49, 341-361.

[197] Soares, J. C., Mann, J. J. (1997). The anatomy of mood disorders--review of structural neuroimaging studies. Biological Psychiatry, 41, 86-106.

[198] Kendler, K. S., Walters, E. E., Truett, K. R., Heath, A. C., Neale, M. C., Martin, N. G., Eaves, L. J., (1994). Sources of individual differences in depressive symptoms: analysis of two samples of twins and their families. American Journal of Psychiatry, 151, 1605-1614.

[199] Tochigia, M., Hibinoa, H., Otowaa, T., Katoa, C., Maruia, T., Ohtania, T., Umekagea, T., Katoa, N., Sasakia, T. (2006). Association between dopamine D4 receptor (DRD4) exon III polymorphism and neuroticism in the Japanese population. Neuroscience Letters, 398 (3), 333-336.

[200] Settle et al. (2010).

[201] Ben Zion, et al. (2006).

Chapter Twenty

[202] Webster, J.P. (2007). The effect of Toxoplasma gondii on animal behavior: playing cat and mouse. Schizophrenia Bulletin, 33 (3), 752–756.

[203] Berdoy, M., Webster, J. P., Macdonald, D.W. (2000). Fatal attraction in rats infected with Toxoplasma gondii. Proceedings of the Royal Society, Biological Sciences, 267, 1591–1594.

204   Webster J.P. (2001). Rats, cats, people and parasites: the impact of latent toxoplasmosis on behaviour. Microbes and Infection, 3, 1037–1045.

205   Flegr, J. (2007). Effects of toxoplasma on human behaviour. Schizophrenia Bulletin, 33 (3), 757–760.

206   Alvarado-Esquivel, C., Alanis-Quinones, O. P., Arreola-Valenzuela, M. A., Rodriguez-Briones, A., Piedra-Nevarez, L. J., Duran-Morales, E., Estrada-Martinez, S., Martinez-Garcia, S. A., Liesenfeld, O. (2006). Seroepidemiology of Toxoplasma gondii infection in psychiatric inpatients in a northern Mexican city. BMC Infectious Diseases, 6, 178.

207   Lafferty, K. D. (2006). Can the common brain parasite, Toxoplasma gondii, influence human culture? Proceedings of the Royal Society, Biological Sciences, 273, 2749-2755.

208   Hofstede, G., McCrae, R. (2004). Personality and culture revisited: linking traits and dimensions of culture. Cross-Cultural Research 38, 52–88.

209   Treier & Hillygus, (2005).

210   Jost (2006).

211   Haidt, J., & Hersh, M. (2001). Sexual morality: The cultures and emotions of conservatives and liberals. Journal of Applied Social Psychology, 31, 191–221.

212   Garcia et al. (2010).

213   Tomkins (1963).

214   Stibbs, H. H. (1985). Changes in brain concentrations of catecholamines and indoleamines in Toxoplasma gondii–infected mice. Annals of Tropical Medicine and Parasitology, 79, 153-157.

215   Melzer, T. C., Cranston, H. J., Weiss, L. M., Halonen, S. K., (2010). Host cell preference of Toxoplasma gondii cysts in murine brain: a confocal study. Journal of Neuroparasitology, 2010, 1, 19-24.

216   Vyas, A., Kim, S.K., Giacomini, N., Boothroyd, J.C., Sapolsky, R.M. (2007). Behavioral changes induced by Toxoplasma infection of rodents are highly specific to aversion of cat odors. Proceedings of the National Academy of Sciences of the United States of America, 104, 6442–6447.

217   Henriques, J. B., Davidson, R. J. (1991). Left frontal hypoactivation in depression. Journal of Abnormal Psychology, 100 (4), 535–545.

218   Martinot, J. L., Hardy, P., Feline, A., Huret, J. D., Mazoyer, B., Attar-Levy, D., Pappata, S., Syrota, A. (1990). Left prefrontal glucose hypometabolism in the depressed state: a confirmation. American Journal of Psychiatry, 147 (10), 1313–1317.

219   Henriquez, S. A., Brett, R., Alexander, J., Pratt, J., Roberts C. W. (2009). Neuropsychiatric disease and Toxoplasma gondii infection. Neuroimmunomodulation, 16 (2), 122–133.

220   Lafferty (2006).

221   Kar, N, Misra, B. (2004). Toxoplasma seropositivity and depression: a case report. BMC Psychiatry, 2004; 4, 1.

222   Stibbs, H. H. (1985). Changes in brain concentrations of catecholamines and indoleamines in Toxoplasma gondii–infected mice. Annals of Tropical Medicine and Parasitology, 79, 153-157.

223 Mattay, V. S., Berman, K. F., Ostrem, J. L. (1996). Dextroamphetamine enhances "neural network-specific" physiological signals: a positron-emission tomography rCBF study. The Journal of Neuroscience, 16 (15), 4816-4822.

224 Berridge, (2007).

225 Berridge, et al., (1998).

226 Melzer, et al., (2010).

227 Berdoy, et.al (2000).

228 Adolphs, et al., (1998).

229 Adolphs, et al., (2002).

230 Broks, et al., (1998).

231 Winston,et al., (2002).

Chapter Twenty One

232 Sergeanta, M.J.T., Dickins, T. E., Davies, M. N. O., Griffiths, M. D. (2006). Aggression, empathy and sexual orientation in males. Personality and Individual Differences, 40 (3), 475–486.

233 Dailey, T. (2004). Comparing the lifestyles of homosexual couples to married couples. Insight, (Washington,DC: Family Research Council), 260.

234 Bell, A.P., Weinberg, M. S. (1978). Homosexualities: A study of diversity among men and women. New York: Simon and Schuster. pp. 308, 309

235 Aaron Sell, A., Hone, L. S. E., Pound, N. (2012). The importance of physical strength to human males. Human Nature, 23(1), 30-44.

236 Petersen M. B., Sznycer D., Sell A., Cosmides L., Tooby J. (2013). The ancestral logic of politics: Upper-body strength regulates men's assertion of self-interest over economic redistribution. Psychological Science, [Epub ahead of print].

237 Camperio Ciani, A. S., Fontanesi, L., Iemmola, F., Giannella, E., Ferron, C., Lombardi, L., (2012). Factors associated with higher fecundity in female maternal relatives of homosexual men. The Journal of Sexual Medicine, 9 (11), 2878–2887

238 See: Hamer, D. (2002). Genetics of sexual behavior. In J. Benjamin, R. P. Ebstein, R. H. Belmaker (Eds.), Molecular Genetics and the Human Personality (pp. 257–272). Washington, DC: American Psychiatric Publishing. p266

239 Rice, W. R., Friberg, U., Gavrilets, S. (2012). Homosexuality as a consequence of epigenetically canalized sexual development. The Quarterly Review of Biology, 87 (4), pp. 343-368.

240 Bocklandt S., Horvath S., Vilain E., Hamer D. H. (2006). Extreme skewing of X chromosome inactivation in mothers of homosexual men. Human Genetics, 118(6), 691-694.

241 Allen, R. C., Zoghbi, H. Y., Moseley, A.B., Rosenblatt, H. M., Belmont, J. W. (1992). Methylation of Hpall and Hhal sites near the polymorphic CAG repeat in the human androgen-receptor gene correlates with X chromosome inactivation. American Journal of Human Genetics, 51, 1229-1239.

242   Liu, T., Dartevelle, L., Chunyan Yuan, C., Wei1, H., Wang1, Y., Ferveur, J. F., Guo1, A. (2008). Increased dopamine level enhances male–male courtship in Drosophila. The Journal of Neuroscience, 28 (21), 5539-5546.

243   Graham Tearse. "Parkinson's Drugs Made Me Gambler, Thief and Gay Sex Fiend." 9 December, 2007. <http://www.guardian.co.uk/world/2007/dec/09/france.health> (21 April 2013)

244   Savic, I., Lindström, P. (2008). PET and MRI show differences in cerebral asymmetry and functional connectivity between homo- and heterosexual subjects. Proceedings of the National Academy of Sciences, 105(27), 9403-9408.

245   Kanai, et al., (2011).

246   *"More masculine women had more sex partners and had a less restricted sociosexual orientation than did less masculine women; less masculine men had a higher sex drive than did more masculine men."*
From:
Ostovich JM1, Sabini J. (2004). How are sociosexuality, sex drive, and lifetime number of sexual partners related? Personality and Social Psychology Bulletin, (10):1255-66

247   Men in today's resource-rich, dopamine saturated world are being noted to be less masculine, perhaps due to less competition, (perhaps an endocrine effect elicited through dopaminergic mechanisms), failing to stimulate sufficient testosterone production. See:
Trumble1, B. C., Cummings, D., von Rueden, C., O'Connor, K. A., Smith, E. A., Gurven, M., Kaplan, H. (2012). Physical Competition Increases Testosterone Among Amazonian Forager-Horticulturalists: A Test of the 'Challenge Hypothesis'. Proceedings of the Royal Society, Biological Sciences, 279 (1739), 2907-2912.

248   Highly sexed women are more masculine:
Mikach, S.M., Bailey, J.M. (1999). What Distinguishes Women with Unusually High Numbers of Sex Partners? Evolution and Human Behavior, 20(3), 141-150.

Chapter Twenty Two

249   Berne, E. (1996). Games People Play: the Psychology of Human Relations; New York: Balantine Books.

250   Schultz, W. (2010). Dopamine signals reward value and risk: basic and recent data. Behavioral and Brain Functions, 6 (1), 24.

251   Berridge (2007).

252   Berridge (1998).

Chapter Twenty Three

253   Jost has done as good a job as is possible of aggregating the characteristics of ideologues. Much of his work is from a left-wing perspective. Then again, the entire field has long been populated with bunnies, which are puzzling over the urges of wolves, given how different they are. So the work he describes naturally carries that bent.

For interest, read the research in this field in the context of it being written by a field of rabbits discussing a wolf's psychology. Imagine all the rabbits puzzling over why the wolf will not just sit in a field peacefully eating grass. Picture the rabbits unable to figure out why the wolf won't spend his day telling all the rabbits how pretty they are, and giving the rabbits all of his stuff to spread around. Suddenly the confusion and bias of these researchers will make much more sense.

We will ignore Jost's examinations of political ideology in the context of system justification, since that is of little use if you understand ideology in the context of r/K. Instead we will focus on those works where he aggregates the observations of others on the traits and characteristics of ideologues. The four papers below are a decent representation of this work.

Jost, J. T., Glaser, J., Kruglanski, A. W., and Sulloway, F. J. (2003). Political conservatism as motivated social cognition. Psychological Bulletin, 129 (3), 339–375.

Jost, J. T. (2006). The end of the end of ideology. American Psychologist, 61 (7), 651–670.

Jost, J. T., Napier, J. L., Thorisdottir, H., Gosling, S. D., Palfai, T. P., Ostafin, B. (2007). Are needs to manage uncertainty and threat associated with political conservatism or ideological extremity? Personality and Social Psychology Bulletin, 33, 989-1007.

Jost, J. T., Federico, C. M., Napier, J. L. (2009). Political Ideology: Its Structure, Functions, and Elective Affinities. Annual Review of Psychology, 60, 307–337.

254   Anti-authoritarianism, which is used by these researchers as a measure of leftism, correlates with the clinical diagnostic criteria of psychopathology. See: Martin, J., Ray, J. J. (1972). Anti-authoritarianism: an indicator of psychopathology. Australian Journal of Psychology, 24, 13-18.

255   Jost et al. (2003) noted the increase in right-wing in-grouping following the attacks of Sept 11th, tying it to a larger fear motivation underlying adoption of the conservative ideology. Notice, the wolves begin fighting, and the bunnies wonder why the wolf with them gets agitated. That is deficient amygdala function impairing threat recognition.

256   Buchanan, p. 205.

Chapter Twenty Four

257   Bouchard, T. J., and McGue, M. (2003). Genetic and environmental influences on human psychological differences. Journal of Neurobiology, 54 (1), 44–45.

258   Cloninger, et al. (1993).

259   Eaves, L. J., Eysenck, H. J. (1974). Genetics and the development of social attitudes. Nature, 249, 288–289.

260   Alford, (2005).

261   Hatemi, P. K., Medland, S. E., Morley, K. I., Heath, A. C., Martin, N.G. (2007). The genetics of voting: An Australian twin study. Behavior Genetics, 37 (3), 435–448.

262   Hatemi, P. K., Hibbing, J., Alford, J., Martin, N., Eaves, L. (2009). Is there a 'party' in your genes? Political Research Quarterly, 62 (3), 584–600.

263   Settle, J. E., Dawes, C. T., and Fowler, J. H. (2009). The heritability of partisan attachment. Political Research Quarterly, 62 (3), 601–613.

264   Roszak, T. (1968). The Making of a Counter Culture. Berkeley: University of California.

265   Levitt, M., Rubenstein, B. (1974). The counter-culture: adaptive or maladaptive? The International Journal of Psychoanalysis, 1 (3), 325-336

266   Lattin, D. (2003). Following Our Bliss: How the Spiritual Ideals of the Sixties Shape Our Lives Today. New York: Harper Collins. p. 186.

267   Douglas, J. D. (1970). Youth in turmoil. Chevy Chase, Md.: National Institute of Mental Health. p. 131

268   Lattin, D. (2003). Following our bliss: how the spiritual ideals of the sixties shape our lives today. New York: Harper Collins. p. 186.

269   Hagopian, P. (2009). The Vietnam War in American Memory: Veterans, Memorials, and the Politics of Healing. Massachusetts: University of Massachusetts Press. p. 66.

270   Sale, K. (1973). SDS. New York: Random House. p. 648-653.

271   Hagopian, p. 66.

272   Bugliosi, V. Gentry, C. (1994). Helter skelter. New York: W. W. Norton & Company, Inc. p. 493

273   Ibid., p. 492

274   US Census Bureau. (2002). Population Profile of the United States. <http://www.census.gov/prod/2001pubs/p23-205.pdf> (retrieved February 24, 2012)

275   Centers for Disease Control. (2004). "Live Births, Birth Rates, and Fertility Rates, by Race: United States, 1909-2003." <http://www.cdc.gov/nchs/data /statab/natfinal2003.annvol1_01.pdf>. (retrieved January 13, 2012)

276   Jost, (2006).

277   Alford, J., Funk, C. Hibbing, J. (2005). Are political orientations genetically transmitted? American Political Science Review 99 (2), 153–167.

278   Hatemi, (2007).

279   Martin, N. G., Eaves, L. J., Heath, A. C. Jardine, R., Feingold, L. and Eysenck, H. J. (1986). Transmission of social attitudes. Proceedings of the National Academy of Sciences 83 (12), 4364–4368.

280   Tesser, A. (1993). The importance of heritability in psychological research: The case of attitudes. Psychological Review. 100 (1), 129–142.

281   Settle et al. (2010).

282   Ebstein et al. (1996).

283   Benjamin (1996).

284   Garcia et al. (2010).

285   Olsson, C. A., Moyzis, R. K., Williamson, E., Ellis, J. E., Parkinson-Bates, M., Patton, G. C., Dwyer, T., Romaniuk, H. and Moore, E. E. (2011). Gene–environment interaction in problematic substance use: interaction between DRD4 and insecure attachments. Addiction Biology. doi: 10.1111/j.1369-1600.2011.00413.x (again, environment interacts with DRD4 to produce a more hedonistic, addictive personality)

286   Kotler, M., Cohen, H., Segman, R., Gritsenko, I., Nemanov, L., Lerer, B., Kramer, I., Zer-Zion, M., Kletz, I., Ebstein, R. P. (1997). Excess dopamine D4 receptor (DRD4) exon III seven repeat allele in opioid dependent subjects. Molecular Psychiatry, 2, 251–254.

287   Jost, (2006).

288   Haensch, S., Bianucci, R., Signoli, M., Schultz, M., Kacki, S., Vermunt, M., Weston, D. A., Hurst, D., Achtman, M., Carniel, E., Bramanti, B. (2010). Distinct clones of Yersinia pestis caused the black death. PLoS Pathogens, 6 (10), e1001134.

289   Austin Alchon, S. (2003). A pest in the land: New world pandemics in a global perspective. Albuquerque: University of New Mexico Press. p. 21.

290   Caferro, W, (2010). Contesting the Renaissance. New York: John Wiley and Sons

291   Jordan, W. C. (1997) The Great Famine. Princeton: Princeton University Press.

292   Monkeys with amygdala damage are also less discriminating in the foods they consume, as discussed (less ability to experience aversive stimulus makes all foods palatable). The disease avoiding trait of disgust may also be an amygdala-mediated cognitive function, and be less present in r-strategists. Both traits could make r-strategists less likely to survive pandemics, and thus make many diseases not only psychologically adapting towards K, but selective for its genetic underpinnings, as well.

293   Stark, R. (2005) The Victory of Reason: How Christianity Led to Freedom, Capitalism, and Western Success. New York: Random House.

294   Gibbons, E. (1909). The History of the Decline and Fall of the Roman Empire. Volume 7. Reprint, 1974, Bury, J. B. (Ed.), New York: AMS Press. p308-309.

295   Ferrill, A. (1986). The Fall of the Roman Empire: The Military Explanation. New York, Thames and Hudson, Ltd.

296   Bartlett, B. (1994). How excessive government killed Rome. Cato Journal, 14 (2), 287-303.

[297] Taintor, J. (1988). The Collapse of Complex Societies. Cambridge: Cambridge University Press.

[298] Nriagu, J. O. (1983). Saturnine gout among Roman aristocrats: did lead poisoning contribute to the fall of the Empire? New England Journal of Medicine, 308 (11), 660-663.

Chapter Twenty Five

[299] Bartels, L. (2013). Americans are more conservative than they have been in decades. <http://www.washingtonpost.com/blogs/monkey-cage/wp/2013/09/30/americans-are-more-conservative-than-they-have-been-in-decades/> (Viewed 30 June, 2014)

[300] Tang, C. F.., Lean, H. H. (2009) New evidence from the misery index in the crime function. Economics Letters, 102(2), Pages 112–115.

Chapter Twenty Seven

[301] Those who are familiar with Strauss and Howe's generational theory will see the parallels here. Under Strauss and Howe's theory, civilizations undergo four generational periods, namely Crisis, High, Awakening, and Unraveling. Each period lasts approximately twenty years, and those raised during it adopt similar psychologies and perceptual frameworks. The chaos of the Crisis period is clearly r-strategists attempting to cope with an environment of K-selection. The K-selected generation it produces generates a period known as a High, through civic responsibility, sense of community, and conscientious work ethic. This is an environment in which K-strategists are not parasitized by r-strategists.

The High period generates an Awakening period, where individuals begin to focus on enjoying the resource availability, and force selfish individuality on a culture of conformity and common purpose. This is clearly the rise of the r-strategy within a population, though here, the r-strategists are able to comfortably parasitize the K-strategist's productivity due to their reduced numbers. This progresses into an Unraveling cycle, as r-strategists exceed the productivity of the population, hedonistic r-morals begin to erode the culture's decency and purpose, productivity and commitment to purpose deteriorate, and civilization begins to collapse. That ultimately yields the chaotic Crisis phase, which begins the cycle anew. Viewed in the context of Strauss and Howe's work, this might indicate that the adherence to r and K are generational, meaning adoption of an r or K strategy may be due less to an individual adaptability, and more due to perceiving cues as one matures, and developing accordingly.

What is less clear is if a period such as a High can be extended through artificially extending free resource availability through means such as conquest or credit, or what effect this would have on the cycles to follow. See:

Howe, N., Strauss, W. (1991). *Generations: The History of America's Future, 1584 to 2069.* New York: William Morrow & Company.

Howe, N., Strauss, W. (1997). *The Fourth Turning: What the Cycles of History Tell Us About America's Next Rendezvous with Destiny.* New York: Broadway Books

[302] Reaction time correlates with general (heritable) intelligence (g), and it is declining. See:

Jensen, A. R. (1998). The g-factor: the science of mental ability. Westport, CT: Praeger.

And:

Silverman I. W. (2010). Simple reaction time: it is not what it used to be. American Journal of Psychology, 123, 39-50.

And:

Woodley, M. A., te Nijenhuis, J., Murphy, R. (2013). Were the Victorians cleverer than us? The decline in general intelligence estimated from a meta-analysis of the slowing of simple reaction time. Intelligence, http://dx.doi.org/10.1016/j.intell.2013.04.006

[303] Genotypic Intelligence has been declining since the mid 1800's:

Woodley, M. A. (2012). The social and scientific temporal correlates of genotypic intelligence and the Flynn effect. Intelligence, 40 (2), 189-204.

[304] Technological innovation has been declining since the mid 1800's:

Huebner, J. T. (2005). A possible declining trend for worldwide innovation. Technological Forecasting and Social Change, 72 (8), 980–986.

Chapter Thirty

[305] Colp, R. (1974). The contacts between Karl Marx and Charles Darwin. Journal of the History of Ideas, 35 (2), 329-338.

[306] Mitchell O. C. (2008) Hitler's Storm Troopers and the Attack on the German Republic. Jefferson, North Carolina: McFarland & Company, Inc. pp. 46-56.

[307] Hilter, A. (1925) Mein Kampf. Reprint 2010, Bottom of the Hill Publishing

[308] Fodor, M. W. (1936). The spread of Hitlerism. The Nation, 142 (3683), 156.